ems should be returned on or before the last date
hown below. Items not already requested by other
orrowers may be renewed in person, in writing or by
elephone. To renew, please quote the number on the
barcode label. To renew online a PIN is required.
This can be requested at your local library.
Renew online @ **www.dublincitypubliclibraries.ie**
Fines charged for overdue items will include postage
incurred in recovery. Damage to or loss of items will
be charged to the borrower.

Leabharlanna Poiblí Chathair Bhaile Átha Cliath
Dublin City Public Libraries

Rathmines Library
157 Lr. Rathmines Road
Dublin 6

Dublin City
Baile Átha Cliath

Date Due	Date Due	Date Due
10. FEB 09		
11 MAR 09		02 MAY

COME ON SHORE AND WE WILL
KILL AND EAT YOU ALL

Come on Shore and We Will Kill and Eat You All

An unlikely love story

Christina Thompson

BLOOMSBURY

First published in Great Britain 2008

Maps prepared by C. Scott Walker, Digital Cartography Specialist, Harvard Map Collection, Nathan Marsh Pusey Library, Harvard University.

A version of "Turton's Land Deeds" was originally published in the Australian literary journal *Meanjin* and was reprinted along with part of "Nana Miri" in *The Best Australian Essays* 2000. An early version of "Hawaiki" appeared in the *American Scholar*, while a version of "Smoked Heads" was published in *Salmagundi* and subsequently reprinted in *The Best Australian Essays* 2006.

Permission to reproduce an extract from the poem "Landfall in Unknown Seas" by Allen Curnow courtesy of the copyright owner, Jenifer Curnow, and Auckland University Press.

Bloomsbury Publishing Plc,
36 Soho Square,
London W1D 3QY

A CIP catalogue record for this book
is available from the British Library

ISBN 978 0 7475 8252 6

10 9 8 7 6 5 4 3 2 1

Printed in Great Britain by Clays Ltd, St Ives plc

www.bloomsbury.com

The paper this book is printed on is certified by the © 1996 Forest Stewardship Council A.C. (FSC). It is ancient-forest friendly. The printer holds FSC chain of custody SGS-COC-2061

FSC
Mixed Sources
Product group from well-managed
forests and other controlled sources
Cert no. SGS-COC-2061
www.fsc.org
© 1996 Forest Stewardship Council

For Aperahama, Matiu, and Dani Matariki

Time is a flattened landscape, a land of unlinked lakes seen from the air.

—Annie Dillard, *Living by Fiction*

CONTENTS

The South Pacific
and the Polynesian Triangle

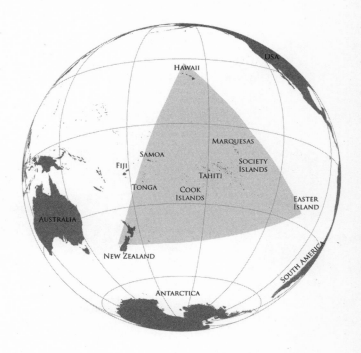

Australia

NEW ZEALAND

TASMAN SEA

BAY OF ISLANDS

WHANGAREI

AUCKLAND

NORTH ISLAND

MURDERERS' BAY

WELLINGTON

CHRISTCHURCH

SOUTH ISLAND

SOUTH PACIFIC OCEAN

DUNEDIN

AUTHOR'S NOTE

THIS WORK IS a mixture of history and memoir and, as such, it adheres to the truth in some areas and deviates from it in others. I have tried to be completely scrupulous with regard to the historical material both from New Zealand and the United States, and have used real place names and real historical figures in these parts of the text. Any errors or discrepancies here are my mistakes. I have also felt free to use real names and places in the case of my own family, that is, my husband, my children, my parents, my grandparents, and so on. When it comes to my husband's family, however—and by this I mean not his distant ancestors, whose lives are a matter of historical record, but his living relatives and those recently deceased—I have handled the material differently. It is not their story I am telling; it is mine. It would no doubt be very different if they told it and I feel that it would be improper to tie them too closely to my text. I have, therefore, disguised their names, the names of the places from which they come, and the details of their stories.

It may be objected that this distinction is overfine and that what applies to one side should apply to the other. But I have spent all these years thinking about and living with the consequences of colonialism, and I believe that this small gesture of respect, the offer of this small protection, is the least I can make to a group of people who have been unfailingly kind and generous to me, and who, when they talked to me and told me stories, never expected to find themselves cast as characters in a book.

PROLOGUE: NEW ZEALAND, 1642

IT IS THE evening of December 18, 1642, about an hour
after sunset, ten, perhaps ten thirty at night, with the sky still
holding the last vestige of light on the western horizon. The
crews of the two ships *Heemskerck* and *Zeehaen* see the light
of many fires on shore and four canoes, two of which come
toward them through the deepening gloom. It is not their first
indication that this island or continent—they know not
which—is inhabited, but it is the first time they have been
close enough to make out the people.

For five days they have been following the coast, running
north with a wide, open sea to their left, rolling in great billows
and swells, and a high, mountainous land to their right,
masked by low-lying clouds. They have been keeping well
out to sea lest the wind, which is predominantly from the
southwest, should freshen and drive them onto the shore. They
are looking for a landlocked bay or sheltered harbor where
they might safely go ashore and see what kind of country this is
they have discovered. They want wood and water, fresh food,
game, and greens. When they find a long, low sand spit curving
round to the east enclosing a large, open bay, they call a
meeting of the ships' council and make a resolution to land.

The two ships set sail in August from the Dutch outpost
of Batavia, now the Indonesian city of Jakarta. They were
under the command of Abel Janszoon Tasman, a captain in
the service of the Dutch East India Company, and were

commissioned to explore what lay south of Java between the Indian Ocean and the coast of the New World. Sailing west and south with the winds to Mauritius, Tasman's ships described a great arc through the Indian and Southern oceans. When they turned east in the high southern latitudes, they passed into a region that was largely unknown. They sailed south of mainland Australia, missing the continent entirely, and made their first landfall on the island now known as Tasmania, which they named Van Diemen's Land in honor of the governor-general of the Dutch Indies.

Here they landed long enough to see smoke and signs of fires. They heard people singing and playing a gong somewhere in the forest. They found notches cut into a tree at five-foot intervals and, believing these to be steps, concluded that the people must be giants. But the Tasmanian Aborigines remained hidden in the bush, "with watching eyes on our proceedings," or so the nervous Dutchmen believed. There was, in any case, nothing of interest to the Company and so Tasman set sail again to the east. Eight days later they sighted "a large land, uplifted high": the first recorded European glimpse of New Zealand.

The evening of December 18 finds them anchored in fifteen fathoms. The wind dies with the setting sun and there follows an hour of glassy calm, broken only by voices and the splash of oars. The *Zeehaen*'s boats have been sent to reconnoiter the bay and, when they return with the fading light, they are followed at some distance by two canoes. These come within a stone's throw of the Dutch ships and lie there, riding on the swell. Each of the canoes carries a dozen well-made men of average height with skin of a color between brown and yellow and thick black hair tied up in the fashion of the Japanese. Their chests are bare but around their waists they wear some kind of mat or clothing.

After a while, a man in the prow of the larger canoe stands and calls out in a guttural voice words that no one on board the ships can decipher. The master's mate calls back in Dutch and then the man in the canoe lifts something to his lips and blows a blast on what sounds to the sailors like a Moorish trumpet. The second officer of the *Zeehaen*, who has come out to the Indies as a trumpeter, is sent to fetch his horn and ordered to play a tune. This exchange is repeated a number of times and, when it finally grows too dark to see, the canoes turn and paddle back to shore. Uncertain of the natives' intentions, Tasman sets a double watch and sees that the men have muskets, pikes, and cutlasses to hand.

Early the next morning, a canoe carrying thirteen men approaches. The Dutch sailors lean over the rails, showing white linen and knives and trying to indicate by signs that they want to trade. But the natives keep their distance and eventually they leave. Tasman calls a council of his officers and resolves to bring the ships inshore, since, as he notes in his journal, "these people (as it seems) are seeking friendship."

But barely has this decision been reached when seven canoes set out from shore, speeding across the water. The *Zeehaen*'s skipper, who is on board the *Heemskerck*, grows nervous about having left his crew unsupervised and sends his quartermaster, Cornelis Joppen, back in the cockboat with instructions to the junior officers to be on their guard. The canoes, meanwhile, having reached the ships, take up positions on either side.

Joppen delivers his message and gets back in the cockboat, ordering his rowers to return to the commander's ship. As if on cue, the nearest canoe begins paddling furiously in his direction. Joppen has his back to the canoe and, at first, he does not see it coming. The sailors on board the ships begin to shout, but the natives in the other canoes are also shouting and waving their paddles in the air. The canoe, now flying over the water, rams the cockboat so violently that two of the sailors are tossed into the sea. Joppen reels and grabs for the gunwale but a native jabs him in the neck with a spear and hurls him overboard. The rest of the natives leap from their canoe and fall upon the sailors with clubs, beating them so furiously about the head that three sailors are killed instantly; a fourth lies bleeding in the bottom of the boat.

Joppen and the two sailors manage to swim away and the shallop is sent to rescue them. The natives drown one of the bodies and drag another into their canoe. The Dutch fire heavily with muskets and guns but miss their mark and the natives retreat to shore without suffering any casualties. The *Heemskerck*'s skipper is sent to recover the cockboat with its grisly cargo of dead and dying men, and Tasman gives the order to set sail, since "no friendship could be made with these people."

The ships weigh anchor and begin to move but the sailors can see a fleet of twenty-two canoes massing like storm clouds in the distance. The canoes, which are much faster and more mobile than the heavy ships, advance with alarming speed, obviously intending to cut off the intruders before they can escape from the confines of the bay. The Dutch wait until the natives are within range and then fire, this time rattling the canoes with shot and hitting a man in the leading canoe who is standing with a little white flag in his hand. The natives abruptly stop paddling. The Dutch spread what canvas they have and the *Heemskerck* and *Zeehaen* sail away, leaving behind the Maori armada and the bodies of two of their men.

Tasman calls a meeting of the ships' council and then goes below to commit his account of what has happened to paper.

"Since the detestable deed," he writes, "of these inhabitants, committed this morning against four of the Zeehaen's crew, teaches us a lesson, we consider the inhabitants of this country as enemies." And to this place he gives the name of Murderers' Bay.

I

PAIHIA

IF YOU STICK a hatpin in at Boston and drive it through the center of the earth, you come out very near the Bay of Islands. The first Europeans to go south of the equator expected to find a sort of looking-glass world, backward but recognizable, like people who resembled them but walked on their hands. This, of course, is not how it was, though there were birds that scuttled and animals that flew, trees that lost their bark and kept their leaves, pools of bubbling mud and other wonders. But even today there is something about the antipodes that makes one feel estranged, as if time had stopped or begun reversing, as if under a different heavens one were breathing a different air.

The first time I was in New Zealand it was as a tourist. I had been living in the Pacific for about three years, studying at the University of Melbourne, and I was on my way back to Australia after spending Christmas with my family in the States. I was traveling alone with no real plans, only that I wanted to spend a week somewhere, and New Zealand, like Tahiti or Rarotonga, was conveniently on the way. I had been to the islands on previous trips and I was looking for something uncomplicated, someplace I could just relax before starting the new academic year. At the tourist bureau in Auckland they suggested I try the Bay of Islands. "It's beautiful up there," said the girl at the counter with a sigh. So I took a bus to Whangarei and got up early the next morning to catch the milk run going north.

There were only a handful of passengers on the bus, all half-asleep. The front two seats were stacked with mailbags and parcels. I took a seat halfway back and watched as we pulled away from a Victorian country railway station on a defunct stretch of line. The sun was climbing into the sky and the day promised to be hot and bright.

We left town by the industrial quarter, a series of low, corrugated aluminum sheds, chain-link fences, boats on blocks, and the hulks of rusting machinery. We passed a three-story Victorian corner hotel painted blue, the Golden Dragon Chinese Restaurant, the vast, empty parking lot of Pak 'n Pay. Then we were on the outskirts of town, row after row of little wooden houses, yellow and white, each with a concrete step and a patch of yard and a Hill's hoist gleaming in the morning sun. Every couple of blocks there was a corner store already open for business, the day's headlines blaring in four-inch type from posters propped outside—FINANCE MINISTER SACKED; FRENCH EMBROILED IN DIPLOMATIC SCANDAL. I caught a glimpse of dim interiors behind strips of fluttering plastic, the poor man's fly-screen door.

For nearly four hours we ground our way up steep, volcanic hillsides between dense patches of native bush, thickets of manuka and giant fern. Then down the other side, the engine whining in protest and the landscape opening out before us like a nineteenth-century painting. The names of suburbs and towns rolled by: Kamo, Hikurangi, Whakapara, Waiotu, Moerewa. I looked them up in my dictionary of place names: *Kamo*—to bubble up, descriptive of hot springs; *Hikurangi*—point or summit of the sky; *Whakapara*—to make a clearing in the forest; *Waiotu*—spring or pool of Tu, the god of war; *Moerewa*—floating like a bird in sleep or, perhaps, to sleep on high. In between, the country was empty. Stripped of its native covering, it looked smooth and bald. Sheep the color of dust grazed on hillsides covered with a stubble of grass and the scoria of ancient volcanic explosions. In the vales and clefts the grass was startlingly green; on the hills it was burnt golden brown by the fierce antipodean summer. There were farms every so often and once or twice a view of the sea, glimmering far off.

At Puketona we left the main road and made a steep descent through a twisting, deeply shaded ravine, emerging suddenly into a blinding world of sunlight and water. WELCOME TO PAIHIA, said a sign by the roadside, JEWEL OF THE BAY OF ISLANDS.

Paihia is not a Maori name. It is widely believed to be a pidgin expression: *pai* means "good" in Maori, while *hia* is thought to be a transliteration of the English word "here." According to a popular story, the Reverend Henry Williams, who established a mission there in 1823, was so enchanted by the site that he exclaimed, "*Pai* here!" meaning "What a good place this is!" or "How good it is to be here!" The experts, though, cast doubt upon this explanation, arguing that it seems too good to be true. At least two other early commentators had spelled the name differently, referring to it as *Pahia*, which, in Maori, means "to slap."

Today Paihia is a tight half mile of chip shops, milkbars, seaside motels, and concrete condominiums, a pale, patterned grid of balconies and awnings set against a backdrop of brooding, prehistoric bush. Across the road is the Pacific Ocean. Not the open sea, but the Bay of Islands, a sublimely beautiful stretch of water with dozens of islets and a complex, meandering coastline, named in 1769 by Captain James Cook, who was the first European to see it.

My bus rumbled to a stop at the edge of the wharf. The passengers all got off and stood outside, blinking and stretching and putting on hats and shading their eyes with their hands. I stayed where I was for a moment, staring out at the glittering sea and thinking about the long January arc of the sun as it made its way across the southern hemisphere. In Boston, where I had just come from, it was pitch-dark at four thirty.

After a minute the bus driver stuck his head back in. "You need any help there?"

I got off the bus and walked out onto the pier. To my right an arm of the coastline reached out into the bay, enfolding a little harbor. A number of yachts and launches bobbed at anchor and I caught the faint, melodic clanking of wires hitting the aluminum masts. To my left and beyond was the open bay and the myriad islands like the hills of a drowned continent sticking up out of the sea. There were dozens of boats out on the water, their brightly colored spinnakers bellied out in the breeze. But the air on shore was still and the sun hot in a cloudless sky.

In Australia I often used to stand on the beach and look out to sea and think about what it must have been like to see these places for the first time. It was a curious thought, since the view from where I stood was exactly the opposite of what those first Europeans saw. They, seeing land from sea, recorded it in gently undulating profiles, taking note of any distinctive formations that might prove useful to future navigators. To them it was a stretch of rocky coastline, miles of inscrutable gray-green bush, a series of possible landfalls, inlets and bays where one might get water, reefs and sandbars to avoid. To me, standing there with my back to the cliffs, it was a great reach of emptiness, a stretch of possibility, the gentle curve of the horizon at the edge of the sea. Still, I thought I understood something of the sense of expectation those early explorers must have felt as they approached an unknown coastline for the first time.

The Pacific was an enormous challenge for Europeans. It was so far away, so difficult to get to, and, when they finally reached it, so unexpectedly immense. The early explorers suffered terribly from scurvy, hunger, thirst, not to mention disorientation in the course of voyages that often lasted for years. But it was not just the size of the Pacific that confounded them. It was its emptiness, a reality all the more distressing for the fact that it was not at all what they had imagined they would find.

For centuries the map of the world showed a huge mysterious landmass to the south peopled by men with funny hats or the heads of dogs, wielding spears and praying to idols. It was known as *Terra Australis Incognita*, the Unknown South Land—or sometimes, more optimistically, *Terra Australis Nondum Cognita*, the South Land Not Yet Known—and its existence was an article of faith among European geographers for fifteen hundred years.

The theory, first articulated by the ancient Greeks, was that the landmasses of the northern hemisphere must be counterbalanced by an equal weight of continental matter in the south, or else the world would topple over. But although European explorers crisscrossed the Pacific, beginning with Magellan in 1520, the great South Land remained stubbornly elusive. There were tantalizing hints, rumors of sightings: an island auspiciously named *Austrialia del Espiritu Santo* by Quirós in 1605, something called Davis Land in the eastern Pacific, sighted by an English buccaneer in 1687 and never seen again, suggestions of continental shadows, of land birds too far out to sea, of unexpected cloud formations in places where they shouldn't be. There were bits of Australia, a tip of Tasmania, a coast of New Zealand, islands scattered here and there, but few complete outlines well into the eighteenth century. And in the absence of conclusive proof to the contrary, many continued to cherish the idea of a strange and marvelous country somewhere in the South Seas.

But if Europeans in the Pacific were always hoping to stumble upon some great good place, experience often disappointed them. The Solomon Islands, named for the biblical King Solomon (and his gold) by the sixteenth-century Spanish explorer Alvaro de Mendaña, turned out to be inhabited by cannibals. Australia, first visited in the early seventeenth century by the Dutch, was, in the view of Jan Cartensz, "the most arid and barren region that could be found anywhere on earth," while New Zealand was inhabited by a people so treacherous and belligerent that anyone hoping to land there would, at least according to Abel Tasman, have to fight his way to shore.

Of course, none of this stopped Europeans from coming—far from it—but it did occasionally give them pause as they peered into the early-morning mist, trying to decide if that smudge on the horizon were the coast of some undiscovered country or a bank of low-lying cloud, or wondering, as they drew near some unknown coastline, what manner of men they might find.

I took a long last look out across the bay and made my way back up the pier to where the bus was idling. All the other passengers had vanished, merging into the crowd of tourists and shoppers on the opposite side of the road. For a moment I thought about following them. It was an appealing sort of place, touristy but recognizable in the way that resort towns often are, an easy sort of place to imagine staying. But the ticket I was holding was not for Paihia. It was for an inland agricultural center called Kerikeri, where, in an effort to economize, I had booked a bed at the local youth hostel.

The driver was already in his seat and he gave me a nod as I climbed back on the bus. It was just the two of us, and as soon as I was settled, he yanked the door shut and we pulled out into the stream of traffic snaking through the town.

We passed a series of gift shops and tearooms, a couple of real estate agencies, a one-hour photo lab, some restaurants, a hairdresser, and a bank. There were signs for at least a dozen motels that I might have stayed at: the Dolphin, the Outrigger, the Nautilus, the Admiral's View. There was one with a nice ring to it called Cook's Lookout and another with the oddly ironic name the Abel Tasman Lodge. But it was not a big place and before long we had reached the end of Paihia proper. Then trundling over the Waitangi Bridge, we left the motels and spinnakers behind us and climbed back into the green and shadowed bush.

Kerikeri, known to the missionaries as "Kiddy-kiddy," lies upriver from the Bay of Islands just beyond the navigable head of the Kerikeri River. There is a famous mission house there and the oldest stone building in New Zealand and, not too far from either of these, the ruins of a Maori *pa*, or fortified village, known in pre-European times as *Te Waha-o-te-riri*, or the Mouth of War.

At thirty-five degrees south latitude, well watered, and protected from the prevailing winds, the inland Bay of Islands is a gardener's paradise. Charles Darwin, visiting the region in

December 1835 on the homeward leg of his voyage in the *Beagle*, described crops of barley and wheat standing in full ear and fields of potatoes and clover. "There were large gardens," he wrote, "with every fruit and vegetable which England produces; and many belonging to a warmer clime . . . asparagus, kidney beans, cucumbers, rhubarb, apples, pears, figs, peaches, apricots, grapes, olives, gooseberries, currants, hops, gorse for fences, and English oaks; also many kinds of flowers." Kerikeri, which means, literally, "dig, dig," still produces all this and more, including many fruits unknown to Europeans in Darwin's day, like passion fruit, feijoas, and tamarillos.

Like most ordinary towns, Kerikeri is made up of concentric circles. It has a small retail center with a handful of shops, a newsagent, a couple of banks, a Laundromat, a supermarket, a post office, and a pub. Outside this is a ring of marine and agricultural businesses: tractor sales and tire centers and places to get a boat engine overhauled. Then there's a suburban belt of ranches and bungalows on quarter-acre blocks, beyond which lie the commercial orchards and farms.

Kerikeri is a prosperous town with an air of solid, middle-class well-being. A sizable chunk of the population is made up of local farmers and businessmen, some of whose families have lived in the area for generations. In recent years it has attracted a large number of new arrivals: rose growers and hobby farmers and well-heeled retirees, drawn to the region by the gentle climate and the pleasant way of life. Somewhat less expectedly, Kerikeri is also home to a thriving alternative fringe. Tucked in between the farm stands on the road to Whangarei are pottery barns and woodworking studios. You can easily find someone who does shiatsu massage or aromatherapy, and at least one store in town sells Indian cottons, crystals, and healing CDs.

On certain days of the week there are great congregations of Maoris in Kerikeri. They sit in parked cars and chat through the window. They buy fish-and-chips at the takeaway and eat it off butcher paper in the park. They splurge on lotto tickets, tailor-mades, pies with sauce, cream buns, and cases of beer. You can see them in the Laundromat, folding and gossiping while the kids play video games, or queueing up at the supermarket, their trolleys piled high with staples: flour in twenty-kilo bags, sugar, tea, milk, potatoes, pumpkins, butter, eggs, and jam.

Most of the Maoris in Kerikeri live out beyond the smaller landholdings, beyond the orchards and the farms, past where the tarmac ends and the gravel takes over, on small residual blocks of tribal land. Some of these communities are inland, but most of them are on the sea, cupped in a sheltered bend of the coastline or perched at the back of a cove. Many of these settlements are ancient by New Zealand standards, dating from long before the arrival of any Europeans, and many of the people who live there today are directly descended from those who occupied them hundreds of years ago. Although they are not exactly hidden, these places are not easy to locate. A lot of Maori history can be found in the local tourist brochures and guidebooks, and there are maps showing how to get to the ruins of Kororipo *pa* or the recreation of Rewa's village. But there are few, if any, signposts to the places where most of the local Maoris actually live.

I spent just under a week in Kerikeri, much of it on my own. I hiked the trails to Rainbow Falls and walked down the hill to Waipapa Landing to see the Kemp House and the Stone Store. I visited the arts-and-crafts cooperative and a nursery specializing in lavenders and culinary herbs. I hung out in the tearooms and in the newsagent, where I found a surprisingly good supply of books.

I was always on the lookout for books when I traveled, and never went anywhere without some of my own. One, in particular, I took with me whenever I crossed the Pacific: a battered 1949 anthology called *The Spell of the Pacific* that my brother had given me when I first left the States. It had a worn, rather lurid dust jacket showing the mauve mountains of a high island with its green coastal plain and, in the foreground, a cluster of lateen-rigged canoes sailing on a coral sea, all framed with a bit of beach grass and a fringe of black palm. It was filled with accounts of poets and explorers, missionaries, sailors, scientists—travelers of all kinds—arranged geographically and prefaced with an epigraph from *Moby-Dick:* "There is one knows not what sweet mystery about this sea, whose gently awful stirrings seem to speak of some hidden soul beneath . . ."

Plainly sensational in its presentation—the flap copy was addressed to "those whose hearts can thrill to romance and adventure," while the back promised "Natives," "Shipwreck," and "Treasure"—it was nevertheless a serious, even a scholarly work, containing an astonishing array of European writings about the Pacific, from an eyewitness account of the death of Magellan in 1521 to a wartime dispatch from the Philippines in 1944. Anyone who was anyone was represented—Conrad, Melville, London, Maugham, Tasman, Darwin, Cook, and the unhappy Captain Bligh—over a thousand thin, brittle pages between fraying cloth-covered boards. My copy, which my brother had found at an estate sale in Santa Barbara, had been at some previous time inscribed on the flyleaf: *For your travels.* I packed it in my hand luggage and carried it with me, reading as I went.

It was organized by region: Melanesia, Polynesia, Australia, and so on. The New Zealand section began with Tasman's arrival and the first recorded instance of contact between the Maoris and Europeans at a place thereafter known as Murderers' Bay. This was followed by a couple of Maori myths; an extract from Charles Darwin's *Beagle* journal; a grim uncharacteristic story by Katherine Mansfield about madness on the colonial frontier; some poems, including one with a dirgelike refrain that began, "Morning in Murderers' Bay, / Blood drifted away"; and an excerpt from a curious book called *Old New Zealand*, written in 1863 by a "harum scarum Irishman" named Frederick Maning. This last was titled "A Maori Ruffian," and it told the story of a fight between the author and "a bullet-headed, scowling, bowlegged, broad-shouldered, Herculean savage" who had "killed several men in fair fight, and had also—as was well known—committed two most diabolical murders, one of which was on his own wife."

None of this correlated well with the magazine in the seatback pocket of my Air New Zealand flight or any of the other popular representations of New Zealand as a land of panoramic beauty dotted with sheep. Nor did it seem to have much to do with places I had visited like Kerikeri or Paihia, and I began to wonder about the history of the country and the undercurrents that might run through its society.

I was booked on the late bus back to Auckland and, looking for a way to spend my last few hours, I wandered over to the pub. It was a Saturday evening at the height of summer and the place was full of smoke and people sitting at sticky tables crowded with pitchers of Lion and DB. At one end of the room, a jukebox was playing a loud mixture of reggae and rock. At the other stood a pair of pool tables surrounded by players waiting for their turn. There were a number of counter-height tables scattered around the room. The women perched on barstools and drank rum and Coke; the men stood and drank their beer straight from the jug, as if even the largest glasses were too small for their hands. Slumped in the corners of the room were a handful of people who'd clearly been there all day, but most had been trickling in since late afternoon, and by the time the fight broke out, there was standing room only.

How they all knew something had happened I have no idea, but the minute the punch was thrown, every head in the place swiveled in the fighters' direction. A space had opened up in the middle of the room and in the center of it were two young men, one of whom was standing stock-still with a hurt expression and blood running down his face.

The hitter was a Maori, a half-caste, with a compact body and fair, freckly skin. He could hardly have been more than eighteen, probably he was younger. The bleeder was a Pakeha, a New Zealander of European descent. He was blond and wiry and older than the Maori boy, with a face already weathered by the southern sun. He was wearing blue jeans and a red plaid shirt, which was handy, I remember thinking, since he was using the sleeve of it to mop up his face.

For an instant there was silence. And then it was over, just like that. The Pakeha vanished into the bathroom, the Maori sat down with a thump, and everyone else turned back to his beer.

"What happened?" I asked the fellow standing nearest, a tall, solid Maori with cropped hair, sunglasses, and a bright pink shirt. "What's going on?"

"Guess someone said something someone didn't like," he said. "Gotta light?"

He was very big, I realized, studying him more closely. Not just tall but heavily muscled and dark, or maybe that was the shirt. His face was broad and perfectly impassive. I could see nothing behind the glasses, the lenses of which looked black.

I handed him my lighter.

"Ta," he said. "You here on holiday?"

I explained that I was living in Australia, though, as he could tell from my accent, I was obviously a Yank. "How about you? Are you from around here?"

He said he was a foundryman and that he made boat parts in Whangarei. He pronounced it the Maori way—FAHNG-ah-day—so that even though I'd just spent a night there on my way to Kerikeri from Auckland, I didn't recognize the name. He'd come home for the Christmas holidays. His family lived out in Mangonui, about fifteen miles away.

I told him I'd been in Kerikeri for a week, staying at the youth hostel, and that I was headed back to Auckland that same night.

"Hmmm," he said, looking past me in a manner I found oddly reassuring.

"My name's Christina," I volunteered.

"Tauwhitu," he said, pronouncing it TOE-fee-too. "But everyone calls me Seven."

"Why's that?"

"*Tau whitu*. In Maori it means 'seven years.' "

But this, like everything else, was curiously misleading. He was not called Seven because his name meant "seven years." He was called Seven because he was the seventh of ten children and because some wag among his cousins had nicknamed him "Number Seven" when he was a kid.

The way he told it, it was only an accident that he was even in the pub that night. He said he'd been out on the water all day diving for crayfish with his cousins—by which I understood him to mean the piratical-looking crew of Maoris at the next table. They were all wearing sunglasses and close-fitting jeans and some had leather jackets. "We only came into town for cigarettes," he was saying. "We didn't plan on stopping at the pub."

The problem, it seemed, was that none of them had any money. But then someone had the bright idea of taking the crayfish, which they were supposed to bring home, and hawking them in the pub. At the last minute, the crays were saved when Seven found a twenty-dollar note on the men's room floor. He laughed as he mimed handing it over to the bartender with the very tip of his forefinger and thumb.

Just then the noise in the pub, which had once again risen to a steady roar, died abruptly for a second time. A group of policemen, five or six, in hats and uniforms with handcuffs and billy clubs dangling from their belts, were standing in the door. They shouldered their way through the crowd to where the Maori who'd been in the fight was sitting. "Outside," said one of them roughly. "Outside with yer mates."

The boy and his two companions, one with dreadlocks and a crocheted cap and a thin, grizzled fellow in his forties, got to their feet and left, followed by the police.

"Excuse me," I said. "I'll be right back." And, leaving my drink on the table, I slipped out after them.

By this time night had fallen. The police had their suspects lined up against the wall and were barking questions at them: What were their names? Where did they come from? What were they doing here? They told the Maoris to empty out their car, a battered old Falcon stuffed with clothing, blankets, fishing gear, and trash. As the one with the dreadlocks went to open the door, a Doberman leaped out and he grabbed it by the collar. I took in the scene from the doorway—the police beacons flashing in the night, the whining dog, the staccato nonsense of the radio, and the dark mutterings of the men, whose disheveled belongings were now strewn around the parking lot—and wondered if this were normal for a Saturday night.

At last the police decided to take the oldest, most inoffensive member of the trio to the station, leaving the other two to stuff their things back into the car.

"You can pick him up later," they told them. "Then you're on your way."

I went back inside, if anything even less clear about what had actually happened. Why were there so many policemen? Why did they take the wrong guy? Why did they even bother to turn up when the fight was over? What had happened to the Pakeha? And why was there no buzz about it in the pub?

I headed back to where I'd left my beer and put my questions to Seven.

"Ah," he said, "they're just troublemakers. They're not from around here."

2

ABOMINABLY SAUCY

I HAVE OFTEN thought of that night as a contact encounter. "Contact" is what we call it when two previously unacquainted groups meet for the very first time. It is what happened when Christopher Columbus reached the Bahamas in 1492 and encountered a tribal people henceforth known as "Indians" from his misconception about where in the world he was. Or when the Leahy brothers, trekking into the interior of Papua New Guinea in search of gold, came upon a group of highlanders who in 1933 still knew nothing about the outside world. It describes a moment of sudden wonder, a tectonic shift, that undermines old certainties and opens up whole new views.

Of course, there have been thousands, perhaps tens of thousands, of such moments. Contact, after all, has taken place in all corners of the world between all kinds of people, most of whom have left no written record of the events. Documented instances are comparatively rare and this, perhaps, is why so much glamour attaches to these moments—that and the fact that they no longer happen. *First contact,* unless it is with someone in outer space, is a scenario that will not be repeated on the terrestrial globe, and this naturally adds to its attraction.

But contact, as a generalized concept, is still a very useful idea. In the context of the last five hundred years, the age of

European expansion, contact has often been understood as an asymmetrical event, an act, in which someone *contacts* someone else. But historians and anthropologists tend to speak rather of a "contact period" or "contact zone," meaning a time and space in which two groups of people come together, part, come together, part, and come together again in a strange, unsettled period of uncertainty, like a dance that none of the performers has had a chance to fully learn.

Because contact, whatever else it is, is a matter of confusion. One side may have technological superiority; the other maybe have numbers on its side. But when they first come together, there is, for a limited time, a kind of parity, the parity of incomprehension. Each side constructs hypotheses, tries to assess the other's strength, to parse the other's utterances, to deduce the other's purpose and intent. Neither fully understands what's happening and neither can say with confidence what's going on.

The absolute truth of this, and its applicability even to contemporary situations, was impressed upon me that evening after I left the Kerikeri pub. My bus to Auckland had been scheduled for ten o'clock, but somehow ten had come and gone and, before I knew it, the pub was closing and there I was with all my gear and no place to go. "You can come with us," said Seven. And so I did.

Our destination, it turned out, was a house that belonged to somebody's uncle. The owner was away at the time and in his absence the place had become a sort of flophouse for those of his relations who could not be bothered, or were too drunk, to drive back out to Mangonui. You could walk to it from the pub, which is what we'd done, stumbling through the schoolyard and across a lumpy paddock to a surprisingly suburban-looking street at the bottom of a hill.

It was a plain, rectangular timber house, sparsely furnished, with a living room, a kitchen, three small bedrooms, and a bath. Inside, it had a hard-worn, barren feeling, no knick-knacks or decorations, but all the surfaces were immaculately clean. When we arrived, the place was already filled with people, draped in various postures about the room. At one end of the lounge a couple of girls were playing cards at a table, at the other a bunch of guys were sprawled in front of a TV. Between them, pushed up against the wall, was a sagging couch, which is where, as the evening advanced, I found myself sitting.

Beside me on the sofa was a scruffy-looking guy in his midtwenties whom I'd seen earlier in the pub. He had a surly sort of expression and a handsome mop of curly black hair. He was wearing a singlet and a pair of black jeans and his hands were covered with homemade tattoos.

We'd been sitting there for a while when out of the blue he said, "I've been looking for an earring."

From the kitchen came the smell of frying onions and the sound of the kettle coming to a boil. A lean and wispy character with several missing teeth was strumming a Bob Marley song on the guitar. On the coffee table in front of us stood a half-empty bottle of whisky and an ashtray full of butts.

I fingered the earrings I was wearing, a pair of large engraved silver hoops that I had bought for myself at a shop in Melbourne. I wore them often and considered them my favorite pair. On impulse I took one off and handed it over. "Here," I said. "Have this."

He looked at me for a moment and then held the earring up and ripped the silver hoop from the ring that attached it to the wire. Then he tossed the hoop into a corner and put the wire in his ear.

I sat perfectly still, thinking about what had just happened.

I had left the pub in the company of these strangers because I wanted to know more about them and because I trusted the fellow in the bright pink shirt. It was instinct and nothing more, and now I wondered if perhaps I'd misjudged the situation.

Maybe it was because I was a tourist. Maybe it was because I'd come to the party with someone he didn't like. Maybe there was something insulting about my giving him the earring, as though I were making a display of the fact that it was easy for me to give something valuable away. Maybe he thought I was trying to placate him or buy him off. Maybe he just didn't like the hoop. Maybe he thought it looked like something for a girl. I wasn't even all that sure of my own motives, but I had absolutely no idea what was going through his mind. All I knew was that something had gone wrong.

Later the memory of this moment was like a flash going off inside my head. It was exactly the kind of thing, I realized, that had happened over and over in those early years when Maoris and Europeans were first coming into contact with one another. Not that this was anywhere near as serious—it was easy enough for me to get up and walk away, to seek out people in whose company I felt safer, to sneak back later when no one was looking and retrieve my silver hoop. But if you ramped up the risks and the consequences, you could see in this the sort of encounter that had so often been repeated in the history of New Zealand and had so often ended badly for one or the other side.

All the early accounts of contact in New Zealand have an air of peril about them. The Maoris, so numerous and brooding, seem perpetually on the verge of attack. The Europeans, full of uncertainty, sail in and out in a state of chronic trepidation. Neither side seems clearly in command.

After Tasman's misadventure in Murderers' Bay, no European ship reached New Zealand for 127 years. Then, in rapid succession, came Cook and the Frenchman Jean de Surville, separately but simultaneously in 1769, Marion du Fresne in 1772, Cook again with Tobias Furneaux in 1773–74, and then Cook once more on his third and final voyage in 1777. Of these expeditions, not one escaped New Zealand without confrontation and, in some cases, significant loss of life.

Surville, who reached New Zealand at virtually the same time as Cook, approached New Zealand only with the greatest unease. He had made a long and pointless passage through the Coral Sea with a crew that was dying of scurvy, and he desperately needed someplace where he could go ashore. New Zealand seemed to him the best of bad options. "According to the report of the travellers who have preceded us there," he wrote, "the natives of the country are ferocious and bloodthirsty." But it was the closest known landfall and the one he thought they would be able to find. And, "anyhow," he added, "we have no alternative in the state in which we are."

As it was, the Maoris treated him civilly. They came out in their canoes and traded fish for cloth and knives, led the visitors to a place where they could get water, and even helped them care for their sick on shore. But Surville did not trust them. "They stand close to you with marks of friendship," he wrote, "and if you relax and they think they have time to flee after striking their blow, they will not fail to."

Still, for a week all went well. Then one night a storm arose and a boatload of invalids returning to the ship was forced back to shore. The ship dragged her anchors and had to be moved, leaving behind a yawl that had sunk in shallow water.

When the wind subsided, Surville spotted the yawl, which the Maoris had in the meantime refloated. He set off to retrieve it, but when he arrived, the yawl was gone. Determined to revenge himself for, in his words, "the theft which had just been committed under our very noses," Surville seized the first Maori he could lay his hands on, confiscated a large canoe, and set fire to some thirty dwellings and storehouses full of food. Then, clapping his captive in irons, he sailed out of the bay. The prisoner, who later died of scurvy at sea, turned out to be none other than Ranginui, a local chief who—in the ultimate proof of the maxim "no good deed goes unpunished"—had fed and sheltered the sick Frenchmen when they were stranded by the storm.

Surville's behavior, which seems not only wicked but bizarre, cannot possibly have made sense to the Maoris. But they themselves were often just as baffling: witness the story of Marion du Fresne. Marion's view of the Maoris was exactly the opposite of Surville's. An idealist and a romantic who had come under the influence of Jean-Jacques Rousseau, Marion believed that the Maoris were nature's children. "As I do only good to them," he told his lieutenant, "assuredly they will do me no evil."

Marion spent five weeks in the Bay of Islands in May and June of 1772. Relations there were quickly established, the local people expressing great interest in and apparent friendliness toward the French, who, in turn, described the Maoris as "a fine, courageous, industrious, and very intelligent race." Both Marion's lieutenant and the commander of his storeship, however, felt that their captain placed too much confidence in the Maoris' goodwill. The lieutenant, particularly, thought he detected "a species of underlying ferocity" in their behavior. They "treated us to a great many endearments," he wrote, but "when we permitted them to place their lips, either upon our hands or our faces, they sucked the flesh with a surprising greediness."

One day, when the French had been in the bay for about a month, two chiefs took Marion to the top of a hill where a great many people were gathered. There, they embraced him and placed a crown of greenery upon his head. Marion understood these gestures to mean that they acknowledged him as their sovereign, but this is patently not what was going on. "Whatever these ceremonies may have meant," writes the anthropologist Anne Salmond, "they sealed his death warrant."

The next day Marion went on shore in the company of several Maoris. He told his lieutenant that he was going fishing in a nearby cove and that none of his soldiers need accompany him, since they would just be in the way. And that was the last that anyone ever saw of Marion du Fresne.

When the full scale of the tragedy became apparent—a reconnaissance mission to the cove reported that both Marion's cutter and the longboat that had been sent after him were on the beach, that all but one of the longboat's crew had been massacred, and that one of the chiefs had been seen wearing Marion's velvet waistcoat and carrying his silver-mounted gun—the lieutenant led a punitive expedition against the local Maoris. Three hundred or more were killed, including women and children, some of whom were shot in their canoes as they tried to escape. The Frenchmen then set fire to three, perhaps four villages and, naming the spot "Treachery Bay," sailed for Île-de-France.

Many years later, in the late 1820s, a traveling Englishman reported that he had met a Maori in the Bay of Islands who claimed to have been among the party that murdered Marion.

"They were all brave men," the Maori said, "but they were killed and eaten."

Even Cook, undoubtedly the most experienced and capable navigator to visit New Zealand in these years, found relations with the Maoris tricky. Cook spent a full six months circumnavigating New Zealand in the course of his first voyage round the world. He had the distinct advantage over other commanders, not only of this cumulative experience but of having a Tahitian on board who was able to serve as a translator. And even so there was confusion, misunderstanding, even death.

In their very first encounter at a place called Poverty Bay, Cook's men, perceiving that they were about to be attacked, shot and killed a Maori, one of the very first they had met. A similar altercation the next day left three Maoris wounded, one mortally, and a fracas at sea that same afternoon resulted in four deaths, all Maori, and the capture of three adolescent Maori boys. Cook and his officers were not happy. "Black be the mark" for this day, wrote the young gentleman Joseph Banks, who sailed with Cook as an observer, "and heaven send that such may never return to embitter future reflection."

All up and down the coast, whenever the *Endeavour* was sighted, Maoris would set off in canoes, sometimes no more than two or three, sometimes as many as fifty at a time. Paddling as fast as they could, they would come to within earshot of the ship and cry out, "Come here, come ashore, and we will kill you!" waving their weapons in the air and hurling stones at the vessel. The British replied by firing small shot over the Maoris' heads. Sometimes the Maoris turned around and paddled back to shore. Sometimes they put down their weapons, entered into conversation, and began to trade: fish and *kumara* (sweet potatoes) for nails and cloth, weapons and cloaks for paper and hatchets. The daring and distinguished among them went aboard and examined everything in the ship, tasting the food, trying on the clothes, inspecting such novel instruments as telescopes and compasses. Cook, who became quite fond of the Maoris during his long circumnavigation, found their behavior remarkable.

At times they would dance the war dance, and at other times they would trade with and talk to us and answer such questions as were put to them with all the calmness imaginable, and then again begin the war dance, shaking their paddles, patoo patoos, etc., and make strange contortions at the same time. And as soon as they had worked themselves up to a proper pitch, they would begin to attack us with stones and darts and oblige us whether we would or no to fire upon them.

Cook had been coasting New Zealand for about a month when he reached the Bay of Islands on a fine spring day in late November. It was immediately apparent to everyone on board that this was no ordinary inlet. There were signs of occupation everywhere: plantations on all the larger islands, houses, villages, fortifications all along the shore. The people seemed in every respect more prosperous than any they had yet encountered. Their chiefs were better dressed and carried more weapons; their skins were darker and differently tattooed; their canoes were bigger and more elaborately carved; and they came out to the ship in great fleets numbering hundreds of men. The bay itself was safer, deeper, better protected than any Cook had yet seen in New Zealand, with sheltered anchorages and harbors "as smooth as mill pools." Even the fish were unusually plentiful: the men caught sharks, stingrays, bream, and mullet, while the mackerel, wrote Cook, "are larger than any I ever saw in any other part of the world."

It was, in fact, no ordinary place. The Bay of Islands at the end of the eighteenth century was a hotly contested region in political flux. The *hapu*, or subtribes, of Ngati Awa, Ngati Pou, and Ngati Wai were under pressure from Ngapuhi, a tribal grouping from the Hokianga and inland regions, whose rise to supremacy in the area coincided with the arrival of the Europeans. It was Ngapuhi who would later use the Bay of Islands as its base of operations for the first major war of the colonial period—a war fought by Maori against Maori with the use of the Pakeha's guns. It was Ngapuhi who would initiate the trade in timber, flax, and tattooed heads, who would sell the first land and build the first churches. It was a Ngapuhi chief who began the revolt against the Pakeha in 1844, and it was Ngapuhi who now confronted a European ship with European weapons in their bay for the very first time.

As soon as the *Endeavour* rounded the entrance to the bay, several large canoes set out from shore and quickly surrounded the ship. Some of the Maoris came on board but there was tension and misunderstanding. The Maoris seemed unfriendly, tempers began to rise. Sydney Parkinson, the ship's artist, described them as unruly, and complained that while he was greeting one of them in the local manner—by gently pressing noses—the Maori picked his pocket. Joseph Banks pronounced them "most abominably saucy."

Over the course of the day, no fewer than four or five hundred Maoris came out to the ship, their numbers and behavior such that Cook decided to take the *Endeavour* out of the bay before nightfall. They sailed north to the Cavalle Islands, where they bought fish and again were pelted with stones. But with the wind in their teeth they could make no progress and so back they went, determined so long as the wind was contrary to make a closer inspection of the bay.

The next day it was raining. No sooner had the ship come to anchor than three or four hundred Maoris assembled near it in their canoes. At first, wrote Cook, they behaved "tollerable well," but soon a group of youths tried to steal the buoy from the anchor. Nothing would make them stop but musket fire, and one of the boys, reported Cook, was hit. The captain then ordered a great gun fired over their heads, frightening them "not a little," and moved the ship to deeper water.

And then an incident occurred that nearly spelled the end of things for Cook. Cook, Banks, and the *Endeavour*'s naturalist, Dr. Daniel Solander, accompanied by an escort of marines, set off in the pinnace and the yawl to investigate one of the islands in the outer bay. They had only just landed when they discovered that all the canoes that had been gathered about the ship had followed them to the island, landing at different points along the shore. Within minutes they were surrounded by an unruly crowd of two or three hundred people. "Notwithstanding that they were all armed," wrote Cook,

> they came upon us in such a confused straggling manner that we hardly suspected that they meant us any harm. But in this we were very soon undeceived, for upon our endeavouring to draw a line of the sand between us and them, they set up the war dance and immediately some of them attempted to seize the two boats.

Finding themselves cornered and seeing the Maoris advance with what was now plainly hostile intent, Cook, Banks, Solander, and two of the marines fired into the crowd. This gave the attackers pause, but only for a moment, and the Maoris quickly rallied, shouting and waving their weapons in the air. Luckily for the men on the island, the officer in charge of the *Endeavour* had been keeping a close eye on things and he brought the ship's cannons to bear on the island and fired a series of four-pounders over the Maoris' heads. This time they retreated, but it was a dangerous skirmish for the British, and a foreshadowing of the way in which Cook, ten years later in Hawaii, would meet his death at the hands of a different group of Polynesians.

When I say that I thought of that night as a contact encounter, what I mean is that this is what it felt like to me. No doubt it had elements of oddness for the Maoris—they may have wondered what I was doing, going home with a bunch of people I didn't know—but at least I was recognizably a tourist, someone who had appeared on the periphery of their consciousness and would just as certainly disappear. For me, it was different. Seven was almost the first Maori I'd ever met, certainly the first I'd ever talked to, and the situation in which I found myself had all the hallmarks of a contact encounter: the excitement, the anxiety, the bafflement, the humor, the humility that ultimately comes from realizing *you've gotten it all wrong*.

What I thought I'd witnessed that night in the pub was nothing less than the unbridgeable gulf between Maori and Pakeha—a gulf no narrower for all the years that had elapsed since the two first faced each other across a narrow strip of beach. Had not Tasman sailed away leaving behind the name Murderers' Bay and the bodies of four of his men? Were not Cook's first days in New Zealand filled with death on the Maori side and dismay on the part of the Europeans? And what of Surville's irrational reprisals and the death of Marion du Fresne? Were not Maori and Pakeha from the very beginning locked in a belligerent embrace: no justice for Maori in a Pakeha world, no mercy for Pakeha among Maori?

"Nah," said Seven later. "That's not how it was. The Pakeha's a local lad—most of the fellas have known him for years. It was the other ones that caused all the trouble. I told you, they're not from around here."

The real fault lines, it seemed, lay that night between Maori and Maori and not between Maori and Pakeha, as I had assumed. I had been primed to see the incident in terms of a conflict between natives and colonizers, that is, between a fair, freckled Maori boy and a white guy in a red shirt. But, of course, that was far too simple.

The Pakeha who was involved in the fight, and who discreetly disappeared before the arrival of the police, was actually on the home team. He was the manager of an orchard outside town and was well known to most of the Maoris in the pub. The young Maori fighter and his two friends, on the other hand, had come from somewhere down the North Island and had no ties to the area. They were interlopers, "troublemakers," from the local point of view. Their manners were bad and they deserved to be punished. It was fine for the police to take them away. It was even fine for the police to harass them. In a certain, albeit ambiguous, sense, the police were on the home team too.

It was a while, though, before I really understood this. No Maori will tell you everything all at once and Seven was no exception to this rule. And even when I thought I had some of the answers, I was aware that there were things I didn't understand. This feeling of not quite getting what was going on would dog me whenever I was in New Zealand. Indeed, it seemed only to grow stronger with each visit. I like to think this is how astronomers feel: with each new discovery of something curious—quasars, black holes, dark matter—the universe grows not more comprehensible but less, though the hope endures of a simple, unifying explanatory narrative.

But back in the beginning, in the pub, I had only the merest signs to go on: the offer of a light, the flicker of a smile. It was like a code that needed cracking, a language that with effort one might finally comprehend. I was a tourist who should have been on a bus back to where I came from. Instead I found myself in a house long after midnight with a bunch of Maoris I didn't know. That was the night I missed my bus and then I missed my plane.

3

MANGONUI

ABOUT FIFTEEN MILES as the crow flies across the Bay of Islands lies the village of Mangonui. A settlement of some two hundred people, each of whom can claim all the others as his kin, Mangonui occupies a secluded spot on a branch of the Taimarie inlet. The water there is quiet, the fishing is good, the mudflats are full of shellfish, and there are oyster beds nearby. Maoris have lived there, off and on, for centuries. In the old days they probably came there in summer, when the fish and shellfish were fat, and went back to their inland homes at Waimate and Whakataha when the rain came and the chill wet winter wind began to blow.

The road to Mangonui is only paved halfway. After that it's what they call "loose metal," a slippery gravel surface that gives off clouds of dust. The road winds uphill and down, through pastures, over creeks, past long driveways that disappear over the top of a pasture only to reappear again as a ribbon in the distance between two fields. There are pine groves and pockets of manuka and great balls of gorse in the paddocks. The local Maoris, who know the road, drive fast, sliding round curves and flying over bumps. Occasionally someone hits a power pole, but usually only when they're drunk.

About twenty minutes from the end of the sealed road, a narrower, bumpier road turns off and heads down in a sweeping curve toward the tip of a small peninsula that juts out into the bay. Mangonui sits on this finger of land, with one *marae*, or meetinghouse, at the first joint, and another at the knuckle. The presence of two such institutions in so small a place—where you cannot buy a newspaper or a quart of milk, where two or three hundred people have among them four or five surnames—suggests two things: a high degree of religiosity and a long-standing family feud, the one likely having to do with the other. On one side of Mangonui live the Ratana adherents, on the other the Rapana faithful, divided from each other by a consonant, a dirt road, and a lost ideological disagreement. Their dispute, once a matter of principle, has become a matter of habit, and just what originally caused it no one under seventy can now say.

Past the *marae* on either side are houses, sheds, a handful of gardens, a number of abandoned cars, the shingle, and the sea. Though set in a landscape of exquisite natural beauty, the houses are not much to look at. The nicest of them is the one that Seven's father bought from the government in the early 1960s. It had been built for the Mangonui schoolteacher, who would have been a Pakeha, possibly with a wife, and it sat on a section of Crown land given to the government by Seven's grandfather specially for the purpose. When a bigger school was built out on the main road to accommodate not only the Maoris but the children of the local Pakeha farmers, the Mangonui teacher's house was no longer needed and, with the help of a government loan, Seven's father took it up.

It was a beautiful little house, all handmade of kauri pine, with a wide overhang and casement windows and a set of outside stairs leading to the front door. It had a kitchen with a wood stove, a lounge with a fireplace, two bedrooms with a bath in between, an outside toilet, and a pair of water tanks that collected rainwater from the roof. It was perched on the side of a gently sloping hill and gave a view of both *marae* and the road between them, and, beyond that, the inlet and the farther shore. Behind it, going up the hill, was a twisted lemon tree and a shed and a washing line with two forked props, and then, at the edge of the mown meadow, the beginning of the bush. A tangle of trees and creepers marked the top of the embankment, which dropped abruptly on the other side to the flat, where a cluster of houses sat separated from the beach by a shock of tufted grass and flax, like the crest of a giant bird.

This was the house that Seven grew up in. His parents raised ten children in its five rooms, his father working multiple jobs, often far from home, building houses, packing meat, picking vegetables. His mother ran the post office and telephone exchange from a cupboard inside the front door until the government closed the branch and moved the business into town. When I first met them, they were still living there, with the last of their children, a girl, who was then about thirteen years old. She had all to herself the room that had at different times contained every possible arrangement of beds (two sets of bunks; a bunk and a double; a double, a single, and a cot) and slept every possible arrangement of children (two boys in each bunk; four girls in the bed; all the younger children in one bed together, and a cot for whoever was the baby at the time). Her brothers and sisters had grown up and most had gone away, but a few remained in Mangonui, living in houses to either side, married with children of their own.

Seven's father was a man of not very many words, at least not to me. He was a minister of the faith that the people call Absolute Maori, or *Mana Motuhake*, a Rapana offshoot with roots in the Anglican Church. He wore a blue cassock with a white surplice and a red stole and conducted the service entirely in Maori. It was wonderful to listen to—the way any language one doesn't understand is wonderful—moving in a musical, purely emotional way. Seven's mother was a fine singer with a big voice that filled the *marae* on Sunday mornings and kept the faithful on their toes in the *whare kai*, or communal kitchen, whenever there were church events. They were the traditionalists in Mangonui, and referred, in private, to their relations across the road as *paki paki* (meaning "clap clap") because of their Pentecostal inclinations.

The day I arrived in Mangonui was hot and bright. I had gone to sleep in a house full of people and awakened to find the sun streaming in the windows and everybody gone. There were dishes with the remains of breakfast piled on the kitchen counter and cups with the dregs of the sweet hot drink that passes for coffee in New Zealand, a dusty, cocoa-colored powder, mixed with sugar, milk, and boiling water. But there was no one in evidence and the house seemed preternaturally still.

Seven must have heard me, though, because he suddenly materialized in the doorway.

"You want a cuppa?" he said.

We went outside and sat on the steps with our cups of coffee. I had a lot of questions. I wanted to know (again) how he spelled his name and how he pronounced it, and where he had come from, and what he was doing there, and who all those people were in the house, and what his relationship was to them. But I didn't ask any of them just yet. The sun was warm and there were some little birds pecking about in the grass and flitting back and forth between the bushes.

"So," I said, "what are you going to do now?"

"Heading out to Mangonui. Want to come?"

"Okay," I said, "sure."

We arrived at Seven's parents just in time for lunch. They were having fish heads, boiled with slices of onion and salt in an enormous pot, and Maori bread with slabs of butter. Eating a fish head, as it turns out, is not as easy as you might think. The brain, a creamy, gelatinous substance, can get lost if you aren't careful, and you have to suck the insides out of the eyes and spit out the clear thin case and the white marble of the eyeball.

My uncertainty about the process must have been obvious, because, before I knew what was happening, Seven's mother was back at the stove, battering and frying fillets of snapper just for me. She did it out of politeness for a Pakeha who plainly did not know what to do with a head, and I was grateful if somewhat embarrassed.

It was not much like the meals I had growing up. There was no more talking than what was needed to get something passed from the other side of the table. No one chatted about the weather or discussed political events. They ate with enormous concentration, not hurriedly, but with focus, and the only noise was the sound of sucking, as every bit of meat was extracted from the bones, and the clatter of silverware and dishes, and the quiet slurp of someone polishing off a drink, and, finally, the scrape of chairs pushing away from the table.

When the fish heads were all eaten and the bread was gone and everyone had had a big swig of water weakly flavored with powdered lemonade, we finished the meal with cups of tea.

"Milk?" asked Seven's mother.

"Lemon, if you have any," I said.

"Just like Dad. Faith, go get a lemon from the tree." After that it became a point of honor for me to drink my tea with lemon, though I became aware that I was reducing the tiny stock of lemon juice—the tree, being old, was not much of a producer—and potentially, at least, depriving Seven's father of one of his small pleasures.

Seven's parents were discreet in their inquiries about who I was and what I was doing there, and they asked me almost nothing about myself. Finally, after dinner, his father, speaking quietly and looking past my head as though it would be impolite to confront me with a direct question, said "Your family, they're far away?"

"They're in Boston, in the United States," I told him.

"*Long* way away," he said. And then, after a pause, "You must miss your home."

"I'm not sure I know where home is," I replied with the insouciance of a twenty something. To which he said nothing.

I have since wondered what he must have made of such a remark. At the time I was deaf to its absurdity, but now I can't help but think about the way it must have sounded to a man who lived on what could honestly be called ancestral land; who had never been farther than two hundred miles from the place where he was born; who, whether consciously or not, had spent much of his life defending his right and that of his children, against the pressures of commerce, modernization, and Pakeha land-hunger, to remain where he was. It's possible that he pitied me, though more likely that, with the wisdom of a man who had fathered many children, he just recognized that I was young.

But if I was a mystery to them, they were certainly a mystery to me. I knew nothing about how even the most elementary things were done, and was, in the local parlance, completely "useless." Offering to do the laundry for one of Seven's sisters, I washed the dark clothes first instead of the whites and had to throw out a whole tub of water that should, at that dry season, have been used two or three times. Trying to help another sister shuck oysters, I only succeeded in irritating her by breaking the tip of my blade. I can still see her, in her gum boots and apron, a big woman on an upturned bucket, shaking her head and waving me away. I could not dig shellfish without slicing my hands, I could not pry sea urchins from the rocks, even in shallow water. And I inspired hilarity by going about with a sarong draped over my hat to protect my skin from the burning antipodean sun. The smallest children were cleverer, more useful than I. But mostly people were amused by my incompetence, and even I could see that it was funny.

I stayed in Mangonui for a week, camping with Seven in a shack by the sea with no running water, eating snapper that he caught with a hand line and cooked over a fire. When we needed more food, we turned up at a house, his mother's or sister's or sister-in-law's, about the time that someone might be making supper. We had pork bones with dumplings and *puha*, a bitter weed that grows in orchards and along fence lines and sometimes beside the road. We had oysters and *kina*, or sea urchin roe, which is salty and strong, with a flavor like iodine, and addictive to those who are raised on it. We had *pipi*, a kind of sweet little clam, steamed just until they opened, and *paua*, or abalone, minced and sautéed in cream. We had lamb chops, and sausages, and "smashed" potatoes, buckets of loquats and passion fruit and plums.

Occasionally Seven had things to do. One day his father sent him to shoot feral cats in the bush at the bottom of the embankment. Another time one of his brothers wanted him to go out in the boat. They left early and were gone all day, returning about sunset with half a dozen sugar sacks full of crayfish and abalone. I spent much of this time sitting and watching the water. The beach was pebbly down by the waterline and littered with shells. The slope was gradual and the tide went a long way out and crept back slowly, lapping at the mud. Across the inlet the hills were darkly clothed with plantations of pine, and then gold and green where it opened out into pasture with scattered clumps of trees. There were no buildings, or roads, or houses to be seen in any direction and my mind invariably turned to the question of what it must have been like for the earliest settlers, with their European memories and their European eyes.

Sometimes I went for walks, wandering up the road or into the bush beyond the houses. I liked the drone of the cicadas in the midday heat, and the crunch of the dry grass, and the strange, pungent smell of something, an aromatic tree or shrub that I could never locate but that would suddenly surround me like some kind of enchantment and then vanish if I took another step. I got quieter and quieter as the days wore on, one hot, bright, summer day after another, and I found myself talking less and less. One day I said to Seven, "You know, I might stop talking altogether if I stay here too long." He just laughed and said nothing.

It was on one of these days when I was on my own that I first met Kura, the second youngest of Seven's sisters. She was about eighteen at the time, a handsome girl with thick, curly black hair, long legs, and a raucous manner. She had been slightly deafened in her youth, probably by an untreated ear infection, and had a tendency to shout. Perhaps because Seven was her favorite brother, perhaps because she was stuck at home and bored, we quickly became friends.

"I had this terrible dream last night," she told me.

"What was it?"

"I dreamed that all my teeth fell out!"

I laughed. "That's a classic dream, you know. They say it's got something to do with sex."

"Really?" she said. "Uh-oh. Don't tell Mum."

But what I thought it really had to do with was tooth decay. Kura and Seven were among the few young adults in Mangonui who still had all their own teeth. In fact, if anyone over the age of about thirty had a full set, you could be almost certain they weren't real. And a couple of people I met had had all their teeth pulled while they were still in their twenties because it was cheaper than getting them fixed.

I found this very shocking and the irony of it was inescapable, at least to me. One of the first things eighteenth- and early-nineteenth-century European visitors to New Zealand noticed was the Maoris' dazzling white teeth, so very different from their own. But along with guns, germs, and steel, came flour and sugar, and a diet that has led not only to widespread obesity and diabetes but to rampant tooth decay.

The other person I got to know fairly well in Mangonui was an old lady named Nana Miri, who lived on the flat below the embankment, a stone's throw from the sea. She was a small, energetic woman with strong features and a long plait of steel-gray hair, which she wore up in a bun. She had a taste for simplicity, clean lines and dark colors, and was always impeccably dressed. When she went out, she wore a yellow flax hat with a black band and black trousers or a long black skirt with a black or dark gray jersey. She carried a flax kit, or woven bag, a plain one for shopping, a patterned one for church.

Nana Miri was widely acknowledged to be one of Mangonui's finest weavers, but she always asserted that her friend Ngaire was finer still. One day she took me to see some of the things that Ngaire had made. Her kits were yellow and black, or sometimes red, made of fine, flexible flax and exquisitely patterned. They were considered great treasures by everyone who was lucky enough to be given one, as the knowledge of how to make them was disappearing along with the old ladies themselves.

Most of the people in Mangonui were cautiously polite in their dealings with me, though some, like Nana Miri and Kura, were more open and unguarded. But there were a few people in the village who made me nervous. One day Seven took me to see one of his cousins, a big, fearsome man with a lot of black hair who lived in a dark little cabin with his wife and a jumble of little kids. His wife was not, like Seven's mother, a force of nature, but a famished-looking creature who'd been pretty once and who'd had five pregnancies in seven years, including a baby who had died for no apparent reason. To me it seemed that she worked like a coolie: cooking, washing, cleaning, even fetching her own water from the spring. She kept her head down and said little, and, though it might have been my imagination, I thought she kept a wary eye on her husband.

There were a certain number of women like her in Mangonui and a certain number of men like him. But Seven was nothing like them. He may have worn black leather and dark glasses like the rest, but he didn't come across like a gang member. The difference was not so much what he wore as how he carried himself, how he dealt with other people, how he seemed to feel about the world. They said in his family that it was because he was both the youngest and the biggest of the boys. He never had a chip on his shoulder, never had to prove anything or show how powerful he was.

But even he took a certain pleasure in retelling the stories of his various fights: how he'd once hit a guy so hard the skin of his face slid sideways across his skull; how he'd caught another under the chin in the parking lot of a pub and lifted him clean off the ground; how he'd once popped one of his older brothers and run, terrified at what he'd done. He told these stories laughing, without malice, as though he was still surprised that any of it had ever happened, as though none of it, really, had anything to do with him.

Seven was the easiest person to be with I had ever met. He was like someone who fit perfectly in his own skin, someone entirely at home in the world. He was tolerant of others and nonjudgmental and he honestly didn't care what anyone else thought. His calm was something new to me, a lack of striving, an imperturbability that I found curious but magnetic, and I sometimes wondered if it was this quality that lay behind all those eighteenth-century stories about the gentle, easygoing Polynesians.

The days passed in a haze. When we wanted a shower, we borrowed the key to the shower block at the *marae*. When we wanted to go swimming, we caught a lift up the road to the other side of the peninsula where the open ocean crashed on a white sand beach and a handful of offshore islands floated on the sea.

One day the whole family crammed into a couple of cars and made the trek to a little cove where there was a colony of sea urchins. I went, as usual, slathered in sunscreen, with dark glasses and a hat and a long-sleeved shirt and the ubiquitous sarong, now keeping my legs from sunburn, now covering my head. Everyone else was in bathing suits and shorts, their skin almost black from exposure by this time of the year. I waded out with Seven's mother, knee-deep in the water, searching for the spiky, well-camouflaged shells. The idea was to reach in quickly and twist them off the rocks, but the spines were sharp and I was afraid of them and clumsy in my approach. Invariably the creatures felt me and sucked themselves closer to the rock. Once they'd done that, it was impossible to loosen them; you might as well have tried to pry a brick from a finished wall.

Eventually, I wandered up to the top of the beach and installed myself under a large pohutukawa tree. They say that the first Maoris to reach New Zealand, sailing there in canoes from the islands to the north, were so excited by the sight of a pohutukawa that they threw their sacred red feathers into the sea, only to discover that what they had mistaken for flocks of bright birds were, in fact, the tree's red blossoms. It is a story about false appearances and precipitate acts, and if I had known it then perhaps I would have given it some thought. But by then I was more or less caught in a spell woven by the sun and the sea and the strangeness of everything around me.

When I finally shook myself awake and realized I had to get back to Australia, Seven hitchhiked down to Auckland to see me off. We said good-bye at the airport awkwardly, neither of us having any clear idea of what, if anything, might be next. I gave him my address and phone number, though I somehow doubted that he'd call. He gave me a number in Whangarei where he said he could be reached.

I was back in Melbourne within hours, but for weeks I felt as though I'd left some piece of me behind. I wandered around in a fog, finding it impossible to settle down. I wanted to talk about what had happened and, at the same time, I wanted to keep it to myself. Actually, I wasn't quite sure what *had* happened.

One of my friends, a professor of politics, once told me jokingly that it had come to him in a blinding flash that he was trapped in the body of a European when, in truth, he was actually Bengali. This, I thought, was a little like what had just happened to me. It wasn't that I thought I was a Maori trapped in the skin of a New Englander, but something about the place and the people, something about Seven and the inlet and the sea, made me feel as though I had discovered something new and marvelous, as though I had arrived at wherever I was meant to be.

At first, I just sat and wondered what, if anything, I should do. I knew that if I did nothing, the power of these impressions would inevitably fade. But I couldn't stand the prospect of just letting everything go back to the way it had been before. I felt as though I'd been shown something, taught something, offered something, and I wasn't ready to let it go.

After a couple of weeks, I screwed my courage to the sticking place and put a call through to the boardinghouse where Seven said I might find him. It was hard to get through, and when I finally reached him, he sounded kind of surprised.

"So," I said, without too much preamble, "why don't you come to Australia?"

He said he'd been thinking about it. He had in mind to go to Brisbane, where a couple of his cousins lived.

"Brisbane!" I nearly shouted. "What do you want to go to Brisbane for? Come to Melbourne. Just call and let me know which plane you're on. I'll meet you at the airport."

He arrived in Melbourne a month later with a gym bag that he carried on the plane. I wasn't entirely sure I would recognize him and almost called out to another Maori of about his size who was among the first passengers off. When he finally came through the doors, almost the last to disembark, I was seriously considering the possibility that he had decided not to come at all.

In the gym bag he had one pair of shorts, three T-shirts,

some socks, underwear, and two little wooden-handled trow-els that were the tools of his trade. This, plus the jeans, shirt, and jacket that he had on his back, was the sum of his worldly possessions, or at least everything he thought he needed to move to another country. It was the flip side, as I later discovered, of his irresponsibility, but I think it was this that clinched it for me. Even though I quickly burdened him with all the trappings of ordinary life, he never lost the lightness of touch that that gym bag represented.

4

TERRA INCOGNITA

A T THE TIME of this, my first visit to New Zealand, I was about halfway through my doctoral dissertation on the European literature of the Pacific. A dissertation is a demonstration of scholarship, an account of what is already known about a subject to which one adds a contribution of original research. It is a project in which one's own experience, that is, one's *personal* experience, plays no proper part. And yet, although I read and read, it struck me forcibly that it was only when I experienced things firsthand that they acquired real meaning for me.

I mentioned this to the chairman of my department at our first meeting of the new year. I was just back from my trip and the intense impressions it had made on me were uppermost in my mind. I had brought a chapter of my thesis with me. It was a section in which I was trying to explain why the writers I was studying routinely made a point of referring to the events of their own lives, building their stories around what had happened to them. "You know that great line of Conrad's," I said. "*A writing may be lost; a lie may be written; but what the eye has seen is truth and remains in the mind. Melville, Conrad, Malinowski, what would they have been without ships and tents?"

The chairman, an extremely tall deconstructionist, looked displeased. Still, he agreed to look over my chapter, and at the end of the week there was a note in my mailbox saying I could come and pick it up.

The door to his office was shut when I got there. I knocked and heard a voice say, "Come in." He was sitting at a desk piled high with papers, every wall from floor to ceiling was filled with books. He turned in his chair and, without rising, held out the paper for me to take. "I'm sorry," he said, "but I don't think there's anything in this you can use."

"You really think it's that bad?" I asked him.

"I'm afraid so, yes."

Attached to the front of my paper was a one-page critique, which I read as soon as the office door had closed behind me. The piece, the chairman noted, was pleasantly written, but this was, unfortunately, its only virtue. On the downside, there were theoretical difficulties. I had failed to say anything new not only about the authors or their writings, but about "the intertextual processes of establishment of authority via discourses of experience or empirical observation." I had also made the mistake of presenting empiricism "as a form of simplicity," rather than "as a metaphysically complex mode of representation," and of validating the "authority-effect" that writers like Conrad and Melville had tried to achieve at the expense of "exploring the empirical as a reality-projecting mode of textuality."

I had, in other words, taken my writers at face value, naïvely accepting what they had to say and secretly, though obviously transparently, hoping to peer through their words to the world as it had been—or not even as it had been, but as they had experienced it—a world that they had actually lived in but that I could only read about in books.

I knew it was unsophisticated. I knew that I had effectively abandoned the critical project in favor of a hopeless attempt to grasp *what it had actually been like* to be there on the beach. I had been a graduate student long enough to know how this kind of unreconstructed romanticism would be greeted within the academy. But I also knew that I *was* a romantic—not in the ordinary sense of being preoccupied with love affairs and triangles—but in the more specialized, even technical sense of possessing a Romantic sensibility. What I liked was adventure and excitement; I liked Lawrence of Arabia and Sir Walter Scott. I was incurably drawn to heroism and melancholy and anything that smacked of the mysterious, the exotic, or remote. It was what I was doing there in the first place—not in the office of the English department chairman, but in this far-flung corner of the world.

The Pacific was not, on the surface, an obvious place for me to be. I had grown up in Boston and knew almost nothing of islands or the sea, having spent the summers of my youth in Europe visiting museums with my mother while my father taught, and reading a great deal, especially Victorian novels. I imagined myself as little Mary Lennox in *The Secret Garden* or Sara Crewe, and my mind was filled with cavernous and drafty English manor houses and half-formed images of moors.

But if you are raised on a steady diet of Frances Hodgson Burnett, you can hardly come away from it without some feeling for the colonies. The England of my imagination was one that belonged, strictly speaking, to my mother's childhood: a great, sprawling empire that covered most of the map—India and Ceylon, Shanghai and Cape Town, Burma, Barbados, Guyana, Brunei. A world of vast riches and utter squalor, it was where, in the sorts of stories I liked, people went to make their fortunes or to disappear if they were in disgrace. It was where they returned from, *if* they returned, and where, if they didn't, they had either gone native or contracted the cholera and died.

It was all long gone in reality, but even in my own life there were occasional odd eruptions of Europe's imperial past. The visits, for example, of my mother's maiden aunt, who had taken a Grand Tour in the 1920s and who periodically descended upon us in a cloud of tea rose and camphor tar. She was quite deaf and rather strange and I dreaded her arrival, but she always brought me curious things: stiff little boots made of reindeer hide with curled-up toes and woolen tassels, or aromatic cigarette boxes inlaid with ivory and mother-of-pearl. It was enough to make one nostalgic for the days of ocean travel, for deck chairs and steamer trunks and the idea of *going abroad*.

"Abroad" had mostly meant Europe and the mysterious East, but for me it turned out to be Australia. I had been working as a secretary since leaving college and I was desperate to get away. On impulse I applied for a fellowship to study in Australia. I was not going to study mining and metallurgy, or marine biology, or veterinary science, or any of the fields for which Australia is known, however. I was going to read Australian literature.

"Hah," said my brother. "That won't take long."

But the novelty of it must have struck someone on the fellowship committee, because they awarded me a grant.

The whole process took almost a year of planning, and for much of that time I slept in a room with a map of Australia pinned to the sloping ceiling above my bed. The land on the map was yellow and the sea was blue. A tracery of red lines indicating roads and a scattering of thin blue rivers stretched inland from the coasts for a few inches and petered out. There was a network of large lakes in the interior, depicted, interestingly, not in the blue of water but in the white of salt. Not really lakes at all, they represented huge salt pans, the crystalline dregs of an ancient inland sea. Across the open expanse of the map's middle were scattered a handful of names: the Great Sandy Desert, the Little Sandy Desert, the Stony Desert, the Nullarbor Plain.

I had heard about the Nullarbor from my father, who had done a stint in Australia during World War II. It was not a name like so many others—Wagga Wagga, Wollongong, Moranbah, Kalgoorlie—not an Aboriginal name at all. "*Nulla arbor*," he told me, "Latin for *no tree*."

My father was in the submarine service and he spent the early part of the war training crews in Chicago until, finally, he could no longer stand it and asked to be transferred to active duty. He was sent out to the U.S. naval base in Brisbane, Australia, as a relieving officer for one of the Pacific fleet's submarine crews. From there, the men were transported by rail to Fremantle, just south of Perth. This meant crossing from one side of Australia to the other, a distance, as the crow flies, of some 2,300 miles. On the ground, though, it was much longer. They followed a route that hugged the coast—all the way down through New South Wales, around Victoria, up through South Australia, and across the western desert—a journey of over 4,000 miles. At Port Augusta, about halfway, they left what passed for civilization. The land around them was broken and stony, the clouds were thin and high.

It was hot along the Nullarbor and the train periodically stopped to water. The men would get out to stretch and smoke and eat a meal of the mutton stew that my father grew to hate with an enduring passion. When they had finished, the mess crew would take the big cooking pots and dump what was left on the ground beside the tracks. One time, my father told me, as the train was pulling away, he looked back and saw a group of people—men, children, women, dogs—materialize out of the bush and gather up the remnants of the food. "They must have been there all the time," he said, "watching, waiting for us to go away."

During that year leading up to my departure, I kept a book on my bedside table. It was the only book I had actually read about Australia, and I had found it quite by chance in a secondhand bookshop near where I worked. It was called *Voss* and it had been written by Australia's Nobel laureate, Patrick White. The cover showed a detail from a nineteenth-century painting by Frederick McCubbin called *Down on His Luck*. In it a bearded man in moleskins and a battered hat sits looking despondently at a small fire. Behind him the bush looms, not dense and dark like the forests of a German fairy tale, but thin and dappled and disorienting. It was easy to imagine thin, brown people standing perfectly still with their tall, thin spears, half-hidden in the spindly trees.

Voss is the story of an explorer who walks out into the blazing Australian desert and dies. The novel, which was first published in 1958, is based on a famous nineteenth-century overland expedition. In 1848 a German scientist named Ludwig Leichhardt attempted a direct route from Brisbane to Perth—the same route my father would have taken had there been a railway or a road—across a landscape dotted with names like Mount Hopeless, the Moon Desert, and Lake Blanche. But it was no more possible to travel straight across the parched interior of Australia in 1944 than it had been a century earlier.

Leichhardt's party consisted of seven white men mounted on horses and two Aboriginal guides who walked. Last seen leaving a sheep station on the Darling Downs, the entire expedition vanished without a trace. Nothing was ever found of them, not a stirrup, not a button, not a bit of leather strap. Various theories surfaced: that they were washed away in a flash flood, or burned up in a bushfire, or speared by hostile Aborigines. But the most likely scenario is that they simply struggled on, farther and farther into country that proved increasingly inhospitable, through spinifex and stunted forest and a maze of dry creek beds, hoping always for higher ground and for water until, finally, it was too late to turn back.

Voss, the Leichhardt-figure in the novel, similarly sets off on a long slog toward death. "He is going on this great expedition," says one of the characters. "You know, to find an inland sea. Or is it gold?" In fact, Voss's quest is not for wealth or power or even information about the height of Australia's mountain ranges or which way the rivers run. He is a Romantic hero driven by some internal need to cross great tracts of difficult land, to expose himself to risks and dangers, to suffer, and ultimately to die.

The sensibility was familiar to me but the setting was entirely new. Exploration was not something we thought much about in Boston, where our stories were of Pilgrims and Minutemen and hanging lanterns in the church. I myself was descended from settlers, who were not the same as explorers, and although there must have been explorers who came before them, I had no idea who they were. Of course, there *were* American explorers who had crossed the plains and the Rockies and discovered the source of the Mississippi and the Great Salt Lake. But that was all in the West and had little to do with New England. The only other explorers I knew of were Spaniards (well, Italians, actually) whose names we dutifully chanted at school—*In fourteen hundred and ninety-two, Columbus sailed the ocean blue*—and a handful of

Norsemen who had, purportedly, set foot somewhere in Canada in the exceedingly distant past.

But something about White's operatic treatment of the quest—a journey, as one of the characters puts it, "of dust, and flies, and dying horses"—struck a chord in me. I was all of twenty-three and White's themes of alienation and longing, of risk taking and rebellion, were like music to my ears. I identified, above all, with White's fixation on the unattainable. "Places yet unvisited," writes White, "can become an obsession, promising final peace, all goodness." This was something I thought I understood.

Perhaps the effect on me of this novel would have been less profound had it not dovetailed so neatly with the handful of Australian films that were playing in American cinemas at the time. These movies—films like *Breaker Morant* and *Walkabout* and *Picnic at Hanging Rock*—were mostly set in the nineteenth century and featured girls in frocks and men on horses and children who got lost in the bush. The stories were bleak and unresolved: crimes were committed and the wrong man punished; the children who got lost were never found. But the settings were spectacularly beautiful and the films made me want to set out immediately for a place that was, as I understood it, mysterious, empty, and exotic in a hot, dry sort of way.

There was one film, in particular, that impressed me, a made-for-television movie called *The Plumber*, directed by Peter Weir. It was unlike all the other Australian movies I had seen in that it took no advantage whatsoever of Australia's panoramic potential. It was the story of a graduate student in anthropology, who spends all her time alone in a tiny high-rise apartment, studying videotapes and photographs of Melanesian men. Her husband is a young, ambitious doctor who spends all *his* time at the lab and seems not to be paying very much attention to what is going on at home. One day there's a knock on the apartment door and a big guy with a lot of curly black hair is standing in the hallway. He's wearing blue jeans and a utility belt hung with tools that bounce against his hip. "I'm the plumber," he says. And she says, "What plumber?" And he says, "I'm here to check the plumbing." And she says, "I didn't call for anyone to check the plumbing." And he says, "It's just a routine thing." And she hesitates a second and then she says, "OK," and lets him in.

The fact that *Voss* was an inane guidebook for someone going to live in late-twentieth-century urban Australia, or that *The Plumber* was more about class warfare than transgressive sex, had no effect whatsoever on my enthusiasm. Nor did the fact that virtually every other American or Canadian graduate student I met, and a fair few of the Germans, Dutch, and Scandinavians, was also writing about explorers. It was as though we had all found copies of the same novel and were all giddy with the excitement of traveling to a place from which, we imagined romantically, we might never return.

Our professors, who were, of course, Australians, viewed us with varying degrees of humor and contempt, as did most of the Australian students, who were bent on deconstructing the colonial system in which they considered themselves mired. But, as I had been trying to explain to my chairman, we were all just working from experience. We, who came from else-where, were drawn to stories about other people who had come from someplace else. They, who had always been there, were completely uninterested in the idea of discovery. They had other things to think about, like, for instance, getting away.

It was sometimes frustrating to be so out of sync with the general tenor of the department, but I was lucky in that the thesis advisor assigned to me was a poet. A good-natured bon vivant with a shock of wiry gray hair, he was quite unconcerned by the seeming naïveté of my approach. "Don't fret," he would say cheerfully, "all dissertations are autobiographical."

Perhaps this is more true in Australia, where graduate school is conducted on the English model, in a manner quite unlike that in the States. My degree was "by thesis only" and I had no obligation either to take any classes or to pass any exams. This left me entirely free to determine my own course of study and, since I was comparatively unsupervised, I ranged all over the map.

I filled my study carrel and my bibliographies with books that had almost nothing in common with one another. They were not bound by period, or genre, or discipline; they were not written by the same sort of people, or at the same time, or even under circumstances that were remotely similar. There were seventeenth-century Dutch travelogues, French anthropological classics, British pulp fiction from between the wars, and contemporary Australian novels. True, they had a certain geographic logic, but one could hardly make a thesis out of that—*Everything Ever Written About a Certain Place*? No, what appealed to me about these books was something I found difficult to explain, much less to justify academically, though I thought it had something to do with what Conrad, in one of his last essays, called "the great spirit of the realities of the story."

A lot of the titles I liked began with a preposition suggesting movement—*On the Wool Track*, *Towards New Holland*, *Under Tropic Skies*—or named a body of water—*The Blue Lagoon*, *The Spanish Lake*, *The Merry-Go-Round in the Sea*. I liked the panoramic feel of *The Peopling of the British Per-*

ipheries or *The Fate of Adventure in the Western World*, and
the intimacy of *A Diary in the Strict Sense of the Term* or
Letters from the Field. Sometimes, when I was stuck somewhere, I would arrange them into little poems:

> *The Fateful Voyage of the St. Jean Baptiste*
> *Men Against the Sea*
> *The Enchafèd Flood, The Fatal Shore*
> *Leaves of the Banyan Tree.*

Or I might make lists of alliterative titles—*South Sea Super-
cargo, Travelers and Travel Liars*—or titles of only one
word—*Victory, Tracks, Typee*. What I liked was the enormous sense of possibility, a sense not only of what had
actually happened, but of what had almost happened, what
might have happened, what might still happen to someone,
namely me.

I would set myself up in my favorite spot in the university
library, an armchair on the second floor with a view across
the tops of the plane trees to a range of smoky blue hills in
the east, and think about the adventures that had brought
these books into being. I thought about the explorer Charles
Sturt, who rode into the searing heart of Australia with a
whaleboat in pieces that he planned to launch upon an inland
sea. Or poor Burke and Wills, who walked all the way from
Adelaide to the Gulf of Carpentaria and almost all the way
back. I envisioned clouds of pink galahs, glittering white salt
pans, basins strewn with rust-colored rocks. All of Australia
seemed laid out before me, and beyond Australia, the Pacific,
the islands, and the sea.

My friends all thought I was ridiculous, though in an
endearing sort of way. "You're such a *dag*," they would

say to me when I showed them my maps with the routes of the explorers plotted in several colors of ink. But I don't think any of them appreciated how seriously I felt about it or how profoundly—especially once I had come back from New Zealand—my scholarship was entangled with my life.

5

PRESENT PERFECT

SUMMER WAS COMING to an end when Seven arrived in Australia. At the time I was living alone in a three-room flat in a residential neighborhood near the university. Mine was one of four apartments in what had once been a single-family Victorian home, and up until then I had thought it perfectly comfortable. But Seven was over six feet tall and broad in the shoulders. With him in it, my flat suddenly felt tiny. The showerhead was so low he had to stoop to get under it, and if we sat together at the kitchen table, one of us had to leave the room if the other wanted something from the fridge. The chairs were rickety and creaked when he sat on them, and my couch, a cheap affair made entirely of foam rubber, simply collapsed under his weight. There was, however, a nice little balcony, and during the waning days of summer and those first crisp autumn weeks, we often sat with our feet up on the railing and ate grilled octopus and stuffed grape leaves from the Greek takeaway down the road.

We settled in together amazingly quickly, and after a couple of weeks, Seven decided to get a job. He was hired at the first place he applied: a foundry out on the edge of the city where they made cast-iron gratings and veranda lace. It was a large, smoky factory filled with immigrants who all kept to their own ethnic gangs. The Italian Australians warned him about the

Greek Australians, who, in turn, told him to keep an eye on the Turks. Seven was the only Maori and he moved easily among them. But it was a far cry from the neat little engineering shop he'd worked in back in New Zealand, where they made bronze and aluminum parts for luxury yachts, and he began to think about doing something different. I, of course, continued to go to school.

But it was a whole new life for me. I started getting up at five to eat breakfast with Seven before he went off to work. It was still dark then and beginning to get cold in the mornings, and we ate large hot breakfasts of porridge and eggs, instead of my usual coffee and a slice of toast. He was home by three in the afternoon, when normally I'd have been at the library. It was not a schedule that any of the other graduate students kept and I began to drift away somewhat from the life of the university.

Then, late that autumn, we decided it was time to find a house. The flat was just not big enough, especially with winter coming and the balcony out of use, and Seven wanted to be closer to the sea. So we left the neighborhood where I had lived ever since coming to Australia and headed for the beach.

The bayside suburbs were expensive but eventually we found a house we could afford to rent. It was what is quaintly known as a "workingman's cottage"—three rooms and a hall with a bathroom tacked on at the back and a long, narrow backyard full of weeds. It was deceptively pretty from the outside, with a bit of lace on the veranda and a picket fence all wound about with a pink climbing rose. But, on closer inspection, it was really kind of a wreck. The inside had been recently carpeted and slapped with a coat of chalky gray paint, but otherwise it was almost as basic as it had been in the 1890s— with the addition, perhaps, of electricity and plumbing.

Winters in Melbourne are cold and damp and quite unlike the rest of Australia. The English, who settled the country, replicated the housing they had at home—as unsuitable on one side of the world as it was on the other—and built rows and rows of cold brick houses with inadequate heating and little light. Ours was no exception; although smaller than many, it was as damp and chilly and dark as the best. The only source of heat was a shallow fireplace in the front room, which I used as a study and which, I thought, must once have served as some poor workingwoman's parlor. The fireplace smoked horribly, and when we moved out, all my books had a brownish tinge, as though they'd been lightly toasted.

The next room, going down the hall, was the bedroom. It was a small room with a single window and a view of the laundry line and the cracked concrete. It had just enough space for a bed, which was pushed up against the wall that it shared with the front room. When the fire had been going all day, you could feel the heat of it in the bricks. Once, when I put my hand on the wall, it felt so hot I thought it might burst into flame, but it did have the advantage of warming the pillows nicely.

At the end of the hall was the third and final room: a combined kitchen, living room, dining room, and bicycle workshop. It was furnished with a kitchen table and four mismatched chairs, the foam rubber couch from the previous apartment, and an ancient, garishly painted refrigerator. At the very back, next to the sink, was the entrance to the bathroom. Obviously an afterthought, it was only half the size of a normal door, and Seven had to turn sideways to go through it. Needless to say, when it rained, the roof of the bathroom leaked.

But we liked it down there by the beach. We could ride our bikes to the market and the water was only a block away.

Seven quit his job at the foundry and became a bicycle messenger, riding with a rugged group of Canadians and Australians and New Zealanders. They were a tight-knit tribe, all young and fit, easy to spot as they swooped through the city in their fluorescent green and black Lycra with their radios and their bags.

There was, despite the comparative squalor, a lot that was charming about this life: the tie-dyed T-shirts on the line, the yard-sale crockery, the weeds valiantly struggling up through the cracks. I washed our clothes in a machine that I kept in a lean-to and rolled into the yard when I wanted to use it, filling it with a hose from the kitchen sink. It was unlike any washing machine I'd ever seen: a rectangular tin tub with an agitator on one wall and a wringer on the top. Washing machines with wringers—two rollers through which you feed the clothing in order to squeeze out the excess water—had last been seen in Boston about a decade before I was born, and the first one I ever saw was in Mangonui. It was all somewhat eccentric, but I had a taste for the bohemian life, and, as for Seven, well, I never could make out if he just didn't notice or if it wasn't all that different from the way he'd always lived.

He was the one, in any case, who had what it took to make living like this fun. Take, for instance, the way he fixed the doorbell. Early on, we discovered that the doorbell on our cottage didn't ring and that, if we were out back, which we mostly were, we couldn't hear anyone knocking. So Seven decided to make us a doorbell out of a block of wood, a toy motor, a bicycle bell, two bamboo skewers, three corks, a pair of paper clips, and two keys.

The contraption, which was mounted on a wooden crate in the kitchen, was wired to the buzzer at the front door. When someone pushed the buzzer, it made the motor turn. Stuck upright on the motor was one of the bamboo skewers to which the second skewer was perpendicularly affixed by means of a cork. On either end of the crosspiece was another cork, from which dangled a paper clip hung with a key. A bicycle bell was mounted next to the motor and, as the motor turned and the skewers rotated, the keys swung around and hit the bell. *Ding, ding, ding, ding.*

I later learned that they have a name for this in New Zealand: it's called a "number eight fencing wire approach" and refers to a particularly versatile gauge of wire—the kind you might use to tie up your muffler if it happened to come loose on a bumpy road, the kind that, in a rural country, you can easily enough lay your hands on if you don't mind snipping out a section of some farmer's fence. New Zealanders pride themselves on "Kiwi ingenuity" and a "do-it-yourself" approach to life. It's no doubt an attitude born of isolation; one can easily imagine how important it might have been in the days when replacement parts and special materials had to come all the way from England by ship.

But I thought it was a Maori thing and had even heard (though it may be apocryphal) that one of New Zealand's prime ministers had once joked: "What would the Maori do without number eight wire?" It was, as I understood it, an admiring if somewhat backhanded remark that combined a fond affection for Maori ingenuity with the vaguely racist suggestion that Maoris were not too particular about whose wire they used. But it made sense to me that the people in New Zealand who had the least would be the best at making do. And even though I, too, came from a family in which this sort of creativity was highly valued—my father had once fixed a car with the button from a baby's jacket—I'd never met anyone more ingenious than Seven in this respect. He was not only a tremendous scavenger, always finding whatever he needed in the junk that other people threw away; he was expert at thinking outside the box. In fact, as time went on, I began to wonder if he ever thought inside it.

There was a lot about this new life that I found fascinating, and I threw myself into it, not quite forsaking the old but, from the point of view of my colleagues at the university, more or less disappearing from view. I was still enrolled and receiving a stipend, however, and eventually I had to resurface. "Maybe you could call it fieldwork," I suggested, when I finally fronted up to my supervisor.

I wasn't entirely joking. Part of what I loved about Seven was how utterly different he was from me. This was not just a matter of looks or background or even what one might call worldview. It was deeper than that, I thought, maybe older. The Maori author Patricia Grace once wrote that "there's a way the older people have of telling a story, a way where the beginning is not the beginning, the end is not the end. It starts from the centre and moves away from there in such widening circles that you don't know how you will finally arrive at a point of understanding, which becomes itself another core, a new centre." I often felt like this about Seven when he tried to tell a story or give an account of something he knew; it was as though he told it inside out or explained it starting in the middle. His narratives, like his ingenuity, seemed part and parcel of a larger sensibility, the logic of which twisted and turned like a set of French curves or the coils and branches of a Maori carving.

He had a lot of weird ideas—some good, some bad, but all unexpected. He was a great believer in conspiracies and was inclined to see the hand of an unknown agency in any kind of unexplained event (and even in some that were not so difficult to account for). He was deeply suspicious of official explanations, a fact that I attributed to his general mistrust of authority figures—who, as he pointed out, had never been particularly on his side—but perfectly willing to countenance supernatural possibilities.

Maoris are famously leery of the dead and I could never get Seven to wander around old graveyards with me to look at the stones. His views on the subject were not clearly formulated; he couldn't explain it, it was just a feeling he had. But he did tell me once about a time when he'd woken in the middle of the night with a powerful sensation that something was clinging to his back. He tried to shake it off, but no matter what he did, it held on to him. The next morning he learned that a friend of his had died during the night. "That's what it was," he told me. "It was Pete, paying me a visit."

Now, I myself am a rationalist. I have never believed in ghosts or extrasensory perception or that the earth etchings in the Peruvian desert were left there by beings from another world. And while, for the most part, I appreciated Seven's open-mindedness, there were times when his willingness to countenance outlandish explanations drove me quite mad. "How can I listen to you?" I would say. "You think that Earth has been visited by aliens!" His response to these outbursts was so mild, however, that anyone observing us would certainly have concluded that he was the reasonable one.

Once, when we were having one of these conversations, I accused him of being superstitious.

"No, I'm not," he said calmly.

"Yes you are. You believe in UFOs."

"Are you going to tell me that there is no other intelligent life in the universe?"

"No," I countered. "There probably is intelligent life some-where in the universe. I just don't think it's been here. You watch those programs about unexplained phenomena, you get visited by the dead."

"Not regularly," he said.

Many of Seven's virtues seemed like things that might have been advantageous in another place and time. He had many of the qualities Maoris prize in a man—lateral thinking, independence, bravery, tremendous cool—and I sometimes thought it was a pity that he hadn't been born two centuries earlier. He was a great avoider of implications and seemed to consider it unmanly to appear too interested in what things meant. He had no taste at all for competition—except, of course, in sports—and he never did anything just because it was what he was "supposed" to do. He had a disregard for convention so complete (I still remember the first time he drove up onto the sidewalk in order to get around some obstacle in the road) that it could only have been a form of rebellion in anyone else, though in him it seemed more like a kind of innocence. He was easy to please, difficult to anger, and utterly uncritical. He never judged others and seemed not to care—or even particularly to notice—if they judged him.

But the thing about him that I found most intriguing was the way he thought (or didn't think) about the future. Seven was constitutionally incapable of planning: he was a fatalist and an optimist at the same time. If he set out for someplace without directions, he would find it anyway by chance. If he wanted to go somewhere crowded—a hotel by the sea on a holiday weekend, say—he would just turn up and there would be a sudden cancellation. He never decided where he was going, he just ended up wherever he was. He could never commit to a meal in advance, because how could he be sure, when the time came, that he'd be hungry?

While I adored this dedication to spontaneity in the abstract, in practice it could be trying. I was inclined to want to survey the field, to consider the options, to make informed, rational decisions about what ought to be done. But this involved projecting possible outcomes, something Seven was either unwilling or unable to do. If, for example, we were traveling and arrived at dinnertime in a country town, I would want to look at each of the restaurants before choosing one in which to eat. Seven would pick the first one that he came to. "Some people map out their lives like an arrow," he once told me. "I just wait for an arrow to drop in front of me."

It was not, I came to think, merely a matter of impulsivity, but of a different way of looking at the world. I had been raised, for example, to believe that if a conflict arose between what I wanted and the expectations of others, I didn't *have* to fall on my sword, but I certainly had to consider it. But this kind of thinking was entirely foreign to Seven. It was not that he was unwilling to do things for others; on the contrary, he was generous to a fault. But the idea of doing something as a matter of duty—rather than of choice—seemed to him nonsensical. It was almost as though the idea offended him, as though in subordinating his own impulses he would be giving way to some kind of oppression, as though maintaining his right to do as he wanted were a matter of personal pride.

To be fair, Seven extended this ideal to everyone and never expected other people to modify their behavior on his behalf. He was content to let the chips fall where they may and assumed that everyone else was also. And over time I came to feel that this lightness of being defined him as completely as any single characteristic could.

It is, of course, one of the great clichés of European colonialism that natives can be distinguished from colonizers by the way they think about time. We still speak of "island time," a kind of slow time or even no time, but the idea has antecedents in Western thinking that go back at least to the ancient Greeks. There were numerous legends in the ancient world of lands of perpetual summer where miraculous fertility gave abundance without toil and people passed their days in pleasure, free from tyranny, disease, and war. Such stories belong to an enduring, maybe even universal, mythology of escape—from work, from duty, from cold and hunger, from time itself, from death. For most of history these are understood to be imaginary places. But every once in a while they get mapped onto something actual and people suppose for a moment that these mythic Elysiums are real.

Tahiti lies in the middle of the Pacific Ocean, just south of the equator, almost equidistant from Australia and Peru. It is the largest of what are known as the Society Islands, so named by Cook for their close proximity to one another in the middle of a large and largely empty sea. Tahiti had been occupied by Polynesians for perhaps two thousand years when it came to the attention of the European world in the mid-eighteenth century. It was discovered in 1767 by Captain Samuel Wallis of the *Dolphin*, in the course of an expedition to the South Seas.

Wallis reached Tahiti ten months after setting out from England. He'd had an arduous crawl through the Straits of Magellan, seventeen weeks with the wind in his teeth in the narrow, perilous waters. Parted from his supply ship along the way, he was short of everything, especially food, and his crew was suffering badly from scurvy. The first sign of relief came in the form of a scattering of low coral atolls—the Tuamotu Archipelago. A few days later the first of the high islands appeared on the horizon. It was a sight that "made us all rejoice," wrote the master of the *Dolphin*, "and filled us with the greatest hopes imaginable."

Tahiti, in the eighteenth century, was everything that Europe was not. It was warm and tranquil, salubrious, unspoiled. Food fell literally from the trees: coconuts, breadfruit, bananas, and vi-apple, also known as Tahitian quince. There was fish and pork in abundance and the valleys and gardens produced wild ginger, sugarcane, taro, and yams. Polynesians generally conformed to European ideals of physical beauty, but many travelers considered Tahitians the most beautiful people they had ever seen. The islanders were tall and well-proportioned with regular features and long dark hair. Early observers remarked their fondness for bathing, the "singular beauty of their teeth," and their habit of dressing their hair with oil scented with "something like roses." They had no predators and few pests, and the islands they inhabited were not plagued by the diseases of crowded, unsanitary European cities, or fever-ridden tropical ports like Batavia, where so many Europeans died. No wonder that to the tired, grubby, hungry sailors who discovered it, Tahiti seemed a paradise on earth.

Wallis and his crew stayed five weeks and sailed on, observing regretfully that some would have remained if they could have been sure of a ship to come and get them in a few years' time. They claimed the island for the British Crown, naming it in honor of King George III. But before Wallis could even get home to tell the story, Tahiti was discovered and claimed again—this time by France. Unaware that he'd been preceded, Louis-Antoine de Bougainville took possession of Tahiti in the name of his Most Christian Majesty, Louis XV and, in a fit of Gallic enthusiasm, named the island New Cythera after the place at which Aphrodite had risen from the sea. As Bougainville, too, took his leave, he remarked that the worst consequence of shipwreck in this remote corner of the world "would have been to pass the remainder of our days on an isle adorned with all the gifts of nature, and to exchange the sweets of the mother-country, for a peaceable life, exempted from cares."

It was not long before news of these discoveries began circulating back in Europe. The first published account of Tahiti, written anonymously and printed in France, told of an island of haunting beauty inhabited by people who lived "in peace among themselves and know neither hatred, quarrels, dissension, nor civil war." They did no work, they had no industry, they knew nothing of private property or trade. They ate and drank whenever they wanted, had sex with whomever they liked, and danced "naturally and without any set order." The theme of the narrative was innocence, sometimes negatively portrayed as backwardness, sometimes positively as freedom from constraint. But at the heart of it all was the observation that "the New Cytherians know nothing of the duration or of the origin of their existence, and, caring little about the past, concern themselves only with the present."

It has always struck me as one of the great ironies of this particular moment in history that the apparent discovery of a people for whom time did not exist should coincide with a frantic race in Europe to develop a seagoing clock. At issue was the problem of longitude. Mariners had long been able to tell just how far north or south they were at any given moment, but it was almost impossible to figure out where they were from east to west. There were complex calculations that could help but few knew how to perform them. There were astronomical observations that would answer but they could not be taken at sea. A clock—or chronometer, as it was called—that would allow a comparison between local time anywhere in the world and that of the prime meridian (Greenwich) would tell sailors in an instant where they were. But until the middle of the eighteenth century, no clock had been invented that could survive the rigors of being at sea.

Here, then, we have the basic dichotomy. On the one hand, Europeans, energetic, obsessed with progress, relentlessly focused on what lies ahead, and on the other, islanders, who know what it means to *be here now*, indolent maybe, inconstant perhaps, whimsical, capricious, impulsive, rash. It was this character of fickleness, wrote Bougainville, "which constantly amazed us. Everything strikes them, yet nothing fixes their attention. It seems as if the least reflection is a toilsome labour for them, and that they are still more averse to the exercises of the mind than to those of the body . . . I shall not, however, accuse them of want of understanding."

It would be easy to portray these depictions of Tahiti as the workings of a fevered European mind. There is so much that is inaccurate about them. It was not true, for instance, that the Tahitians knew nothing of war. They had, in fact, attacked the *Dolphin* initially, pelting the ship with volleys of stones and challenging the sailors to come ashore with "many wanton gestures." And it was clear, even to the earliest visitors, that they frequently engaged in battle with their neighbors. Similarly, while there were elements of communalism in Polynesian society, there were also rigid social hierarchies and degrees of privilege and access to wealth. There was work, there was trouble, there was even disease. And, as for social mores, well, as the long-running argument over Margaret Mead's account of adolescent Samoan sexuality attests, Polynesian societies are as rife as any with rules about who can sleep with whom.

But if there is spin in these early descriptions, there are also flickers of what feels like truth. Eighteenth-century European observers were influenced by political convictions, including a growing impatience with a remote and narcissistic aristocracy, and by popular philosophical ideas like those of Jean-Jacques Rousseau. And there is certainly a sense in which they tended to perceive only that which confirmed the views they already held. But the eighteenth century was also the age of empiricism, the first perhaps genuinely scientific age. It was full of encounters with new plants, new animals, and new landscapes, hundreds of which were enthusiastically cataloged by adventurous, curious, and comparatively dispassionate Europeans.

Voyagers grappled with all kinds of things they had never seen—kangaroos, icebergs, giant ferns, bottle brushes, molten lava—and made conscientious efforts to document them as faithfully as they could. They were scrupulous observers who took copious notes and brought artists along on their voyages to make visual records of what they discovered. Of course, they were selective and mistook much of what they found— one has only to look at the earliest drawings of a kangaroo to see how wrong they could get it. Of course, they tried to fit their experiences into the framework of what they understood. But within these limitations they still came back with reports of the world, not just as they had expected to find it, but as they had actually seen it with their own eyes.

A large part of my training as a graduate student had been aimed at making me skeptical about everything Europeans had reported in the course of empire's long march. And the claim

that Polynesians—not only Tahitians but the Tongans, Samoans, Marquesans, and Maoris who were their close cultural
kin—lived in some kind of continuous present was exactly the
sort of thing one might have expected. Europeans were always
representing themselves as models of Apollonian reason and
order and depicting everyone else (Orientals, natives, islanders)
as feckless and bizarre. But what was funny about living with
Seven was the way these musty paradigms, so easy to dismiss in
theory, would periodically spring to life. Those elements of
communalism? Somehow they seemed related to the fact that
Seven gave everything away. That particular kind of physical
beauty? It was there before my eyes. And as for that business
about time—*are you kidding*?

One day he said to me out of the blue, "I think about food all
the time."

"You *do*?" I said, finding this hard to imagine.

"Yeah."

"*Really?*"

"Well, I think I do," he said. "Maybe I'm just hungry right
now."

6

THE *VENUS*

WHILE WE WERE living down by the beach, the replica of
Cook's ship, the *Endeavour*, came to Melbourne. I had
seen the notice in the paper and I made Seven go out early with
me to stake out a spot on the esplanade where we could watch
the ship sail up into Port Philip Bay. Port Philip is a long bay,
about thirty miles from the heads to the harbor, and we had
our first sight of the ship while she was still quite far away, the
first flash of white resolving gradually into tier upon tier of
sails, as she made her way toward us. I tried to imagine what it
had been like when there were no smokestacks behind her, no
bridges, no other ships, no jetties, no buildings, no busy roads,
no noise of engines, no airplanes overhead—when nothing of
this kind had ever appeared on this stretch of water before.
Eventually, the ship approached the pier, trailed by a flotilla of
smaller vessels. Everyone on the beach was waving, the sun
glittered on the sand. Then, suddenly, there was a puff of
smoke at the *Endeavour*'s side and a hollow boom rang out
across the bay. We all jumped—unprepared for cannon fire—
and then laughed, realizing what it was.

Every day the imaginative leap required to comprehend such
a journey becomes greater: to have sailed aboard a ship in the
eighteenth century for years on end in uncharted waters, with
only men for company, and the same ninety men at that, day

in, day out, with nothing to eat but the sort of thing that could be kept salted or dried or gradually rotting in the hold for months at a time, with the ever-present possibility of shipwreck on some distant shore or death at the hands of some strange people, and still the cruel boredom of the daily routine.

I have, in my library, a book that describes the rhythm of a long Royal Navy voyage: decks scrubbed and swabbed at dawn, hammocks piped up at seven bells, hands piped to breakfast at eight. Then, at midday, the ceremony in which all the officers and midshipmen took the sun's altitude. The master reported noon and the latitude to the officer of the watch. The officer of the watch, stepping across the quarter-deck and taking off his hat, reported it to the captain, who would reply, "Make it twelve, Mr. ————," a ceremony so excessively ritualistic it would surely be mistaken for a religious event by an alien observer.

The same collection includes a children's book that depicts an eighteenth-century man-o'-war in cross-section—not quite what Cook sailed in but not that different either. It shows where the sailors ate and where they slept, how many barrels of grog there were and how iron shot was stored near the keel to keep the ship from tipping over. A third describes the *Endeavour* in minute detail: her cables, her anchors, her cannons, her masts, how long she was, how broad, how deep, how much water she drew, how she behaved in a variety of winds. These are the sorts of things we are reduced to when we try to understand the past: picture books, diagrams, and models.

Inside the Whaling Museum in New Bedford, Massachusetts, there is a half-scale model of a whaler so strangely proportioned that it makes you feel like Alice in Wonderland when she grew and grew and had to bend her head to keep from hitting the ceiling. I had heard that the full-scale replica of the *Endeavour* was similarly disconcerting. The height of a marine's quarters on the lower deck was four feet seven inches; the cabins for the master, surgeon, gunner, and second and third lieutenants were barely five feet square. I wanted to see this for myself and I mentioned to Seven that, according to the newspaper, they were going to be giving tours.

"You'll come with me, won't you?"

"I don't think so," he said.

"Oh, come on. Why not?"

"I don't like boats."

"What do you mean you don't like boats? You come from the greatest seafaring people in the world. Besides, you've lived your whole life on the water."

"I never liked them," he said.

"Don't be absurd. Anyway, the ship's at anchor. We're not going for a sail."

"No," he said, and that was the end of it.

Perhaps I should have known better than to ask. It was easy for me to romanticize the voyage, to cast myself in the role of explorer setting out for places unknown. Envisioning oneself as the *object* of discovery does not have quite the same appeal.

I went anyway by myself and bought a key ring and a T-shirt printed with the *Endeavour* logo, which Seven, to my surprise, appropriated for himself. I thought it looked good on him and said so.

"It's a bit tight," he said. "I think it shrunk."

"No, it didn't shrink," I told him. "It's a small. I didn't have you in mind when I bought it. Still, it looks good. Kind of ironic though, isn't it? I mean, the *Endeavour* and all."

"I know," he said. "Sometimes I wonder if I should wear it."

*   *   *

There was another ship, besides the *Endeavour*, that I often thought about in those days. Unlike Cook's famous vessel, this one had almost escaped mention in most of the standard histories of New Zealand—a fact I found surprising since this, too, was a ship of "firsts." It was not the first European vessel to visit to New Zealand, or the first to circumnavigate it, or the first to land a European who would, even temporarily, call New Zealand home. It was the first ship to leave a white *woman* in New Zealand—an Australian convict who arrived in the Bay of Islands in 1806, eight years before the first official white settlement, and who twice refused to be rescued by the British and American captains who offered to take her away.

The ship was called the *Venus* and the convict was Charlotte Badger. I had come across a handful of references to the story, but the details were frustratingly sketchy. In the hope of uncovering more, I sent a letter to the research service at the Mitchell Library and one to the Archives Authority of New South Wales.

Dear Sir/Madam,

I am trying to locate information regarding the piratical seizure of the colonial vessel (brig) *Venus* at Port Dalrymple on the 17th of June, 1806, on her way from Port Jackson (via sealing grounds at Two-Fold Bay) with supplies for the settlements in Van Diemen's Land. Any information relative to this episode would be of interest, especially any mention of it in the ship's logs of the *Britannia*, *Brothers*, or *Elizabeth* in the years 1806–08.

I am also looking for information concerning a female convict named Charlotte Badger (possibly Edgar), known to have been aboard the *Venus* when it was captured. She is described as very corpulent with a full face, thick lips, and

light hair, and is said to have had an infant child with her. I
am particularly interested in knowing where she came from,
what ship she arrived on, what she was transported for,
what her movements were in Australia before June 1806,
and whether there is any further record of her after 1808.
Many thanks for your assistance in this matter.
Sincerely yours.

About three weeks later I received a large envelope containing photocopies of the assignment list from the colonial
secretary's correspondence and the convict indent for the ship
Earl Cornwallis, both showing Charlotte Badger's name. Also,
from the Mitchell Library, copies of two cards from the
manuscript index catalog, one of which was intriguingly
marked, "VENUS, ship, seized by mutineers . . . blame attached to captain for event." From these and other sources I
pieced together the following story.

Charlotte Badger was most likely born in Worcestershire,
England, in 1778. Little is known of her before the age of
eighteen, when she was convicted of the crime of house-
breaking, an offense punishable by death. She was tried at
the Worcester Summer Assizes in July 1796 and was sentenced to be transported to Australia for the term of seven
years. She arrived in Port Jackson (Sydney) on June 12, 1801,
on the ship *Earl Cornwallis*. There were 287 other prisoners
aboard, 94 of whom were women, most transported for
varieties of theft.

In 1806, with two years of her sentence left to serve,
Charlotte gave birth to a child at the old Parramatta Female
Factory. Shortly afterward she was assigned, along with an-
other convict named Catherine Hagerty, to the service of a
Tasmanian settler. The ship that was to take them south was

the forty-five-ton brig *Venus*, a colonial vessel used to supply sealing gangs and run provisions up and down the Australian coast. On this occasion, it was loaded with grain, flour, salt pork, and other stores for the settlements at Port Dalrymple (Launceston) and Hobart Town.

It was not a happy voyage. They stopped en route at Two-Fold Bay, where the master, Samuel Chace, discovered that the crew, a mixed lot of seamen and convicts, had been stealing the ship's stores. He accused the first mate, Benjamin Kelly, but Kelly denied the charge. Chace later told an official inquiry that he had every reason to believe, from Kelly's conduct, that the ship was "in danger of being run away with" and that, with the crew robbing and plundering her, he did not think his life safe.

Nevertheless, they arrived safely in Tasmania, where they anchored in the river at Port Dalrymple on the morning of June 16. Chace promptly left the ship and did not return until the following morning, when, to his consternation, he found the *Venus* underway. The sudden appearance of five members of the *Venus*'s crew confirmed his worst suspicions. Kelly, they reported, along with the pilot and a soldier of the New South Wales Corps, had knocked down and confined the second mate and taken command of the vessel and was now in the process of taking her out to sea.

For six months the *Venus* disappeared from view. Then, in early 1807, she was sighted in the Bay of Islands, where two women and a child had reportedly been put ashore, along with Kelly and a convict named John Lancashire. It is unclear whether they had been marooned or had left the ship voluntarily but the *Venus*, in any case, sailed on under the command of a black man who, it was said, was incapable of piloting her. The last we hear of her, she was "supposed to be still wandering about the coast . . . and no possible prospect can present itself to those that remain in her, but to perish by the hands of the natives or to fall into the hands of justice"—which is more or less what came to pass. Within a matter of months, Catherine Hagerty was dead, Kelly had been taken prisoner and was en route to England, and Lancashire, also in irons, was on his way back to New South Wales. The ultimate fate of the ship remains a mystery, though it is presumed that she was finally wrecked and plundered by Maoris somewhere on the New Zealand coast.

And what of Charlotte Badger? She alone remained at Rangihoua, alive and presumably well, for when Captain Bunker of the *Elizabeth* volunteered to take her aboard a year later, she declined the offer. She would, no doubt, have been concerned about returning to either England or New South Wales, as she was listed among those who had "by force of arms violently and piratically" taken a colonial vessel filled with stores belonging to His Majesty King George. But it is interesting to note that Bunker did not arrest her. And, according to at least one contemporary historian, when she was offered a second chance to leave a year later, she responded by saying that "she would prefer to die among the Maori."

What could it possibly have been like for her, alone in the Bay of Islands in 1806? There were no other Europeans to speak of; aside from the occasional runaway sailor, it was, for all intents and purposes, an entirely Maori world. She could not possibly have spoken the language; she would not have been accustomed to the food. She would probably have had to surrender every stitch of her clothing and anything else that she possessed. It cannot have been physically comfortable; it must have been terrifying at times.

It was "a rainy, miserable night," wrote the traveling artist Augustus Earle about two decades later. Earle, who spent nine months touring New Zealand, had been traveling cross-country in the Hokianga—just across the northern peninsula from the Bay of Islands—and had arrived at dusk at a Maori village, whose inhabitants invited him to stay for the night. "We were a large party," he wrote, "crowded into a small smoky hut, with a fire lighted in the middle." Around the fire sat a dozen large, athletic men,

> their huge limbs exposed to the red glare of the fire; their faces rendered hideous by being tattooed all over, showing by the fire-light quite a bright blue; their eyes, which are remarkable for their fierce expression, all fixed upon us, but with a look of good temper, commingled with intense curiosity.

The missionary Samuel Marsden describes a similar night spent inside a *pa*, or fortified village, on the coast near Whangarei in 1820. The *pa* sat on the summit of a high conical hill. At high tide it was almost completely surrounded by water and the only way in was by a path so steep and narrow that Marsden had to be helped up. "When I reached the top," he wrote,

> I found a number of men, women, and children sitting round their fires roasting snappers, crawfish, and fern-root. It was now quite dark. The roaring of the sea at the foot of the [*pa*], as the waves rolled into the deep caverns beneath, the high precipice upon which we stood, whose top and sides were covered with huts, and the groups of natives conversing round their fires, all tended to excite new and strange ideas for reflection.

Was this what it was like? The crackling fires with their sparks dancing up into the dark night sky; the stars blotted out by clouds; the wind from the sea rattling at the palings; the Maoris, huddled under their cloaks, talking quietly among themselves; a laugh somewhere; the thump of a log thrown onto the fire; the acrid smell of burning fish bones; the rustle of a child turning in someone's lap. Was this the New Zealand that tempted Charlotte Badger? It is possible that she felt safer in New Zealand, despite the Maoris' reputation for ferocity. Maybe she enjoyed a kind of freedom that among her own people she was almost sure to be denied. Maybe she just *liked* the Maoris, or is that too twentieth-century an idea? What was it that made her feel as though New Zealand were a place where she could reasonably stay?

There is nothing in the historical record that will definitively answer such questions. What is clear, from other stories of lone Europeans living in places like New Zealand at this time, is that no European, male or female, could have survived without the personal protection of a chief, or *rangatira*. Someone had to feed and protect her; someone had to allow her to remain. Within that framework there were a number of possible roles open to Charlotte Badger. She might have been a wife or a concubine or possibly some kind of slave—a *taurekareka*, a menial slave, or maybe a *mokai*, which can be translated as something closer to "pet." Or she might have begun as one thing, a slave, say, and earned her way to higher status as, perhaps, a wife.

Maori society was hierarchical, but it was still comparatively fluid by European standards. Position, while inherited, could also be earned, and traditions existed both for adopting and enslaving people from outside the tribe. Slavery, too, meant something rather different from what we understand. Slaves were people of low status or those who'd had the misfortune to be captured in war. They were often killed or mistreated, but they could also, under certain circumstances, become integrated into the clan. Charlotte's fate would thus have depended both on how much *mana*, or charisma, she was able to project and how useful she succeeded in making herself to her *rangatira* and her tribe.

There were a number of Europeans in situations like this throughout the Pacific during this period, though, of course, almost all of them were men. Commonly known in the islands as "beachcombers," they were called "Pakeha Maori" in New Zealand, that is, "strangers turned into Maori" in Trevor Bentley's turn of phrase. Some were castaways and some were convicts and some were sailors who'd absconded from ships, and their fates were as varied as their characters. Those who survived and prospered learned to abide by the local rules—infringements of *tapu*, or sacred law, in New Zealand routinely resulted in death—and to treat their hosts with the proper degree of courtesy. It was, writes the historian O. H. K. Spate, "a necessary condition of [their] existence that they should be relatively free from feelings of racial superiority, should see Islanders not as savages noble or ignoble but as fallible human beings like themselves."

This seems obvious enough to us, but to Europeans in the late eighteenth and early nineteenth centuries it was not self-evident. "A man who chose to 'live among natives,'" writes I. C. Campbell,

> was not merely an emigrant; he was regarded in European society as a renegade. To have "gone native" was a mark of degeneration, an act of a man who turned his back on progress, enlightenment, civilization, order, law, and

morality and preferred a life of savagery, immorality, pagan-
ism, and lawlessness. This was not only personal decadence;
it was an affront and a challenge to the ethos of Western
society, which assumed and asserted a moral and existential
superiority over savagery or life in the "state of nature."

For a man to make such a choice was contemptible, but for a
woman to do so begged understanding. White women did not
"choose" to live with natives; they were "captured" by them,
according to seventeenth-, eighteenth-, and nineteenth-century
European thinking. Accounts of white women cast away
among or captured by "Indians" (a term commonly used to
refer to indigenous people all over the world) were a staple of
frontier literature and were enormously popular in both Europe and the United States. The women were generally pitied,
since they had been "ruined," but there was also a prurient
fascination with their fate and much interested speculation as
to whether they could ever be redeemed. But the idea that a
woman might voluntarily place herself in such a situation was
inconceivable, and there was no narrative or explanation for a
woman who did.

In Charlotte's case, part of the story undoubtedly had to do
with the class she came from and the sort of life she had already
led. But part of it must also have had to do with her personally—the way she looked, the way she acted, the way she
thought. There can be little doubt that she was a woman of
some physical strength. She is described as "very corpulent"
and may have been comparatively tall in an age when people of
her class were often small and undernourished. The average
height of the men aboard the *Venus* was five feet six inches,
and her companion John Lancashire, a pockmarked, ema-
ciated man of sallow complexion, was only five foot four. She

was, in any case, clearly robust—consider, too, that she was nursing a baby—and this no doubt served her well among the Maoris, who, like most Polynesians, valued size and strength. There is even something vaguely Polynesian about her physical description, with her "full face [and] thick lips." Disparaged, possibly, by Englishmen for these features, she may well have been considered unusually handsome (for a Pakeha) by the Maoris.

Still, neither beauty nor physical stamina alone would have been enough; she must have had strength of character as well. Perhaps something of this can be deduced from the circumstances of her life: charged and convicted at the age of eighteen, confined for years to hulks and English prisons, she survived the crowded, disease-ridden voyage south and incarceration in the infamous penal colony of New South Wales. Captain Chace described the women on board the *Venus* as enthusiastic participants in the debauchery and drunkenness that plagued his ship, and convict women of the period were commonly, almost routinely, depicted as abandoned (meaning immoral), drunken, dissipated, impudent, vicious, violent, sullen, and deceitful.

But shift the lens ever so slightly and it seems obvious that, simply to survive, they must also have been resourceful, hardy, vigorous, feisty, and resilient. Certainly some of the stories of the convict period suggest this—the historian L. L. Robson relates an incident in which a group of convict women, being addressed by an ecclesiast at the Hobart Town factory, "reacted by drawing up their gowns and, in unison, smacking their buttocks." And sauciness, seen from a different angle, is also a kind of nerve. On the whole, life as a transported felon might almost be viewed as a sort of basic training, a brutal initiation period, beyond which almost anything else might seem comparatively nice. And any woman who was not crushed by it must have had something going for her.

It was enormously tempting to me to romanticize the story of Charlotte Badger, to see her as a heroine, a bold and independent woman taking fate into her own hands, and to imagine her hosts as kind and generous people who opened up a space for her in their world—even to think of her *rangatira* as someone with whom she might have fallen in love. The academic in me strongly resisted this kind of thinking, but the traveler kept trying to project into this fragment of history a sense of what it had actually been like to stay, albeit briefly, among the very descendents of the people who had sheltered Charlotte Badger, not six miles from where she'd lived.

Maybe if I'd never been there, I would have seen the story in a different light. But, as it was, I could so easily imagine their interest in her, their discreet curiosity, the way they might have benignly ignored her many missteps. I could imagine the patience with which one or two might have taken her aside and helped her, and her growing awareness of whom she could count on and whom she had better avoid. I could imagine the pleasure she might have taken in their gaiety, their generous laughter, not to mention the comparative freedom of movement that, even as a slave, she would have had, and the affection that both men and women would undoubtedly have shown toward her child. It might all have been so completely different from what the documentary record, with its nineteenth-century biases, its litany of dramatic and shocking events, its insistence on the waywardness of convicts and the ferocity of Maoris, its preoccupation with violence and terror, might lead one to conclude.

But there was just no way to know. What I finally decided was that she was probably one of those people, a shape-shifter, a transculturite, a person who could slide from one world to another and back again with ease—like the anthropologist Bronislaw Malinowski, who is famous for having invented the fieldwork method in 1914 by setting up a tent in a village in New Guinea and staying there for as long as it took get a handle on what was going on. Some people, it seems, just have this ethnographic impulse, a powerful curiosity about people who are very different from themselves and a willingness to surrender themselves to a flow of experience they do not necessarily understand. Malinowski once half-jokingly suggested that his success might have had something to do with his being a Pole. "Perhaps," he wrote, "the Slavonic nature is more plastic and more naturally savage" than that of the Western European. Maybe, I thought, it was Charlotte's plasticity, maybe she—maybe I—was a little more naturally savage than others of our kind.

7

A Natural Gentleman

LIVING IN New Zealand was not in the cards for me, however, nor would it be again for Seven, not for many years. But Australia proved a surprisingly good place for us, and I've often wondered if we'd have been as happy living in New Zealand or the States. Australia was a neutral territory. We had friends but no family and there was no one who questioned our decisions or argued with us about what we ought to do. But there was also a sense in which Australia connected us to each other, triangulating our relationship in an interesting way. We were about equally distant from the local culture. I, though white, was not as English as people from Australia or New Zealand tend to be. I didn't eat Vegemite or drive on the left and I couldn't tell a cricket bat from a wicket, at least when I arrived. Seven was culturally much closer to the Australian mainstream, having grown up watching *Coronation Street* and spending Christmas at the beach. But being Maori—that is, black but not Aboriginal—set him apart in a different way.

Then, too, Melbourne was a good city for people like us. It was culturally and ethnically diverse and many of our friends were also expatriates, or else they were the kind of locals who gravitate toward people from someplace else. It was an easy place for us to be together and we were happy there, which, I guess, is why we decided to get married.

We did it the way we did everything, quickly, lightheartedly, the way you do things when you're young. The kicker was that we told no one—not our parents, not our siblings, not our friends. We just got up one hot, bright summer morning, almost a year to the day from when we'd met, packed our bags, dropped a house key with the neighbors, and took a taxi to the Mint.

The Melbourne branch of the Royal Mint was a large, handsome building that fronted onto William Street not far from Flagstaff Gardens. It had been built in the late 1860s, when Melbourne was awash in gold, and was styled after a Renaissance Italian palazzo. The building itself was set back from the street in a large lot surrounded by a wrought-iron fence with a pair of great gates opening onto a courtyard, rather like a foreign embassy. There was a gatehouse and a guard and it was possible to drive right in, but the taxi driver dropped us at the sidewalk and we entered the compound on foot, carrying our bags.

Inside the building it was cool and dim and it was hard, at first, to see anything. We were the first wedding of the morning and there was no one about when we arrived. We stood around in the foyer for a while wondering what to do, until finally a young man came out and ushered us into a formally furnished room. It was clearly the room for the smaller weddings—I could see a larger similar room across the hall—but it was still big enough to feel empty with just the three of us in it. After a few more minutes we were joined by a middle-age man who shook our hands and introduced himself as the registrar.

"Um, do you have any witnesses with you?" he asked, as though perhaps we had just forgotten to bring them in.

"No, sorry. I'm afraid we haven't."

There was a short, awkward pause and then he said, "No problem." He whispered something to the younger man, who promptly disappeared and returned a few moments later with Tony and Tony, the parking attendant and the clerk.

"So, shall we get started?"

It was over almost before it had begun. The registrar said something brief and formal and we said something like "I do." There were no rings to exchange and, since we had also neglected to bring a camera, there is no record of the event beyond the official Marriage Register, now filed away in some cool archive, and the certified true copy they gave us when we left.

I had convinced Seven to buy a suit for the occasion, the first, I think, he'd ever owned. It was black and beautifully cut and almost silky. It cost him two weeks' wages and he looked so spectacular in it that everyone in the store stopped what they were doing when he stepped out of the dressing room with it on. I had much more trouble figuring out what to wear. After a week or so of desultory looking, I ended up with a little black-and-white print dress made, improbably, of cotton jersey. It had bell-shaped sleeves and a scoop neck and the faintest hint of a flare. It came to just above the knee and I wore it tied with a belt of the same fabric and a pair of little black flats. It was nobody's idea of a wedding dress, and one day, many years later, I came across it in a trunk when my eldest son happened to be standing nearby.

"Look, this is the dress I got married in."

"Looks like a nightgown," he said.

Of course, we eventually had to explain to any number of people, including our mothers, why we had not told them what we were planning to do. And not only that, but why, when we saw them all shortly thereafter—we were married at nine in the morning and caught a plane out of Australia at noon—we still didn't tell them what we'd done. In fact, we managed to spend two months traveling, from Melbourne to Auckland to Boston and back, visiting everyone we were related to, without ever telling them that we were married.

The longer we neglected to mention it, of course, the harder it got to explain, and when I finally informed my mother— about four months after the fact and by mail—she said it was the most cowardly thing anyone in the family had ever done. No doubt she was right, but it was such a complex set of motivations that had prompted us, first, to forgo any kind of celebration, and then to keep the fact of it to ourselves.

I, for one, had never wanted to be a bride. The wedding gown, the veil, the walk down the aisle, none of it had ever appealed to me. But even if I *had* wanted a party, where were we going to have it and whom would we invite? Seven's family were all in New Zealand; my family were all in the States; all our friends were in Australia. One couple we knew had gone through the whole performance three times over: once in Australia for their buddies, once in New Zealand for the groom, and once in Canada for the bride's family. But if I couldn't see myself getting through one iteration, how was I going to survive three? Then there was the fact that one of Seven's sisters was getting married in New Zealand at almost exactly the same time—we were actually on our way to her wedding when we left our own to catch a plane—and we didn't want to steal any of her thunder.

Of course, none of that explains why we didn't tell anyone. But I think the answer is we just didn't think it was anybody's business but our own. We liked the privacy and the way the casualness of the performance masked the seriousness we felt. It was, I later came to think, quite Polynesian in this discontinuity between the appearance and the meaning, between the surface and the deep. Maoris, as Europeans have long noted, are skilled dissemblers, and many of the oldest stories are filled with ruses, ambuscades, strategems, and tricks. I myself have never been able to tell when anyone in Seven's family is teasing me or when Seven himself is telling me something untrue. It's a power play but also a challenge: to be able to keep a secret and to know when one is being kept.

I suppose there *was* one other thing though, and that was the fact that a marriage like ours was bound to raise eyebrows in some quarters. We were such an unlikely couple. I was small and blonde, he was a six-foot-two, two-hundred-pound Polynesian. I had a Ph.D., he went to trade school. I liked opera, he liked motorsports. Acutally, he liked opera too, but I never learned to like car racing. I used to enjoy telling the story of our first meeting. It was my story, really; I never heard him tell it. "He thought I was rich," I would say gaily to people we met at parties. "Poor thing, you can imagine how disappointed he was when he found out!" And then I would laugh as if this were the funniest thing, while Seven stood there looking impossibly handsome in his black Saba suit.

It was a complicated bit of banter and no one ever knew just how to take it. *Who was I having on?* But I doubt even I could have answered that question. All I knew was that I was compelled to acknowledge, even if only backhandedly, the heady mix of stereotypes about class and race and sex and power that surrounded a relationship like ours.

"Nah," he would say after a moment. "We didn't think she was rich. We just thought she was a tourist."

Our idea was to get married and then make our way across the Pacific, ending up in Boston, where Seven and my family would meet each other for the first time. We traveled by way of New Zealand, where I wore my own wedding dress to my sister-in-law's wedding and enjoyed myself at her reception as I never would have had it been my own.

She had invited hundreds of people and, in order to feed them, her brothers dug an enormous *hangi*. A *hangi* is an earth oven, also sometimes called an *umu*. It is made by digging a pit in the ground and filling it with firewood and a layer of rocks. When the wood has all burned down and the rocks are hot, wire baskets of food are added—chicken, beef, and pork on the bottom, potatoes, pumpkin, and *kumara* on the top. The whole thing is then covered with wet sheets and buried under a layer of earth and left to bake for several hours.

It was a terrific party, with music and dancing well into the night. At some point, in the early hours of the morning, I found myself sitting at the edge of a large, noisy room with Nana Miri. I had had too much to drink by then and was feeling sentimental. Nana Miri had always been kind to me and, before I knew what I was doing, the secret of what Seven and I had done spilled out. I'm not sure which of us was more startled.

"You have to promise you won't tell," I told her. "*Promise.* You're the only person who knows."

Nana Miri frowned a little. "OK. I'll keep your secret for you. But it won't be easy," she said.

I realized instantly the awkwardness of the position in which I'd put her. "We'll tell them soon," I said. "Don't worry. Then you'll be off the hook."

A few days later we flew to Hawaii, where the clerk at the hotel took one look at us and said, "Honeymoon suite?" We opted instead for a rental car and drove to the North Shore, where we found a rundown old beach club that catered to surfers. For nine dollars a night we got a room in a dilapidated bungalow with a mattress on the floor. There was an open-air kitchen and a communal bathhouse and a pair of enormous banyan trees at the edge of a wide, white beach. I bought myself a hibiscus-print muumuu and Seven borrowed a Hawaiian sling—a kind of hand-powered spear gun propelled by a heavy-duty rubber band—and dove into the sea, emerging a few minutes later with a fish skewered on the thin steel rod.

From Honolulu we set out on the last leg of our journey. I don't know if Seven was nervous, probably not, but I was apprehensive about this part of our trip. While they had, of course, heard about him, no one in my family had ever met Seven. In fact, no one had ever met a Maori, or been to New Zealand, or even thought very much about that part of the world.

The Pacific laps the west coast of America, and when you are standing in California, you feel as though you could almost island-hop your way across—Los Angeles to Honolulu to Papeete to Auckland—and that, while everything would become progressively less familiar, it would do so in a recognizable way. But the east coast faces in the other direction: to England, Ireland, Portugal, and Spain, to the Azores and the Canary Islands. The view from the coast of New England in winter is of the cold, gray, storm-tossed North Atlantic, a beautiful ocean in its own way, but very different from the turquoise of Tahiti or the Bay of Islands' cobalt blue. The landscape is different, the people are different, the history is different. In New England, one can only describe the islands of the Pacific by analogy—*like the Caribbean, sort of, but with Indians*—for the older, harsher colonial history of the region has left few traces of a world that still exists in other places.

We arrived in Boston on a bleak late-winter's day. From the air, the city and all the land around it was a mottled grayish brown, a tangle of roads and buildings and bare, leafless woods. There were patches of snow to the north and west and, as we banked and came in to land, the Atlantic glinted beneath us with a metallic sheen. Coming, as we had, from high summer in the southern hemisphere, the contrast was particularly vivid. *I* knew that spring was coming to New England and could see in my mind's eye the pale new green that in just a few months would blanket the entire region. But to Seven, who had never seen a landscape go completely dormant or felt the grip of a really hard frost, everything looked cold and lifeless.

My family met us at the airport: my mother and father, my brother, his wife, and their two children. While I knew they were happy to see me, I also knew that what they really wanted was to see whom I was with. Meanwhile, I was secretly worrying about what kind of impression Seven would make. I had introduced plenty of boyfriends to my family over the years, but I'd never brought home anyone to whom I was secretly married. I worried about both sides of the equation: how my family would seem to Seven and whether he'd pass muster with them. I worried that they would have nothing in common, or that they would fail to locate the few points of experience and knowledge they actually shared. What would they talk about? Sports? Seven was a rugby man, a game no one in my family had ever played. Travel? He'd never been to Europe or Canada or any of the places they usually went. Food? I supposed that was a possibility, though no one in Boston had the faintest notion of *kina* or *puha* or rotten corn. Politics, I knew, was a nonstarter. Seven knew almost nothing about world events, and my family knew nothing about the antipodes. But, as it turned out, I needn't have worried. There was only one subject that interested anyone and that was Seven himself.

For many people in Boston, Seven was the first person they had ever met of his kind. Most had difficulty identifying his ethnicity: he wasn't recognizably Indian or African American or Asian or Hispanic. People who had been to Hawaii sometimes picked him for Polynesian, and occasionally his accent would tip someone off. "Wow," they'd say, "are you a Maori?"—pronouncing it may-OR-ee, which always surprised me, since no one had any trouble with the identical vowel combination in "Mao Tse-tung." But the absence of familiarity was understandable. There aren't very many Maoris to begin with—the total global population is just over half a million—and they are, with the rarest of exceptions, all on the other side of the world.

Even to me, who was used to him, Seven seemed exotic in this setting. From the airport we went directly to my parents' house. It had been built at the tail end of the 1950s and designed by an architect strongly under the influence of Frank Lloyd Wright. It was long and low and everywhere you looked there were large expanses of glass. The feeling one had in it, both summer and winter, was of being indoors and outdoors at the same time; the constant drama of falling snow, or light on the pine needles, or rain pouring off the eaves in sheets was always there in front of you. It was filled with an eclectic assortment of Danish furniture, a few American antiques, and a lot of ethnic bits and pieces, including a number of tribal rugs that my mother had carried back from Morocco wrapped in brown paper and string. There were potted palms and art books, and piles of pillows on the window seat. The walls were covered with paintings and prints, which my parents rotated seasonally, when they put on or took off the summer slipcovers and swapped the red and orange and turquoise rugs for white grass matting.

In summer the house was cool and shady and the paintings were mostly green. But in winter it was a riot of color. I had never seen Seven before in an environment like this, dressed in his suit or a charcoal sweater, his hair now long and tied back in a ponytail, his skin a dusky brown from the summer we had just left. Sometimes I would catch a glimpse of him against the plum-colored linen velvet of my mother's sofa, the corner of a saffron cushion peeking out from behind his back, the big red Japanese painting on the wall behind him, and think, *my God, it's an Ingres.*

In 1775 the great English portraitist Sir Joshua Reynolds painted a man known as Omai. The portrait depicts a tall, exotic-looking figure with a broad, handsome face, black hair, and light brown skin. Barefoot, draped and turbaned in white, he stands with one arm outstretched, the other clasped against his body, showing clearly the tattooing on the back of his hands. Behind him tower masses of cloud and moody shadow and, in the far distance, a little landscape with palms and mountains and perhaps a beach. The body is that of a man, but the face is young, with a full, sensuous mouth, soft cheeks, and strong black brows. In the figure's dark, almond-shaped eyes there is a contemplative, unfocused look, as though he had drifted into some reverie or meditation.

It is hard to say exactly how good a likeness the Reynolds portrait is; other contemporary sketches, even some by Reynolds himself, suggest that it somewhat idealizes the subject. But that, in a sense, is neither here nor there, for what Reynolds aspired to paint was less a likeness than a representation of some quality or idea that the sitter was supposed to embody—wit, for example, or innocence, or understanding. In the case of Omai, the idea was nobility, specifically the nobility of man in his natural state.

What many people do not realize is that almost from the very beginning there were Polynesian adventurers who took passage on European ships and traveled back in the opposite direction to England, America, and France. They were, in many ways, the inverse of figures like Charlotte Badger—ambassadors rather than renegades—but they too served as intermediaries and go-betweens on what Spate calls "the grinding edge" where two cultures meet. By the first decades of the nineteenth century, islanders from most of the major groups—Tongans, Hawaiians, Marquesans, Maoris—were crisscrossing the great oceans of the world, many of them, like Herman Melville's Queequeg, on whalers or sealers or other types of commercial vessels. But the earliest of these voyagers sailed in the late-eighteenth century on the very first expeditions into the Pacific with explorers like Bougainville and Cook.

Omai was a Polynesian from the Society Islands. He had been brought to England by Tobias Furneaux, who was captain of the *Adventure*, the ship that accompanied Cook's *Resolution* on his second Pacific expedition. Still driven by the specter of the Unknown South Land, Cook's aim on this voyage was a circumnavigation in the highest southern latitudes he could manage, through the only remaining region in which *Terra Australis Incognita*, if it existed, could lie. After a first pass through the Southern Ocean in the summer of 1772–3, Cook decided to winter over in the islands of central Polynesia. There each of the ships picked up an islander. At Raiatea, northwest of Tahiti, the *Resolution* was joined by a young Bora-Boran known to the English as Odiddy, while at nearby Huahine, a Raiatean named Mai—or Omai, as he would come to be known—joined the *Adventure*'s crew.

It was Cook's intention to return both of them to the islands the following winter. Two previous attempts to bring Polynesians to Europe—one by Cook himself on his first voyage, the other by Bougainville—had both resulted in the islanders' deaths, from dysentery and malaria in one case, from smallpox in the other. Odiddy was duly deposited at Raiatea when Cook finally headed for home. But a series of misadventures, including a storm that separated the two ships and the murder in New Zealand of a boatload of his crew, prevented Furneaux from returning Omai to the Society Islands. Distressed, dismayed, and shorthanded, Furneaux decided to abandon the voyage and, instead of following Cook into the Southern Ocean as he had planned, he headed for home with the young islander still on board. And thus it was that Omai arrived in London in the northern hemispheric summer of 1774.

Omai was not only the first Polynesian to reach England, he was the first to be exhaustively described by a wide range of observers, including several women, who took a keen interest in the exotic young man. Pacific Islanders had been depicted before by seamen in the course of their voyages, but even the best of these accounts are comparatively superficial. Omai, on the other hand, remained in England for two full years. He was described by Cook and Banks and Lord Sandwich, who was his host for much of that time, as well as by Dr. Johnson, James Boswell, and Mrs. Thrale. One of his most enthusiastic chroniclers was the diarist Fanny Burney, whose brother had sailed with Omai in the *Adventure*. He was presented at court and discussed by members of the Royal Society. His likes and dislikes, his habits and manners, the way he moved and ate and laughed—all were recorded for the benefit of posterity. And although these accounts are by no means objective—they are not even particularly consistent—taken together, they constitute an extraordinary portrait of an eighteenth-century Polynesian face-to-face with the eighteenth-century European world.

Omai was probably about twenty-one when he arrived in England. He was tall by European standards and muscular, with broad flat shoulders and strong, well-shaped legs. He had a flattish nose, a full mouth, a dark complexion (even by Raiatean standards, apparently), and long black hair. By some he was considered "very good looking," while others argued that his features "conveyed no idea" of Polynesian beauty. He was tattooed on the hands and buttocks and dressed, depending upon the occasion, in flowing white tapa-cloth robes or the waistcoat, breeches, and stockings of an eighteenth-century gent.

He was described, especially at first, as having an active and restless temper. "When he desired to sit, he threw himself at full length on a sofa and only with difficulty learned the use of a chair," and it was suggested that he might want exercise. He enjoyed all kinds of sports and athletic activity, including shooting, horseback riding, and ice-skating, and showed a marked aptitude for dancing, making, according to Fanny Burney, *remarkably* good bows." A man of "uncommon spirits," he reportedly took the liveliest interest in everything around him, exhibiting, as one wit put it, "that enthusiastic zeal which Britons talk of [and] Otaheitans feel." But while this led some to depict him as a man of "quick parts"—Johann Forster cited as a mark of Omai's intellectual ability "his knowledge of the game of chess in which he had made an amazing proficiency"—to others it merely proved him "a *Sensationalist* of the first kind."

Omai, it was often said, had a penchant for "immediate corporeal gratifications." He delighted in toys and "trifling amusements" and was intensely interested in anything new. According to one observer, he once entertained himself with a magnifying glass—the first he'd ever encountered—throughout the course of an entire Royal Society dinner. He liked wine, especially Madeira, and all types of animal food, and was said to partake "promiscuously" of soups and vegetables. He had a passion for the theater, which he attended as often as he could, and enjoyed the outings, games, and parties with which his patrons filled their days. It was said that he was openly bored when he had nothing amusing to do.

This absence of gravitas—Cook noted that he had "a tolerable share of understanding" but that he "wanted application and perseverance to exert it"—was frequently ascribed to Omai's childlike nature. And here one detects the conventions of an age in which natives were first beginning to be viewed as people at an earlier stage of historical development, children, as it were, in the family of man. "His judgement," wrote Forster, "was in its infant state, and therefore, like a child, he coveted almost every thing he saw, and particularly that which had amused him by some unexpected effect." It was a charge that Cook and others often laid at the feet of Polynesians, arguing that "this kind of indifferency is the true character of [their] nation."

But for all his apparent lack of diligence, there was one respect in which Omai excelled almost beyond measure. "Indeed," wrote Fanny Burney, "his manners are so extremely graceful, & he is so polite, attentive & easy, that you would have thought he came from some foreign court." Good-

natured, agreeable, and charming, he managed in all sorts of
situations to seem entirely at home—whether bowing "with
the address of a well bred European" to a new acquaintance or
"gallantly handing about cake and bread-and-butter" to the
ladies at tea. Either because of some quality in himself—
"openness of countenance," "natural good behaviour," "native politeness"—or because of the society in which he had
been raised, or perhaps because he so quickly absorbed the
manners of those around him, Omai was considered by all who
encountered him to be perfectly "genteel."

This is, of course, precisely the sort of thing that preoccupied
the upper classes of England, but it was also an observation
very commonly made in the eighteenth and nineteenth centuries about Polynesians in general. Even Melville's cannibal
harpooner Queequeg, who is described in the opening scenes
of *Moby-Dick* as a most terrifying barbarian, is revealed to
have a great deal of the "natural gentleman" about him. "The
truth is," writes Melville, "these savages have an innate sense
of delicacy, say what you will; it is marvellous how essentially
polite they are."

What is *really* marvelous, however, is the staying power of
these conceits. The idea of a Noble Savage may sound con-
descending to modern ears, but by eighteenth-century standards it was the highest kind of praise. Nobility was a quality
that every European aspired to; *natural* nobility was something
even they could not achieve. Reynold's portrait, Fanny's zeal,
even Forster's grudging comments, reflect a broad and general
enthusiasm not just for Omai in particular, but for Polynesians
as a whole.

Perhaps I should hardly have been surprised, then, to find
that when Seven arrived in Boston, he attracted a similar sort

of admiration. Far from being snubbed or patronized, everywhere we went he was the belle of the ball. People peppered
him with questions about who he was and where he'd come
from, what he did for a living, where he'd grown up, what kind
of foods they ate in New Zealand, what languages they spoke.
Women, especially, gravitated to him, though he was also
popular with men. And while they sometimes seemed to be at
cross-purposes in their conversation—it was often hard for
people in Boston to tell what Seven was thinking and equally
difficult for him to decode them—they appeared delighted with
one another.

I had worried that, in some way, Seven would be unac-
ceptable, or that someone would be rude to him, or that they
would all be so baffled by one another that everyone would
just give up. He, after all, had little idea how things were done
among people like my parents and could no more have been
expected to know what passed for good manners among them
than they would have known the protocol for being invited
onto a Ngati Rehia *marae*. But I gave them all too little credit.
My family was genuinely interested in him and he acquitted
himself admirably. Whether by temperament, training, or
tradition, or some happy combination of all three, he appeared, as Fanny Burney once put it, "in a *new world* like a
man [who] had all his life studied the Graces . . . *politely easy
& thoroughly well bred!*"

"A natural gentleman," said my mother.

"Errghh!" said my brother, rolling his eyes.

"Oh, dear. Well, you know what I mean."

8

A DANGEROUS PEOPLE

MANY YEARS LATER, just after my father died, I came across a letter when I was clearing out his desk. It was, by then, almost fifteen years old and was dated to a period not long after Seven and I were first married. It had been sent to him by one of his cousins in California and most of it had to do with family news. The final paragraph, however, referred to an article from a New Zealand magazine, a copy of which was still attached.

> You may recall meeting at Harvard our friend J— of New Zealand, the same age as our Tom. He much appreciated your receiving him—at lunch, I believe. The enclosed article tells the appalling story of his murder—tragic from every point of view, as he was a gentle man and his father and grandfather had done a lot for the Maoris.

It was, indeed, a tragic story. The victim, a white, middle-age New Zealander, unprepossessing though actually very rich, was murdered at his beach house in the course of a bungled burglary by a group of Maori youths. The perpetrator was a fifteen-year-old half-Tongan, half-Maori boy from a large, dysfunctional family. Both his parents were described as alcoholics and the children had been removed from their custody multiple times. "It was like *Once Were Warriors*," said a relative, "If you've seen that film, that was it."

The killing was entirely senseless. The four young men had entered the house while the victim, his wife, and their children were sleeping. They had started to grab things apparently at random—some golf shoes, bizarrely, and a cotton bag—but they made too much noise and the victim woke and rushed out to see what was happening. Two of the intruders bolted as soon as the lights came on, but one remained long enough to get caught, at which point the fourth and youngest grabbed a knife off the kitchen counter and drove it into the victim's chest.

The Pakeha bled to death on the way to the hospital and the four youths ran off through the dunes. They buried the shoes and the bag on the beach and then headed for a friend's, where the fifteen-year-old reportedly told the others that he had stabbed the man in the house. "I used a butter knife," he said later to the police. "I used a butter knife," and "I pricked him."

The article was subtitled "Good New Zealand Meets Bad New Zealand" and, as if that were not bald enough, the final paragraph suggested that the root of the crime could be traced not to the perpetrator's social milieu, or any emotional or psychological damage he might have suffered, or even to the effect of both of these combined with the terrible recklessness of youth, but rather to something the writer referred to as "innate evil."

My father never mentioned this letter to me, but he did keep it for a very long time—and that despite the fact that there was a note on it from his cousin asking for the article to be returned. What, I wondered, had he thought about it? What had it meant to him? And why had he kept it all those years? It was too late for me to ask him by the time I found it, but I wondered if I'd have had the courage even if I'd had the chance.

My father was politically liberal. He had supported the civil rights movement and spoken out against the Vietnam War. But he had also grown up in a world when no one married out of either his ethnic group or his class. Seven had no money and hardly any education. He had no prospects, at least as these might be reckoned by someone like my father. He did not bring anything in the way of wealth or assets to our marriage and, although I was oblivious to this at the time, I'm sure my father worried about the burden this would ultimately place on me. What I did know was that my marriage to someone so very different challenged many of my father's most basic assumptions, and I appreciated the fact that he was gracious enough to keep his misgivings to himself. I was less sure about the motives of his cousin, who must have known that my father's son-in-law was Maori. What message, subtle or not so subtle, had he been hoping to convey?

If you pulled back from the details, you could see that this was a story about ethnic and socioeconomic conflict presented as a moral tale. The Pakehas were cool and well educated. They appeared at the trial fashionably dressed and acted with admirable restraint. The Maoris and Tongans were scruffy and unmotivated. They came to court in gum boots and woolly hats, bringing hordes of children with them who ought to have been in school. Though profoundly loyal to their family, they seemed hopelessly disordered. In the terms of the story it was "Good" versus "Bad," but it was also obviously White versus Black and Rich versus Poor.

In one respect, the tragedy was no different from things that happened all the time in places like England and the United States, and there was something rather quaint about the journalist's shock that such things could happen in New Zealand: "It seemed a violation of the trust and good faith that tied the New Zealand that we knew together, and left in its place a country we didn't recognise." But this, it seemed to me, was disingenuous, for there were elements of this story that would have been familiar to any New Zealander. Both the rift and the roles assigned to the respective parties had been part of the story of New Zealand from the moment Abel Tasman sailed out of Murderers' Bay.

When they first sailed into the Pacific, Europeans came armed with various ideas that helped them make sense of what they found. They had abstract ideas about balance and symmetry, as well as ways of ordering the world, frequently structured in pairs of opposites: noble/ignoble; sacred/profane; civilized and savage. Among these many organizing principles was a notion, originally derived from the ancient Greeks, that there were two kinds of primitivism, a "soft" and a "hard."

The soft, or Arcadian, model was a perfect fit for tropical islands like Tahiti, which Europeans routinely likened to "the garden of Eden," "the Elysian Fields," and "the true Utopia." But it was not the only model available to eighteenth-century Europeans. There was also a hard, or Spartan, version, which, in antiquity, sprang from accounts of barbarians living at the edges of the civilized world. Hard primitivism was associated with cool or rugged regions and described an austere, active people, often warlike, sometimes cruel, who valued bravery, strength, endurance, and loyalty to the tribe. To the neoclassically minded Europeans, New Zealand, with its temperate climate and combative natives, seemed the perfect embodiment of this type.

Like other Polynesians, the Maoris were tall and physically imposing. They had a clan-based society with a hereditary

nobility and a culture marked by oratory and elaborate dec-
orative arts. They were hunters and farmers who combined a
certain degree of geographic mobility with settled agricultural
habits. But the land they inhabited was not, like the rest of
Polynesia, tropical; there were no coconut trees or spreading
breadfruits, but heavily wooded hills, broad plains, and permanently snowcapped mountains. Stretching across the for-
tieth parallel of the southern hemisphere, New Zealand was
closer to Antarctica than any other inhabited region of the
world, save only Tierra del Fuego. In climate and topography it
was more like Scotland than Tahiti, and Highlander and
Viking analogies sprang readily to the European mind.

The emblematic figure of this culture was not the Noble
Savage, as it was for much of tropical Polynesia. Maoris were
not often painted as Omai had been, posed like some prince-
ling of a foreign court. When Maoris were painted, it was often
in action, performing a *haka*, or war dance, leaping with
weapons in arms. Or they might be depicted outdoors in
groups, huddled under their capes around a fire or near a
rude hut or barbarous carving. Early portraits typically focus
on their facial tattoos, which were seen by Europeans as marks
of savagery, and present their subjects not in flowing white
robes but in woven flax cloaks with dogskin tassels, sporting
bone or greenstone pendants and feathers in their hair. Where
a European sitter might be posed with a map or a globe (in the
case of an explorer), or a lap dog, or an open book, a Maori
was generally depicted with a weapon: a greenstone club, or
patu; or a carved wooden *taiaha*, the long ceremonial spear.

Not the Noble Savage but the Warlike Maori. As a character, he crops up all over the historical record—now as a
brave and fearless combatant, now as a cruel and savage eater
of men. He is, in many ways, more interesting than the Noble

Savage, who is always pleasing and admirable and never causes any trouble or does anyone any harm. The moral character of the Warlike Maori, on the other hand, is ambiguous and varies depending on who is telling the tale. To Cook, the Maoris were a "brave, open, warlike people." To Surville, they were "ferocious and bloodthirsty." According to Marion du Fresne, they were "fine" and "courageous," though he might have changed his tune if he had lived.

But what is really remarkable is not so much the variation in the way this image is inflected—positively in one place, negatively in another—as its ubiquitousness. Maoris, in early European accounts, are *always* warlike. They seem to live in a state of perpetual preparedness for battle, to see enemies on every quarter, to value heroism above all. They are said to be exceedingly sensitive to slights and obsessed with avenging real or imagined affronts to their honor. They are reputed to be impervious to pain, fearless of punishment, and impassive in the face of death. Their dances, their legends, their customs, their language—all are thought to express an overriding preoccupation with war. Even their material culture is said to reach its highest level of artistry in the design of fortifications, war canoes, weaponry, and other martial objects.

Historians argue that over the course of the nineteenth century there was a gradual hardening of this view. The image of the Warlike Maori became increasingly negative and less complex as what had begun in the late eighteenth century as an attempt at cultural description devolved into a stereotype and a cliché. The fact that similar shifts occurred in other places, for instance Africa and the American West, suggests that this was part and parcel of the colonial process. As more and more Europeans arrived to settle in New Zealand, the opportunities for conflict between the two sides increased, peaking in the

1860s and '70s in all-out colonial war. The fact that the Maoris were feared and admired by Europeans may have stood them in good stead during the dark days of the colonial period, by making them hard to intimidate and control. But this image also served their colonial masters by dignifying the conquest of New Zealand as a heroic struggle waged against a savage foe.

On the evening of December 19, 1835, the crew and passengers of H.M.S. *Beagle* sighted New Zealand. They were four years into a voyage round the world and still one year away from England. Charles Darwin, then twenty-six years old, served as naturalist on this expedition. The coast of New Zealand was a welcome sight to those on board. The ship's last stop had been Tahiti—"the island," as Darwin described it, "which must for ever remain classical to the voyager in the South Sea"—and for weeks they had been out of sight of land. Darwin was weary and rather homesick. He had been charmed by Tahiti but now he was looking forward to the journey's end.

Entering the Bay of Islands on December 21, Darwin noted some small villages scattered by the water's edge, three whalers lying at anchor, and now and then a canoe, passing silently from shore to shore. "An air of extreme quietness reigned over the whole district," he wrote. "Only a single canoe came alongside. This, and the aspect of the whole scene, afforded a remarkable, and not very pleasing contrast, with our joyful and boisterous welcome at Tahiti." The "hovels of the natives," he added, were "so diminutive and paltry that they can scarcely be perceived from a distance," while the scenery was "nowhere beautiful, and only occasionally pretty." There was, however, one aspect of the country that impressed him. "I should think," he wrote, that a more warlike race of inhabitants could not be found in any part of the world than the New Zealanders. Their conduct on first seeing a ship, as described by Captain Cook, strongly illustrates this: the act of throwing volleys of stones at so great and novel an object, and their defiance of "Come on shore and we will kill and eat you all," shows uncommon boldness.

Darwin, I am sorry to say, did not much like the Maoris. He found them dirty and cunning, brutal and uncouth, and thought they compared particularly badly with the elegant Tahitians. The Maoris, while obviously "belonging to the same family of mankind," were, he wrote, "of a much lower order." And he was glad, when he finally left New Zealand, to leave behind "the land of cannibalism, murder, and all atrocious crimes." But he was also an empiricist and a man of science and he was careful to substantiate his views.

On the second day, Darwin went out walking. "I was surprised to find," he wrote, "that almost every hill which I ascended had been at some former time more or less fortified . . . These are the Pas, so frequently mentioned by Captain Cook." Built as a rule upon hills, headlands, and islands and surrounded by high palisades, these defensive fortifications, were among the first things to be noticed by European visitors to New Zealand. When Joseph Banks, who sailed with Cook, caught his first glimpse of the New Zealand coast, he remarked that "on a small peninsula at the NE head we could plainly see a regular paling, pretty high, inclosing the top of a hill." There was a good deal of discussion as to what this might be. "Most are of the opinion," wrote Banks, "that it must be either a park of deer or a field of oxen and sheep." But the fauna of New Zealand is what zoologists call "depauperate," meaning that, as far as animals are concerned at least, there was almost nothing there.

New Zealand was isolated as a landmass for between eighty to a hundred million years and for all but a thousand of these it was unoccupied by humans. When the ancestors of the Maoris began arriving from the tropical islands to the north, they found a large, mountainous land heavily forested with giant ferns. The most significant creature was an enormous flightless bird, standing well over six feet tall, with a razor-sharp beak and tiny wings. They called it—perhaps jokingly—*moa*, after the bedraggled common fowls of central Polynesia, and quickly hunted it to extinction. There were other interesting creatures: enormous flightless ducks and swans and an eagle big enough to carry off a Maori child. There was a peculiar reptile called the tuatara, which, scientists now conclude, has been around for two hundred million years. But while the seas were teeming with mammalian life, there were no land mammals whatsoever, excepting, peculiarly, the bat. The first Polynesians brought dogs and rats, but while they ate both, they did not pen either, and the only use they had for palings was to keep each other out.

Many of the *pa* that Darwin saw were in ruins, but the sheer number of sites (there are thought to be thousands) and the extensive evidence of pits and middens suggested to him that they had been heavily used. This warlike spirit was also evident, he thought, in many of the Maoris' customs. If a man were struck, even by accident, Darwin asserted, he was honor-bound to return the blow. In Paihia, he learned the story of Hongi Hika, the Ngapuhi chief who traveled to England in search of guns, and how "the love of war was the one and lasting spring of [his] every action." In Kororareka, he remarked the "disagreeable expression" that tattooing gave the

Maori face, and "a twinkling in the eye, which cannot indicate any thing but cunning and ferocity."

All of this contributed to Darwin's impression that the Maoris were a dangerous people. But if you look at the way he builds his case, Darwin's principal claim for the Maoris' belligerence rests, at least rhetorically, upon a sixty-five-year-old citation in translation of a sentence shouted by a nameless New Zealander across an open expanse of water at Cook. *Come on shore and we will kill and eat you all* is—like something in a child's game of telephone—what Darwin said that Cook said the Maoris said at that interesting moment when the Europeans first appeared.

But the story does not stop there. For between Cook's actual experience in New Zealand and Darwin's version, there is still another figure: the editor of Cook's *Endeavour* journal, John Hawkesworth.

Hawkesworth was the professional man of letters who had been hired by the British Admiralty to edit the journals of a group of explorers (Philip Carteret, Samuel Wallis, and John Byron, in addition to Cook) who had recently returned from voyages to the South Seas. His was the only edition of Cook's first voyage for most of the nineteenth century; it went through multiple editions and was very widely read, despite the many liberties that Hawkesworth took with the original texts. Hawkesworth's edition is larded with didactic remarks and philosophical digressions inserted for the edification and moral improvement of his readers. He lengthened the sentences, elevated the diction, added transitional material, and combined the words of different writers, most notably Cook and Banks. To add insult to injury, the entire thing was written in the first person. Cook, who set out on his second voyage before the edition went to press, was reputedly "mortified" when he caught up with it two years later.

What Cook had actually written was that whenever his ship was approached by Maoris who had not yet seen a European vessel, the natives would come out in their largest canoes and, as soon as they were within a stone's throw, "they would there lay, and call out, Haromai hareuta a patoo age, that is come here, come a shore with us and we will kill you with our patoo patoo's, and at the same time would shake them at us."

Patu—Cook's "patoo patoo"—is both a Maori verb meaning to strike, beat, thrash, subdue, ill-treat, or kill, and a noun describing a short, flat, paddle-shaped club with a sharpened edge made of wood, greenstone, or bone. It was worn stuck in a warrior's belt and used to deliver the death blow to an opponent, first with an upthrust of the sharpened edge to the temple, neck, or ribs, followed by a downward blow with the butt of the weapon upon the enemy's head. Banks described a "patoo patoo" he examined as weighing "not less than 4 or 5 pounds" and "certainly well contrived for splitting skulls," while an early French visitor called it a "*casse-tête,*" literally a "head-breaker," "*parce qu'ils n'en font pas d'autre usage,*" because there was no other use for it.

The Maori phrase is phonetically incorrect as reported—Cook's ear for languages was not the best—and over the years several variants have been proposed. But there is little disagreement as to what it means. "In peace or war," writes the anthropologist Anne Salmond, "strangers were greeted with the same ritual forms, because an unknown group might always be planning treachery, and a display of strength could dissuade them. Early observers of these encounters remarked that it was almost impossible to distinguish peaceful overtures from warlike ones."

"Come here, come ashore, and we will kill you" is clearly a challenge thrown out at the meeting of two groups whose relationship has yet to be established. It serves both to acknowledge the prestige of the visitors and to demonstrate the *mana*, or authority, of the people on shore. It is not so much a declaration of intent as an opening gambit. The emphasis is less on a particular outcome (the violent death of the visitors on shore) than on the initiation of negotiations. In other words, while the Maoris clearly intended to intimidate their visitors, they did not *necessarily* plan to kill them. And there is no mention anywhere of anyone eating anyone—which, in Maori terms, would certainly have been insulting.

Cook himself clearly grasped the basic import of the phrase. He noted that these words and gestures were not always followed by further displays of ferocity but often by conversation and trade. Banks, too, recognized their performative aspect. "Whenever they met with us and thought themselves superior they always attacked us, though seldom seeming to mean more than to provoke us to show them what we were able to do." But Hawkesworth seems to have seen in this passage the makings of an epic encounter between savagery and civilization. "When they were at too great a distance to reach us with a lance or a stone," he wrote,

> they presumed that we had no weapon with which we could reach them; here then the defiance was given, and the words were almost universally the same, Haromai, haromai, harre uta a Patoo-Patoo oge: "Come to us, come on shore, and we will kill you all with our Patoo-Patoos." While they were uttering these menaces they came gradually nearer and nearer, till they were close along side; talking at intervals in a peaceable strain, and answering any questions that we

asked them; and at intervals renewing their defiance and threats, till being encouraged by our apparent timidity, they began their war-song and dance, as a prelude to an attack, which always followed, and was sometimes continued till it became absolutely necessary to repress them by firing some small shot; and sometimes ended after throwing a few stones on board, as if content with having offered us an insult which we did not dare to revenge.

The effect of Hawkesworth's alterations is to recast the episode as a melodrama, heightening the tension of the stand-off ("here then the defiance was given") and accentuating the Maori threat ("uttering these menaces they came gradually nearer and nearer"), while simultaneously softening and legit-imizing the British response ("till it became absolutely neces-sary to repress them by firing some small shot"). It was Hawkesworth, argues W. H. Pearson, who gave us "the prototype of that hero of Victorian boy's sea fiction, the magnanimous British commander." But he also, as if to accentuate the contrast, painted the Maoris as arrant cowards. They declare themselves from a safe distance, presuming "that we had no weapon with which we could reach them"; they hesitate to launch an attack until they are "encouraged by our apparent timidity"; and they retreat after a few vain and ineffectual gestures, "as if content with having offered us an insult which we did not dare to revenge." So that, by the time Hawkesworth is done with them, the Maoris scarcely resemble the bold and enigmatic people described by Cook.

Of course, there was no way for Darwin to make this comparison. But what is interesting is the way in which he, too, modified the story. Darwin drops the reference to the *patu* but adds a suggestion of cannibalism that seems to be entirely his own. This is not to say that the suggestion that the Maoris might have eaten their enemies was a wild or improbable idea; on the contrary, it was well known in Darwin's day that cannibalism was a traditional Maori practice. Cook and Banks are perfectly clear on the point, as is Hawkesworth, who, not surprisingly, found the subject fascinating.

It is perhaps to Hawkesworth's account of Maori cannibalism that one should look for insight into Darwin's thinking. Since the Maoris depended upon fish as their principal source of food, they must live in constant danger of starvation. This would account not only for their custom of fortifying their villages against marauders, but for "the horrid practice of eating those who are killed in battle." But, although necessity might press a man to eat his neighbor, Hawkesworth argued, "The mischief does by no means end [there] . . . after the practice has been once begun on one side by hunger, it will naturally be adopted on the other by revenge." Instituted in self-defense, the practice of eating human flesh eventually becomes a habit, which leads eventually to general moral erosion. "There is the strongest reason to believe," he wrote,

> that those who have been so accustomed to prepare a human body for a meal, that they can with as little feeling cut up a dead man, as our cook-maids divide a dead rabbit for a fricassee, would feel as little horror in committing a murder as in picking a pocket . . . so that men, under these circumstances, would be made murderers by the slight temptations that now make them thieves.

The Maoris are, thus, to be feared and mistrusted not because they are instinctively murderous but because they have lost the instinct that sanctifies human life. They are not immoral (which is remediable), but amoral (which is not).

For Cook, Banks, Hawkesworth, and Darwin, cannibalism was a profoundly difficult subject and they twisted themselves into knots whenever they tried to explain it. Today, the generally accepted view is that cannibalism among the Maoris was a form of mastery and a means of degradation, a way of turning something sacred into something base. As such, it was a kind of conquest, not unlike capture, enslavement, or death. But the point is not so much what cannibalism meant from the Maori point of view, as how the *idea* of it was used to enhance a particular image among Europeans. Darwin's claim that the Maoris threatened not just to kill but *to eat* anyone who arrived unbidden was part of a story that could be traced right through to the article I had found in my father's desk.

When Darwin arrived in 1835 things in New Zealand were already quite different from the way they had been in the days of Cook. There had been shipping and trade in the Bay of Islands for nearly three decades and missionaries in residence for more than twenty years. In the previous decade, the bay had become a major provisioning stop for the growing South Seas whaling fleet and an active center for trade in timber and flax. There were something like five hundred Europeans living there permanently, including an American consul, a British resident, a doctor, merchants and tradesmen of various descriptions, and an ever-shifting crowd of drifters, deadbeats, and deserters.

But there were fewer Maoris. It is hard to say exactly how many fewer, but the suggestion of native depopulation in Darwin's journal probably reflects the combined effect of contagious disease and a deadly explosion of intertribal war, both of which were direct consequences of contact with Europeans. It was a melancholy period for the Maoris, these years leading up to annexation, and it would get worse before it got better. It is no wonder, really, that Darwin found New Zealand grim; a lot of Maoris in the 1830s probably felt the same way.

What is worth noting, however, is the tendency on the part of European chroniclers to locate this grimness *in the Maoris themselves*, as an essential component of their character, rather than to see it for what it was—the fallout of contact with Europeans. For, while there can be little doubt that the Maoris were a bellicose people, so, quite obviously, were the people who had suddenly materialized at their door. As the early colonialist Frederick Maning, who wrote under the pseudonym "A Pakeha Maori," put it wittily in the 1860s:

If ever there should land on this shore a people who wear red garments, who do not work, who neither buy nor sell, and who always have arms in their hands, then be aware that these are a people called soldiers, a dangerous people whose only occupation is war.

9

SMOKED HEADS

IN THE ROOM that I called my study in the house down by the beach there were three pieces of furniture: an office chair scavenged from the university, a desk that Seven had made from a piece of plywood, and a two-drawer filing cabinet. At the very front of the top drawer of this cabinet was a thick file marked "Illustrations" that contained a number of photographs that I used in my work. There was one showing the butt of a rifle that had been carved in the Maori style and another depicting an array of Maori weapons. There were several pictures of Maori men, reproductions, for the most part, of nineteenth-century paintings, in which the artist had carefully picked out the tattoos, some landscapes and seascapes, and several photos of groups of people posed in that stiff, old-fashioned way. There was one picture, however, that I kept carefully wrapped, both because I didn't want any harm to come to it and because the subject was, well, difficult.

It was a picture of General Horatio Gordon Robley seated on a cloth-draped bench in front of a wall mounted with thirty-four Maori heads. The photo had no date but was probably taken when Robley was in his midfifties, about 1895. What remained of his hair had been combed carefully across the dome of his head, his eyebrows and mustache were slightly grizzled. His dress and posture were casual but correct; he wore a collar and tie and some kind of ornament in the buttonhole of his lapel. He was sitting, legs crossed, one hand slipped into a trouser pocket, his jacket open below the top button, a watch chain visible across his vest. In his other hand he held a wooden weapon, a short, fiddle-shaped Maori club called a *wahaika*, which lay casually across his lap. He was posed front-on to the camera, head turned slightly to one side, gazing into the middle distance with an expression that was difficult to read.

About half an inch to the left of Robley's right eye, which due to some trick of the camera gleamed slightly, was the empty eye socket of a preserved Maori head, a particularly striking Maori head with a tousled mass of hair, broad cheekbones, and a square jaw. It was, in its way, a handsome face. It was clearly the head of a young man and there was something tender about it and ghoulish at the same time. Above, below, and on either side were more heads ranged in rough, uneven rows: grim, black, disembodied objects with hanks of hair and greenstone ornaments hanging from their ears. Their skin was dark and shiny like leather, on some you could just make out the *moko*, or tattoo. Their eyelids were sewn shut—except for one whose glass eyes gave it a mournful cast—but their lips were open, stretched back as far as they could go to reveal perfect sets of clenched white teeth. They looked as if they were snarling or sneering or maybe grimacing in pain, though one might almost have been smirking. Samuel Marsden, the missionary, had a name for it: he called it that "ghastly grin." But it was Robley who captured the essence of the expression. They had, he wrote, a look of "life-in-death which once seen can never be forgotten."

The way the picture was composed, one instantly saw Robley's own head as one among many. It lay in the same plane and was on the same scale and occupied the position of the second head from the right in the fourth row down. The difference, of course, was that Robley's head was attached to something at the neck, while the Maori heads floated in space, mounted by invisible means, casting only the faintest of shadows. The message of this composition cut both ways, suggesting, on the one hand, that the Maori heads were also once attached to bodies and belonged to individual men—an idea strongly reinforced by the remarkable preservation of their features. And yet, at the same time, it was obvious that in this context they were objects, specimens in a collection, while Robley was clearly a collector.

At the end of the bench on which Robley sat were two small objects about the size of cantaloupes that looked as smooth as polished stone. They were the heads of children and they had a different look about them from the rest. Their mouths were shut, their eyes were closed, and they looked as if they were sleeping. They were not the first thing you saw in the photo but, rather, almost the last, and they seemed to tell a different story, or perhaps to complicate the story told by Robley and the grown-up heads.

The process by which the heads were preserved has been detailed in various places. According to one account,

The preparation of the skull was called *Paki Paki* or *Popo*, which signified taking out the brain. The heads were then steamed in the oven several times, and after each steaming were carefully wiped with the flowers of the *kakaho* or reed, and every portion of flesh and brain was removed, a small thin *manuka* stick being inserted between the skin and bone of the nose to preserve its form. This over, the heads were dried in the sun, and afterwards exposed to the smoke of

their houses. The eyes were extracted, the sockets filled with
flax, and the lids sewn together . . .

I found these descriptions mesmerizing but not repellant. I
was, strangely, not appalled by accounts of the process, by the
idea of dropping a head into boiling water, or wrapping it in
leaves and steaming it in an earth oven until the skin slips off
the skull. It did not distress me to learn that in the final stages
of preparation the head was heated and basted with fat; I even
found myself wondering what kind of fat they used. But it did
occur to me that perhaps I didn't *really* understand what any of
this meant. The heads seemed a test of my ability to imagine
what I would never know, and perhaps the fact that I was *not*
appalled meant that I hadn't imagined it properly.

In principle, I have always been committed to the idea of
disinterested curiosity and to the way of seeing it represents: an
empirical, purely secular approach to the things of this world.
It is a stance with roots in the Englightenment, one that arose in
the days of Cook, and it is certainly cultural. I would never
expect Seven, for example, to share it with me. But the reason I
value this perspective is that I think it gives me the best possible
chance of understanding what has really happened.

Although it is difficult to look at this photograph and not see
the wholesale exploitation, even slaughter, of one people by
another, it is important to try. Because that is not the story
this picture tells us. This picture tells a story of colonialism,
but it is not a story about the impact of one culture on
another like a hammer on a nail. It is more like the story of
two systems colliding, like trains heading in opposite directions
that have been mistakenly shunted onto the same track. It was
the Maoris who took and preserved these heads; it was
the Europeans who bought and sold them. And it was the

interaction of the two that made possible a photograph in which a man in a morning coat can sit looking unperturbed surrounded by trophies with shining teeth and sunken cheeks and albatross feathers in their hair.

In 1864 Horatio Gordon Robley, then a lieutenant in the 68th Durham Light Infantry, arrived in New Zealand as part of a British imperial force sent to occupy Tauranga. An amateur artist, he took his sketchbook with him and made many drawings of Maori life. He sketched canoe races and storehouses, war dances, cemeteries, funerals, soldiers, forts, churches, and battles. He paid particular attention to Maori art, especially the art of the tattoo, which was even then disappearing under the influence of the missionaries, and he earned a reputation for oddity by going around after battles and squatting in the mud next to Maori corpses in order to copy the designs on the faces of the dead. He was an avid collector of coins, curios, and other objects, including *moko-mokai*, or smoked heads. In 1896 he published a monograph called *Moko; or, Maori Tattooing*, which remains an important sourcebook on the history of the art form.

Although most Polynesians practiced some form of tattooing, the Maoris were famous for their facial tattoos, which were excruciatingly painful and took years to complete. A full facial tattoo was considered a sign of the highest distinction and only the most important and aged chiefs succeeded in acquiring it. The designs might cover every inch of the face, even the eyelids and the lips, with patterned bands and spirals. Each *moko* was unique, and though generally symmetrical, they often varied slightly from side to side. It was considered by its wearer to be a sign of his identity and some of the earliest deeds and contracts entered into by Maoris show, instead of a signature, a drawing of the signer's *moko*, ingeniously represented in two dimensions, as if the head had been flayed and the skin laid out flat upon a table.

The Maori method of applying a tattoo might almost have been designed as a test of endurance. Not content to prick or lightly score the skin, the Maoris carved their designs into the face with a chisel dipped in a solution of charcoal (or, in later years, gunpowder) and tapped with a wooden mallet, a process one early observer referred to as "being chipped." Naturally, it was considered unmanly to groan or writhe or give any other indication of discomfort, but the handful of Pakeha sailors and vagabonds who had themselves tattooed in the early decades of the nineteenth century reported that the process was almost unbearable. The resulting scars left the skin ridged and rough, and sometimes, if the cuts were made too deep, interfered with the facial muscles. But it also gave the wearer an ageless look, making the young look older and the old look young, for "where moko is elaborated," wrote Robley, "time can write no wrinkles." Notwithstanding the difficulties of the ordeal, all men of status underwent some degree of tattooing, as did most women, though less extensively and usually only on the lips and chin.

The relationship between tattooing faces and preserving heads is an obvious one, and in some sense, it was the *moko* that was being preserved. In later years tattooed skin was salvaged from other parts of the body; Robley tells of cartouche boxes made from the tattooed skin of a man's buttocks and thighs. But it was heads that Maoris really valued. Traditionally, the heads of both enemies and friends or relatives were preserved. But, in either case, only the heads of the most exalted, and therefore the most fully tattooed, were considered fit for preservation (although exceptions might be made in the case of a favorite wife or child). The curing of the head, writes Robley, was "an acknowledgment of the nobility of its owner" and served to keep his memory alive. When the head of a family member was preserved, the lips were sewn together in the middle, making an elegant shape of the mouth, like two almonds side by side. This gives the face a comparatively quiet expression, unanimated, almost serene. Heads of this type were considered treasures and were kept carefully hidden away by the family of the deceased and brought out only on important occasions.

It was a different matter with enemies' heads. These were the heads most often seen and described by Europeans, and the ones, generally speaking, that turned up in private collections and museums later on. In the case of an enemy, the mouth was left unstitched—thus the ghastly grin—and the head was treated with a curious mixture of reverence and contempt. Early visitors to New Zealand often reported seeing them fixed on the ramparts of a *pa*, or stuck on poles outside a village, where they were taunted and jeered at by passersby. According to Reverend William Yates, a warrior would stand and address his enemy's head in words that went something like this:

You wanted to run away, did you? But my *mere* [club] overtook you, and after you were cooked you were made food for my mouth. And where is your father? He is cooked. Where is your brother? He is eaten. Where is your wife? There she sits, a wife for me. Where are your children? There they are, with loads on their backs, carrying food as my slaves.

For all this, *mokomokai* served an important political purpose. The central governing concept of Maori political life was *utu*, a word that is often translated as "revenge" but means something closer to "satisfaction" or "reciprocity." *Utu* demanded that both favors and grievances be repaid in kind, but it was the grievances, naturally, that caused the most trouble. Tribes often went to war to settle scores that had been nursed for generations, and this, in turn, laid the foundation for what Marsden called "new acts of cruelty and blood," creating new grounds for *utu*. Heads, in this context, served as bargaining chips in tribal negotiations. In order to conclude a peace treaty the parties might require an exchange of heads. Or if an important chief fell in battle, the deliverance of his head might be enough to bring the hostilities to an end. By the same token, it was said that if a chief destroyed an enemy's head while it was in his possession, it was a sign that he would never make peace with that tribe.

All this changed with the arrival of the Europeans. Among Maoris, heads might be traded, but only for political reasons and not in the commercial sense, as one kind of good to be exchanged for another. One could not purchase potatoes, for example, with a head—an idea that would have struck any Maori as obscene. Heads were highly sacred objects, imbued with a significance or power that could not be converted into something else, particularly something base or worldly. For eighteenth- and nineteenth-century Europeans, however, heads were instantly understood as curios, like dinosaur bones or iridescent beetles, objects of aesthetic and scientific interest.

The first "sale" of a Maori head occurred during Captain Cook's first circumnavigation of New Zealand. Toward the end of January 1770, the *Endeavour* was reconnoitering an area of coastline about seventy miles from Tasman's Murderers' Bay. Going ashore one afternoon, Cook, Banks, and Tupaia, their Tahitian translator, met a family employed in preparing a meal. A dog was cooking in an earth oven and there were some baskets containing food nearby. Looking casually into one of these, Banks reported that they saw two bones, "pretty clean picked," which, upon examination, proved to be those of a human being. Although Maoris up and down the coast had repeatedly and freely admitted to the practice of eating their enemies, Cook and his companions felt the need to be convinced. So Banks began to question the Maoris. "What bones are these?" he asked.

—The bones of a man.
—And have you eat the flesh?
—Yes.
—Have you none of it left?
—No.
—Why did not you eat the woman who we saw today in the water [referring to a body they had seen floating in the bay]?
—She was our relation.
—Who then is it that you do eat?
—Those who are killed in war.
—And who was the man whose bones these are?
—Five days ago a boat of our enemies came into this bay and of them we killed seven, of whom the owner of these bones was one.

Cook then took a bone and asserted that it was not the bone of a man but rather that of a dog. "But [the Maori] with great fervency took hold of his fore-arm and told us again that it was that bone and to convince us that they had eat the flesh he took hold of the flesh of his own arm with his teeth and made show of eating." Which plainly showed, Cook added drily, "that the flesh to them was a dainty bit."

The next day a small canoe came out to the ship and Tupaia questioned the Maoris further. Where were the skulls, he asked, "Do you eat them?" To which an old man replied, "We do not eat the heads . . . but we do the brains and tomorrow I will bring one and show you." A few days later he reappeared, bringing with him four preserved heads. Banks immediately grasped what sort of things these were, describing them as trophies and likening them to scalps taken by North American Indians. The old man, Cook reported, was extremely reluctant to part with any of the heads, but Banks at last convinced him to sell one, that of a teenage boy whose skull had been badly fractured, for the price of a pair of linen drawers.

In the days before the arrival of Europeans, Maoris fought each other in sporadic, limited, intertribal wars, conducted during the summer months by small kin-based parties of perhaps two hundred men. They used clubs and spears of hardened wood, bone, or stone. They had no real projectile weapons, no bows and arrows, no slings except for killing birds, while the spear, or *taiaha*, was twirled and thrust, but not typically thrown. This meant that hand-to-hand combat was the norm. No one expected to be killed at a distance and all the defensive techniques that had been developed over centuries of regular warfare assumed that as long as your enemy could not reach you, he could do you no harm. Thus, the gun, even the unreliable flintlock trade musket that was in circulation at the beginning of the nineteenth century, was greeted by those who first felt its effect, writes the historian R. D. Crosby, with "a deep and widespread despair." Describing a battle in which the attackers were armed with guns while the defending tribe had never before experienced musket-fire, he writes, "The initial reaction of stunned silence was followed by a wail which grew in volume as awareness of the horror of the power of the musket struck home."

The first appearance of guns in Maori intertribal warfare dates to 1807, when they were used in a battle at Moremonui. The guns did not, on this occasion, ensure their owners' triumph. On the contrary, so many of their bodies were left on the beach that the battle came to be known as *Te Kai a te Karoro*, or the Seagulls' Feast. But among those who survived the slaughter was a clever young *rangatira* from the Bay of Islands named Hongi Hika. It was Hongi who first recognized that the key to future success lay in the acquisition of the Pakeha's guns. He was entirely motivated by *utu*, that is, by the desire to avenge his tribe's losses at Moremonui and elsewhere. He was not fundamentally interested in Europeans, except insofar as they were able to provide him with the means of achieving his goal. The accident of history is that Hongi belonged to Ngapuhi and Ngapuhi came from the Bay of Islands and the Bay of Islands was the first major port of call for European vessels, which meant that he was among the very first to have significant access to guns.

Hongi led his first great raid against his southern neighbors, the tribes of the Bay of Plenty, in 1818. The *taua*, or war party, consisted of over nine hundred men, of whom fifty or so were armed with muskets. They returned to the Bay of Islands in January of the following year, bringing with them a thousand prisoners and hundreds of heads—one witness counted seventy piled in a single canoe. The next year Hongi sailed to England with the missionary Thomas Kendall. Kendall was seeking ordination; Hongi was seeking guns. In London, Hongi and his cousin Waikato were presented to King George and showered with presents, including a suit of armor from the Tower of

London. On the way back home they stopped in Sydney, where Hongi sold everything—except the armor, which he liked to wear—and used the money to buy guns.

On the way back to New Zealand he encountered two of his long-standing rivals before whom he laid out his new collection, saying,

> E mara ma! O friends! O Te Horeta! and Te Hinaki! Behold! this gun is "Te Wai-whariki" [the Blood-stained Stream], this is "Kaikai-a-te-karoro" [the Seagulls' Feast], this is "Wai-kohu" [River Mist] this is "Te Ringa-huru-huru" [the Warrior's Arm], this is "Mahurangi" [the Exalted],

naming one by one the defeats that Ngapuhi had suffered and that he intended to revenge. Almost as soon as he returned to New Zealand, Hongi embarked on an expedition of war unlike anything the Maoris had ever seen. He had two thousand warriors and one thousand guns and there was not a tribe in New Zealand that could withstand him.

These were the opening salvos of the Musket Wars, a period of intense internecine warfare that lasted almost three decades and resulted in tens of thousands of Maori deaths, the destruction of whole tribes, and the depopulation of entire regions. Hongi was by no means the only force behind the devastation—by the early 1830s almost every major tribe in New Zealand was at war—but he was one of a handful whose desire to see old debts repaid mutated into a taste for pandemonium. It was, however, a self-limiting disorder. As Ngapuhi proceeded down the North Island, exacting retribution for old wrongs, their victims naturally concluded that they too must have muskets, no matter what the cost. The price of a musket in 1820 was a ton of dressed flax, the principal commodity of

European exchange, and soon whole tribes began relocating to swamps, where the plant grew in abundance. People sickened in the damp and neglected the cultivation of their food crops. The demand for slaves skyrocketed—slaves who could only be had by raiding tribal neighbors—to meet the insatiable need for labor to produce more flax.

It takes almost no imagination to predict what happened next. Maoris soon realized that European traders would pay in guns and ammunition for preserved, tattooed heads. Almost overnight the market for heads exploded, transforming what was once an honor reserved for the few into a base, mercantile affair. No head with a good tattoo was safe, and in order to increase the supply, chiefs began tattooing their slaves with the express purpose of selling their heads as soon as they were finished. All kinds of insane stories began circulating, like the one Frederick Maning recorded of a head that was selected, sold, and paid for while its owner was still alive. Meanwhile, across the Tasman Sea, an item described as "Baked Heads" appeared on the list of imports at Sydney customs. Not surprisingly, Maoris quickly stopped preserving the heads of their friends and relatives, leaving only those of enemies, slaves, and unfortunate Pakehas in circulation.

By the early 1830s this vicious cycle—heads for muskets, muskets for heads—had spiraled out of control. In Sydney, Governor Darling issued a general order prohibiting the importation of heads into New South Wales, and what had begun in 1770 as an exercise in scientific curiosity (tinged perhaps with pleasurable horror) became a capital offense. This effectively stopped the trade, but by then hundreds of Maori heads had made their way out of New Zealand and into the hands of collectors around the world. Robley lists some of the collections in which they were held in the 1890s, including the

British Museum, the Berlin Museum of Ethnology, the Florence Anthropological Museum, the Smithsonian Institute, the Paris Muséum national d'histoire naturelle, and the Royal College of Surgeons in London. There are, or were, Maori heads (and a few tattooed heads of Europeans) in New York, Dublin, Rome, Moscow, Hamburg, Copenhagen, and many other American and European cities, while Robley himself had perhaps the finest collection in private hands.

Simply looking at him in this picture, surrounded by his collection of heads, one could be forgiven for thinking Robley an archetypal colonial: arrogant, cold, acquisitive, smug. *Has he no feeling?* one wonders. Can he not see that these too were men, whose grief and pleasure were no different from his own? Why does he not distinguish between carved inanimate objects, like the *wahaika* he holds in his hands, and the carved human remains on the wall behind him? And yet it should be said in Robley's defense that his treatment of these objects was motivated by respect and admiration for them as works of art, and by a powerful desire to understand them in a scientific sense. Even an untutored observer will recognize the continuity of style between the carving of Maori weapons, canoes, and house posts and the lines on a tattooed face. From an aesthetic or technical point of view, it is all of a piece, and it was Robley's wish to preserve a unique aspect of Maori material culture that was on the verge of vanishing in his lifetime.

I had had a copy of this photo for about a year when I showed it to one of Seven's sisters in New Zealand. She took one glance at it and looked as if she were going to be sick.

I was appalled. She was appalled. But we were appalled for different reasons.

"They're somebody's *tupuna*," she said. "Ancestors. Imagine if it was your grandfather."

But I couldn't. I couldn't see my grandfather, with his snow-white hair and steel gray eyes and his papery old man's skin, decapitated, smoked, and mounted on the wall of a photographer's studio flanked by a Maori warrior in a dogskin cloak holding a Smith and Wesson. There is no precedent for such an image. One can only invent it by inverting the details. Nor, to be frank, could I connect in that emotional way with any image of a man I'd never known. The heads in this picture were not those of her grandparents; they were people who could not be fewer than five or six generations distant. Nor was there any evidence to say that they were Ngapuhi; they were probably not even members of her tribe. In fact, if you wanted to get right down to it, they were probably her ancestors' enemies, victims of the great Ngapuhi, like as not.

None of this made any difference to my sister-in-law. It didn't matter that they were not her relations, that nobody knew whose relations they were, that no matter how vivid they looked, they were basically anonymous. To her there was something deeply shocking, almost pornographic about the heads. What wasn't clear to me was exactly what had upset her: whether it was the heads per se, the horror of them, or the idea of such a collection and such a collector, or the fact that I was in possession of this picture, or that I had been so thoughtless as to show it to her.

After that I carried the photograph back and forth to New Zealand like contraband, tucked inside a book hidden in my suitcase. I thought of showing it to my mother-in-law, who took a keen interest in Maori history and who, I thought, might have interesting information to share. But I was afraid of what she might say, of what she might think of me, as if this would prove conclusively that I was a barbarian, to have so little feeling for the dead. It was like the other things I wanted to know about but didn't dare ask—religious things, customary things, things that conflicted with Christianity, things that had been suppressed. I suppose I could have gotten rid of the photo, but I'd become attached to it over the years. Its discovery had been one of my research triumphs; at first I'd imagined I would use it as some kind of illustration, maybe one day even the cover of a book. But gradually I realized this was not going to be possible and I put the photograph away.

It was almost a decade before I took the photo out again. I had learned that a museum in Boston owned a couple of specimens of Maori *mokomokai*. This was not a well-publicized bit of information but no one denied the fact, and when I asked if I could see them, the curator said yes, it could be arranged.

I wanted Seven to go with me. He had seen the Robley photograph but he had never seen an actual head and he was curious about them—though not perhaps as curious as I was to see how he'd react. Our appointment was for a weekday afternoon, so we took some time off work and made a day of it, allowing time to wander around the museum and go out to lunch. When the time for our appointment came, the curator met us in the lobby. After she had signed us in, she led us down a narrow hallway and through a door to a labyrinthine set of passages, up some stairs, down a corridor, into the freight elevator, and finally into the warehouse through one last set of well-locked doors.

It was a large, cavernous space, or would have been, had it not been stuffed to the rafters with crates and pallets. I looked around in awe, wondering what was in them: *wahaika* like the one in the Robley photo, greenstone adzes, royal Hawaiian necklaces made of human hair? There was a small open area near the doorway in which a little table had been placed. The heads, which had been set out earlier in anticipation of our arrival, were on this table covered with a piece of tissue paper.

"I've been here for eleven years and I've never taken these out of their box before," said the curator, as she put on a smock, a pair of gloves, and a disposable mask.

"Is that to protect you or the heads?" I asked.

"Both, really."

I wondered what the heads, which had been in a perfect state of preservation for almost two hundred years, could do to anyone now.

"There's a lot of weird dust around here," she said. "I don't think you can be too careful."

I walked slowly over to the table. One corner of the tissue paper was lifted slightly and beneath it I could see a couple of teeth. For a minute I felt a shiver of contact with the supernatural. Then the curator lifted the sheet of paper and the feeling vanished.

What I saw were two heads, slightly smaller than I'd expected, the color of oak, with dry, dusty-looking hair. Their ears were shriveled and at first Seven thought they'd been cut off. But, no, I told him, look closer, there they are; it must have been the effect of the drying process. Their teeth were intact but rather yellowed. The *moko*, or tattoo, was much less vivid than I'd expected, just a series of faint, rather delicate blue lines, and I could see why it was so hard to decipher in the photographs. It was not at all obvious to me how one would tell if the tattooing had been added posthumously—making the head a "fake" in nineteenth-century terms—though Robley claimed it was easy to distinguish. Looking closer, I could see that the lines on one of the heads appeared to have been inscribed, though on the other I simply could not tell. One of the heads was in a better state of preservation. Interestingly, this one had its mouth stitched closed—again, something I had not expected to see.

There was almost no information about their provenance. One was received by the museum in 1904, the gift of a physician and art collector. The other, the better of the two, was purchased in 1926 and came, according to the catalog, from an old French collection. "Old," of course, is a tantalizing word, suggesting that it might have been acquired in or around the Bay of Islands, where much of the earliest collecting took place. Many of the oldest heads in European collections were traded by Ngapuhi, though, of course, they probably belonged to people who came from farther south. Curiously, the hair on this head was tightly curled—the catalog suggested that it "[had] been curled," as if the wearer had been fashion-conscious. More likely, the hair was just naturally curly. This is not the classic Maori look— most Maoris have wavy hair, but people can certainly be found whose hair is quite kinky. Seven, for example.

After we left, I asked him what he thought of the heads.

"What do you mean?" he said.

"I don't know. Did you think they were spooky? Did they feel like real people? How did you feel when you were looking at them?"

"I thought they were kind of small."

"Me too. What else?"

"I don't know. I didn't really feel anything."

This was also the experience I was having. I hadn't really felt much at all. After the first flicker of excitement, which seemed to have as much to do with their being covered up as anything, I couldn't seem to generate any reaction to the heads. I was almost more aware of the curator, of her vague distaste for the objects I had asked her to unwrap, of her busy schedule and the fact that we were taking up her time, of an uncertainty on my part about how long I should spend looking at the objects, and whether I should touch them (in the end I did not), and the fact that the curator had never been curious enough to look at them in eleven years. In the swirl of all these other issues, the heads themselves seemed almost to disappear. When I left, I found that already I could not remember many of their details.

"What color would you say their skin was?" I asked Seven, as we were driving home.

"Kind of yellowish brown."

I put my feet up on the dashboard and looked out the window of the car. Seven turned on the radio, which was tuned to some station the children liked, and we merged onto the freeway to the sound of some sweet but silly pop tune. I thought about my sister-in-law and wondered how she would have felt if she'd been there with us in the museum storeroom, whether the experience would have heightened or lessened her revulsion, whether she would even have agreed to go.

And I wondered, too, about Seven: why he didn't share his sister's feelings, why he seemed, like me, nonplussed in the presence of these complicated things. Was it a measure of his assimilation? Did it have something to do with his being a guy? Was he—as my mother sometimes said of me—unfeeling? Or was there nothing there to be felt, nothing to be communicated beyond the facts, the historical circumstances that produced these objects, nothing supernatural after all?

"I suppose it depends on what you think happens after death," the curator said mildly as she closed and locked the warehouse door. "My husband, for example, believes that we just return to the earth, to the physical elements we are made of. These heads would never bother him."

10

Turton's Land Deeds

WHEN SEVEN AND I had been married two years, I
finished my dissertation, and in order to celebrate we
decided to move. What followed was a strange peripatetic
period, during which we lived in a series of cities, moving from
Melbourne to Boston to Honolulu to Brisbane and back to
Melbourne again in the space of about four years. I had a series
of short-term jobs and fellowships and Seven was content to go
where I went, and the only complicating factor was that, as we
set out on the first leg of our journey, I found that I was
pregnant with our first child.

I made this discovery in California, where we'd stopped
en route to Boston to visit my aunt, and after the first flush
of excitement the only thing I could think about was how I
was going to manage the drive. Our plan had been to buy a
car in Los Angeles and set out across the country in the
great, time-honored (if, in this case, reversed) American
tradition. We had done a lot of driving together in Australia,
up to Broken Hill and Port Macquarie, all the way across
the Nullarbor to Perth. And Seven was what I thought of as
a car guy. He read the automotive section of the paper and
never took his car to the garage unless the job required tools
he didn't have.

I was a lot less handy with a wrench but I also liked to drive and had crossed the country several times when I was in college: I-90 from Boston to Buffalo, Chicago, and Sioux Falls; I-70 from Baltimore to Denver via Kansas City; I-40 across the south—Raleigh, Durham, Winston-Salem, Knoxville, Nashville, Little Rock; I-10 from Jacksonville to the City of Angels by way of New Orleans. It seemed like a good way for Seven to see America and, besides, he hated flying and was relieved that we'd now reached a part of the journey that could be conducted on the ground.

The last thing Seven had done before we left Melbourne was to give away our car, a copper-colored, two-door Valiant with a black vinyl top. We had left pretty much everything behind us, apart from my books, his toolbox, and his bike. But the car was our main possession, and as soon as we reached Los Angeles, we started looking for a replacement.

L.A. being what it is, we had to rent a car in order to buy one. And so, while I stood at the counter making coffee and thinking about whether I really wanted to drink it, Seven sat at my aunt's kitchen table flipping through the Yellow Pages.

"*Hires, car hire, motorcar*—why can't I find what I'm looking for?"

"Because that's not what we call it," I told him. "Try looking under *car rental*."

We figured we had about a week to find a suitable vehicle, and every morning Seven would comb through the paper picking out the possibilities. I was in charge of the map.

"How about Glendale."

"OK."

"Long Beach."

"No."

"Montebello."

"Maybe."

Being the expert, Seven naturally made the inquiries. He knew what he wanted—something cheap and solid that would make it to New England—and he definitely knew his automobiles. The only problem was that, on the phone particularly, no one could understand a word he said.

"I undustend you hev a cah for sale?"

"Excuse me?"

"A cah, I'm looking for a cah. You know, a motucah?"

In the end, I had to do the calling. Seven would tell me what to ask and I relayed back to him whatever the seller said and then he would feed me the next question. Once we'd narrowed the search to a handful of possibilities, we set out in our rental to tour the suburbs within reach—Alhambra, Burbank, Altadena—returning home in the afternoon, hot and cranky, and, in my case, increasingly nauseated. At last, however, we found it: a mustard-colored Volvo wagon with about eighty thousand miles. It was an unlovely vehicle, but it was roomy and solid, and Seven was fairly confident it would get us to the other side.

What I mostly rememeber about that drive is the smell of the inside of the Volvo, which I ever after associated with being sick. We stopped in Las Vegas and New Mexico and in Kansas, where we were hustled into a motel basement during a tornado scare. The weather was hot; the air-conditioning in the car was broken; and the country passed me by in a sort of swoon. But, at length, we arrived in Boston.

Perhaps because this was the end of the journey and we were no longer in the surreal limbo in which travelers float, or because we were now within the gravitational field exerted by my family, almost as soon as we reached the Massachusetts Turnpike I felt the first flickers of doubt. Dimly, through the fog of my morning sickness, I began to perceive some of the difficulties that lay ahead.

We were not only unemployed; we were not very employable. Even the taxi drivers in Boston had Ph.D.s and Seven was a blue-collar worker with a nineteenth-century trade. Plus, until we managed to find jobs, we had no health insurance. Seven had never lived in the United States before and he didn't grasp the seriousness of the situation. He had grown up in a country with nationalized health care, and he couldn't even imagine what kind of bind we might find ourselves in if anything went wrong. But I knew all about America. "You're on your own here," I wrote to a friend back in Australia. "I'd almost forgotten what it's like."

But it was hard to stay worried around Seven. Worrying is just envisioning a future in which things don't work out, and Seven hardly ever thought about the future. To the extent that he did, he simply assumed that everything would be fine. I tried to follow his example—it seemed much the nicest way to live— but my instincts, my training, my background were against me, as evidenced by a dream I had not long after we'd arrived.

I dreamed I was driving some kind of bus. I had never driven a bus before and I was nervous. Everything was going well until, all of a sudden, the bus began to roll backward into a parking lot full of cars. It crashed slowly—in that horrible dreamlike way—into a large number of vehicles. People everywhere began to yell at me: "What the hell do you think you're doing?" they shouted.

"I'm sorry," I said. "I'm sorry. I don't know what happened." And then I realized that I had no insurance and that I was going to have to pay for all the damage to all the cars.

In the morning I told Seven about this dream.

"It's a money dream," he said.

"No," I told him. "It's a dream about responsibility. It's about having a lot of responsibility and fucking things up."

He laughed. "We indigenous people never have those sorts of dreams."

This time I told my family about our change in circumstances right away, calling my mother from California as soon as I had my pregnancy test results. I knew we were going to need help—with money, for starters—but there is also something about having a baby that yanks you back into the family fold whether you want it to or not. It's not just *your* baby—the way we had thought of it as *our* marriage—it's *their* baby too. And so, what had begun as a romance of two individuals was transformed by this event into an entanglement of tribes, a web of indebtedness and responsibility that extended not only into the future but back into the past. I had been accustomed to thinking about Maoris and the Pacific from the point of view of an interested outsider. But all that changed with the prospect of a baby. Suddenly I began to think of *their* history as *his* history and *his* history as *my* history and the whole business was suddenly cast in a new light.

I had not even had the baby yet when this came home to me with some force. I had taken a short-term job as a research assistant at an institute in Cambridge. There were no foundries in the area, and Seven was pretty much done with that anyway—"Too dirty," he said. Instead, he cashed in his experience as a bicycle messenger for work with a company making high-end bikes, and began casting jewelry on the side, using the silver spoons that my father periodically dropped into the garbage disposal by accident.

I spent my free time doing one of two things: sending off applications for jobs and fellowships and going to the library.

I had discovered, in one of the university libraries, a small but surprisingly good Oceanic collection that no one ever seemed to use except me. Most of the books had not been taken out for decades, some had never left the shelves. With a handful of important exceptions—Beaglehole's five-volume *Journals of Captain Cook*, McNab's two-volume *Historical Records of New Zealand*—none had been bar-coded. And I came to think, as I stood at the circulation desk filling out little slips of paper—*author, title, publisher, date*—that I was bar-coding the entire collection single-handedly, one volume at a time.

But some of the things I wanted were obscure enough to be available only on microfilm and there came a day—it had been alternately snowing and raining, the sidewalks were treacherous, and the forecast was for more freezing rain—when I found myself in a long, efficient-looking room marked Government Archives and Microforms. It was a late afternoon in the middle of the week and the place was almost empty, just a few serious researchers, none of whom looked up when I came in. The room was inviting in an impersonal sort of way: all that beige furniture, the shadowless light, the metal filing cabinets with their cryptic labels: W1260, Y4750. There were cabinets on three sides of the room, each cabinet with many drawers, each drawer with many fiche, each fiche with many pages, each page with many words. It reminded me of that nursery rhyme: *Kits, cats, sacks, wives, how many were going to St. Ives?*

I had found in the catalog something described as *Turton's Land Deeds of the North Island*, and I asked the attendant to fetch it for me from the stacks. When it arrived, all thirty sheets of it in a little paper pouch, he told me that the index was missing.

"Oh well," I said cheerfully. "I guess I'll just start at the beginning."

I began by reading something called "An Epitome of Official Documents Relative to Native Affairs and Land Purchases in the North Island of New Zealand" compiled by H. Hanson Turton in 1883. There was a letter from James Busby, Esq., Resident at New Zealand, to the Hon. the Colonial Secretary of New South Wales, dated Bay of Islands, June 16, 1837.

> Sir,—
> I have the honour to acknowledge the receipt of your despatch of the 16th ultimo, which was delivered to me on the 27th of the same month by Captain Hobson, of His Majesty's ship "Rattlesnake."

War, it seemed, had broken out again between the tribes of the Bay of Islands, the Ngapuhi and Pomare's people, the Ngati Manu of the southern bay. This time it had something to do with a woman who was murdered and eaten on being landed from a ship, and Busby wrote that he believed the man responsible to be the woman's former husband. He described the parties involved in the conflict as "actuated by the most irritated and vindictive feelings" and said he did not hope for a quick end to the hostilities. As a consequence of the war, he added, little or no land was under cultivation and "it may naturally be expected that the Natives will become reckless in proportion to their want of the means of subsistence."

Busby's purpose in writing was to ask that some paramount authority be established over the people of New Zealand. He warned that if some means were not found to stop their constant warring, the natives would annihilate themselves. The country, he wrote, was being depopulated. "District after district has become void of its inhabitants, and the population is even now but a remnant of what it was in the memory of some European inhabitants." So fast were the people disappearing that it was a matter of debate as to the cause of their decline. Some said that firearms had made their wars more bloody, some that tobacco and grog had made them weak. Some cited the spread of venereal and other diseases, the prostitution of women, and the murder of any half-caste children that they bore. "The Natives," wrote Busby,

> are perfectly sensible of this decrease; and when they contrast their own condition with that of the English families, amongst whom the marriages have been prolific in a very extraordinary degree of a most healthy progeny, they conclude that the God of the English is removing the aboriginal inhabitants to make room for them; and it appears to me that this impression has produced amongst them a very general recklessness and indifference to life.

I turned off the microfiche reader and pushed back my chair. The room seemed suddenly close and airless, the light an unforgiving green. Across the room a binder snapped, someone was getting ready to leave.

There is a hush in serious libraries made up of sounds—a cough, a rustle, the sigh of a pneumatic chair in a thick, enveloping, general silence. It's like the fog in which researchers move, feeling their way through the blur of data, ships in port, tonnage, cargoes, cases of venereal disease. Only rarely does anything leap out at you; mostly it's a matter of accumulation, of evidence accruing like interest until it reaches a critical mass. But every once in a while a piece of the past comes flying through time at precisely the right angle. When this happens, it feels as though you've been contacted by the dead.

I clicked the reader back on and fed in fiche after fiche, reading a paragraph here, a sentence there, making an occasional copy. I had difficulty working the machine and the copies all came out as negatives: rows of thin, scratchy white letters on a page that was otherwise entirely black.

Busby's letter formed an explanatory preface to the material that followed: thirty sheets of microfiche, all deeds to Maori land. The history of Maori land loss is a scandal, albeit a familiar one, a history of rapacious speculators, government seizures, confusion, dishonesty, and naïveté. In the north, where European settlement first started, land was sold by Maori chiefs on behalf of their tribes starting in 1814. The missionaries—of whom it is often said that "they came to do good and did very well indeed"—were among the earliest buyers, acquiring tens of thousands of acres in the Hokianga, Bay of Islands, and far north. Later there were traders, settlers, even Busby himself, who bought fifty thousand acres between 1834 and 1840, a portion of which he intended to subdivide into urban blocks against the day when a government would be established.

At first the sales were piecemeal, but toward the end of the 1830s the acreage began to fly out of Maori hands, nearly ten million acres between 1837 and 1839 alone. Fifty acres here for a double-barreled fowling piece; a hundred there for a musket, a mirror, four blankets, some powder, and a razor with a strop. Six hundred acres for eleven pounds cash, eleven blankets, ten shirts, six pairs of trousers, a gown, two pieces of print, a velvet waistcoat, three Manila hats, one pair of shoes, eight pairs of earrings, five combs, a musket, a double-barreled gun, five fowling pieces, two bags of shot, three casks of powder, scissors, knives, razors, one hoe, and a hundred and fifty pounds of tobacco, divided among eleven chiefly signatories to the deed. That makes one pound and one blanket each, plus a share of the other trade goods. Who got the velvet waistcoat is not recorded.

How would it feel, I wondered, to be descended from these Maoris? To see those deeds with one's own great-great-great-grandfather's signature? Oh, one can understand the allure at first of a pair of yellow breeches, a coat with braid, an ax, an auger. And, in the beginning, who could have known what the Pakeha had in mind? There weren't enough Pakehas in New Zealand in 1815, even 1820, to work the land they purchased, never mind occupy it in any meaningful way. But by 1837 this sort of explanation begins to make less sense. It is not so reasonable anymore to argue that Maoris did not understand what was happening, that they had no concept of private property, that the meaning of a deed was not clear. Nor can the mere novelty of manufactured goods, seductive as they may have been, account for this headlong rush to alienate their birthright.

What, then, can have motivated them? Greed? Willfulness? A conviction, all evidence to the contrary, that the Pakehas' presence was only a temporary thing? Or might it have been, as Busby contended, that everything the Maoris did in those dark days betrayed a recklessness and indifference to life? The words seemed to echo like the tolling of a bell: *District after district has become void of its inhabitants, and the population is even now but a remnant of what it was in the memory of some European inhabitants.*

At the beginning of the nineteenth century there were perhaps a hundred and fifty thousand Maoris in New Zealand. Fifty years later, when the first census was taken, there were only fifty thousand left. In the Bay of Islands, a heavily populated region, the collapse was particularly dramatic. It was certainly clear to Darwin in 1835 that the flora and fauna of New Zealand were under siege by foreign invaders. "It is said," he wrote, "that the common Norway rat, in the short space of two years, annihilated in this northern end of the island the New Zealand species. In many places I noticed several sorts of weeds, which like the rats, I was forced to own as countrymen." And it was no great leap from the fate of the rat to the fate of the Maori people. In fact, by mid-century the idea had become proverbial: "As the white man's rat has driven away the native rat, so the European fly drives away our own, and the clover kills our fern, so will the Maoris disappear before the white man himself." *Kei muri I te awe kapara he tangata ke, mana te ao, he ma*: "Behind the tattooed face a stranger stands, he who owns the earth, and he is white."

By the time I finished reading, everyone was gone, including the attendant. I packed up my papers and left the fiche on the circulation desk. Outside, the promised sleet had started falling, glimmering like snow in the headlights but driving down like rain. It was five o'clock and dark already; the traffic in Harvard Square had slowed to a crawl. I turned up my collar, put down my head, and dashed through the darkness to my car. There was a parking ticket frozen to the windshield, but by my reckoning it was money well spent: fifteen dollars for six black pages and a sightline to the past.

When our first son was born a few months later, I thought he should have a good name, a strong name, a name that would work in both our worlds. I wanted to give him a Maori name, but I knew it would have to be something pronounceable, something my American family wouldn't massacre or turn into a joke. For months I had been asking Seven about Maori names for boys, but he seemed unable to come up with a single suggestion.

"Well, there was a kid on my rugby team called Haircut."

"Oh, come on. What about your uncles, your cousins? There must have been somebody you admired."

But there wasn't, or he wouldn't say, and so I pondered, but insecurely, not confident enough to choose a name in a language I didn't know. Several hours after the birth, we still had no idea.

"How about Manu?" I suggested.

"No."

"How about Kipa?"

"No."

"How about Tame?"

"I never liked Tame. He was a liar and a thief . . . How about Maui?"

"Get off."

At this point my brother walked through the door.

"It's Lincoln's birthday," he said. "How about Abraham?" And so we named him Aperahama, the Maori form of Abraham, a Hebrew name from the days of the evangelists, from the missionary period of New Zealand.

It turned out that there were several Aperahamas in the family already. Our son had an uncle Aperahama in Auckland and a cousin Aperahama in Perth. There was an Aperahama in his great-grandfather's generation, whom Seven remembered as an old man. He had been famous in Mangonui for a table saw that he built out of a diesel motor, a belt, and a blade. It was a dangerous piece of equipment and everyone was always waiting for the day when it would take off one of his hands. He drove a Model A Ford with no brakes and played the violin.

When he died, both hands intact, a son he'd had out of wedlock turned up at the funeral.

"How'd they know it was his son?" I asked Seven.

"Looked just like him," he said.

So there were lots of Aperahamas these days, but there was a time when it had not yet occurred to any Maori father to give his son this name. Among the very first Maori Aperahamas was one born into my husband's family in the first decades of the nineteenth century. He was the son of Tareha, the infamous Ngati Rehia chief whose strange fortune it was to be at the height of his powers when history brought white men to New Zealand.

Tareha was a giant of a man and terrifying to see. He stood over six and a half feet tall and was so broad in the shoulders that there was not an armchair in the cabins of the English ships that would accommodate him. He had a mass of black curly hair and a great bushy black beard. On his face he wore the *moko* of a chief, an intricate tracery of blue-black lines carved into the surface of his skin. All the Pakehas in the Bay of Islands were afraid of him and were careful to keep out of his way. He was accounted "the greatest savage in New Zealand" by the Reverend John Butler, who recorded in his diary for 1821 that only the other week Tareha had killed and eaten three slaves at Waimate for stealing his sweet potatoes.

Tareha's *hapu*, Ngati Rehia, was part of the great Ngapuhi tribal confederation, whose members occupied the inland Bay of Islands in the eighteenth and early nineteenth centuries. Some decades before the arrival of Captain Cook, they had conquered the northern coastal area, occupying Rangihoua *pa* and the villages of Te Puna, Te Tii, and Mangonui. The *pa*, a Ngati Rehia stronghold, was an impregnable fortress in Tareha's day, a mass of terraces, earthworks, and palisades where several hundred people might shelter, safe from enemy tribes.

I had seen it when I was in New Zealand—a great barren, wedge-shaped ridge at the end of a long dirt road through some farmer's property. To get to it, you had to leave your car at the farmer's gate, climb over a stile, and walk about a mile uphill and down, descending finally into the little valley through which the Oihi stream trickles down to Marsden Cross. From a distance it is clear that the earth has been worked, closer up the signs are more ambiguous. The ground is rough and tussocked with grass, and the terraces are invisible on the golden hillside. You come upon them suddenly, climbing over a little rise and realizing that you are standing on the flat. Here and there the suggestion of a footpath snakes along the hill. In some places you can see the outline of a *kumara* pit or a defensive trench. Nothing seems to grow there except grass; there is not a tree or bush anywhere on the hill. A line of scrub at the foot of the *pa* marks the streambed. On the hillside opposite are rows of faint scarring that might have been plantations once upon a time. On three sides a pyramid, the *pa* falls away on the fourth in a sheer vertical drop to the sea. From the top it commands a view of the entire Bay of Islands. It has the unmistakable air of a *tapu*, or forbidden, place, and it is easy to imagine that the whistle of the wind across its summit is filled with spectral voices.

At the beginning of the nineteenth century, Rangihoua was commanded by Tareha's nephew Ruatara, a thoughtful and well-traveled man who had sailed on Pakeha whalers and seen much of the Pakeha world. In 1808 he met the Revered Samuel Marsden, the evangelical chaplain of New South Wales, who considered the Maoris ideally suited to Christian conversion. "Their minds," wrote Marsden, "appeared like a rich soil that had never been cultivated, and only wanted the proper means of improvement to render them fit to rank with civilized nations." Six years later Marsden held the first Christian service in New Zealand on Christmas Day at the foot of Rangihoua *pa*. Lifting up his voice, he sang the hundredth psalm—"Make a joyful noise unto the Lord, all ye lands"— and preached the glad tidings of the Gospel of Christ before a pulpit made the previous day from a section of a Maori canoe. The assembled Maoris stood up and sat down at a signal from their chief, but complained they could not understand a word of what was said. Ruatara told them not to worry, for he would explain it to them by and by. Within a matter of months, however, he was dead of galloping consumption.

I thought of the name *Aperahama* as shorthand for everything that happened in those years. Like most Maoris of his generation, Tareha never converted to Christianity. His support for the missionaries, whom he saw as go-betweens and suppliers of European goods, was purely pragmatic. But as every year brought further transformations—more ships, more buildings, more strangers to the bay—the Pakehas in the Bay of Islands grew stronger and less dependent upon the Maoris, while the Maoris' capacity to manipulate and exploit them diminished. Tareha was among those caught with a foot in each world and his actions have a sort of shimmer or two-sidedness about them.

When, in 1840, Busby circulated a petition among the northern chiefs ceding their sovereignty to the British Crown, Tareha refused to sign and argued vehemently against cooperating with the British. He was in the minority and the Treaty of Waitangi was signed without him, inaugurating British colonial rule. At the same time, deed after deed for the sale of land in the 1830s and '40s bears Tareha's name. I have a black copy of one for 250 acres in the Mangonui District for which he received a great coat, an ax, an iron wedge, ten pounds of tobacco, some shot, a chisel, an auger, two frocks, a razor, and a steel purse.

He was in late middle age when his son was born, the one he named Aperahama. It is a name that signals the shift in political power, the end of one era and the beginning of the next. In one sense, it symbolizes a loss of Maori *mana*, or strength, and yet, it is a hopeful name, a survivor's name, one that speaks of endurance against the odds. Of all the Pakeha names, Abraham is the one that best expresses the aspirations of a Maori chief in a pre-Pakeha world—for land, influence, descendants, and spiritual prestige. I imagined Tareha sitting and listening to the missionary's words: *And the Lord brought Abraham out under the night sky and said to him, Look now toward heaven and tell the stars if thou be able to number them. And the Lord said to Abraham, So shall thy seed be. And I will make nations of thee, and kings shall come out of thee. And I will give unto thee, and to thy seed after thee, the land wherein thou art a stranger for an everlasting possession.*

Perhaps later, when his son was born, he looked around and saw that it was all slipping away. The things that they had always known were no longer to be taken for granted and in their place were new things, some of them wonderful—like beaver hats, razors, gunpowder, frocks, and augers—some of them horrible, like the deep, hollow cough and the diarrhea and the sores and rashes that none of the old people had ever known. And so he called him Aperahama in the hope that his sons would be as numerous as the stars and as strong as the Pakehas' bullocks and that they would be leaders of men and that their enemies would live in fear of the thunder of their guns.

Of course, in Boston, none of this rang any bells at all. When my parents came that afternoon to see the baby, we all agreed that he was an unusually beautiful child. He was fair-skinned and dark-eyed and he had a wise, elfin expression, wide across the cheekbones and pointed at the chin. They cooed and held his fingers and asked us what name we had chosen.

"Abraham," I told them.

My father looked at me with a quizzical expression.

"Isn't that a Jewish name?"

11

Nana Miri

I HAD NEVER had much to do with babies and was surprised to find that I found looking after one quite easy. My mother said I reminded her of the French Canadian mother in a film by Margaret Mead about cross-cultural child rearing, the one who tossed her babies about in a confident if somewhat offhand way. I had long admired the way children were raised in New Zealand; the Maoris I knew were warm and affectionate but they never hovered over their kids. Maori men, in my experience, were also more at home with children than most of the men I had known, and it came as no surprise to me to find that Seven was a calm and unself-conscious father. He had grown up surrounded by children—siblings, nieces, nephews, cousins—and although he studiously avoided changing diapers (that, he said, had always been his sisters' job), he was relaxed and easy with the baby.

What did surprise me though was Seven's enthusiasm for New England, and particularly his enthusiasm for snow. It wasn't the look of it that he liked or the sporting opportunities it presented—though he did eventually take up ice-skating. No, what he liked about snow was *driving in it*. We were living in a little flat in Cambridge at the time, and whenever there had been a snowfall during the night, he would get up really early and drive around the streets in darkness before the plows were out. Of course, we all thought he was mad.

"I don't get it," I said. "You've never even seen snow before. How do you know how to drive in it?"

"It's just like driving in sand."

And, in fact, the only thing he really missed was the ocean, or not even the ocean so much itself as the *kai moana*, the seafood. Within months he knew every fish market in a radius of twenty miles. He bought only from certain places and only at certain times. Soon the guys behind the counters knew him. "Hey, Seven!" they'd say, when he stopped in. "How are you, buddy?" They saved him lobster bodies and striper heads and set aside the freshest mussels. The ways we ate seafood in New England—deep-fried or sautéed with butter or cooked in tomatoes with garlic and parsley—never interested him. He liked his seafood fresh and without sauces; often he just ate it raw.

Boston was an adventure for Seven, and I was glad to be near my family, who helped us out with everything from cutlery to cars. I would remember in the years that followed how much easier it was to raise children with aunts and uncles and cousins and grandparents nearby. But I wasn't quite ready to give up the Pacific and I still pined for the far side of the world.

One night in the middle of winter, the phone rang. We were all in bed asleep and I came to consciousness just in time to hear the answering machine go on. I knew I should have gotten up to intercept it—at that hour it could only be bad news. But I was tired and I let myself drift back toward sleep. Finally, Seven swung his legs out from under the covers. It was three A.M. and very cold. By the time he got back to bed, I was wide awake.

"Who was it?"

"Someone's died."

"Who?"

"Nana Miri."

It was my sister-in-law's voice on the tape. She was speaking, curiously, to me and not to Seven. She didn't seem to realize that it was the middle of the night in Boston—for her in New Zealand it was dinnertime—and she seemed to think we were all out.

"I just wanted to call and tell you that last night Nana Miri passed away. I knew you were specially fond of her and I thought you'd want to know. Well, I hope you're all fine back there. Bye."

There was little point in calling back. It was too cold to sit up and she wasn't the one I had to talk to anyway. She'd only have known the story third- or fourth-hand. I wanted to talk to Seven's mother and I knew we wouldn't be able to reach her until after the weekend. There were so many deaths (or was it so many relations?) that my mother-in-law was at a funeral almost every weekend. All Saturday and Sunday she would be at the *marae*, talking, singing, sitting with the body, doing the business of death.

To my mother-in-law, her neighbor for over forty years, she was the Old Girl. My husband and his siblings called her Nana, though she was not really any relation of theirs. Other people of my in-laws' generation called her Auntie. For years, I called her simply Miri, not realizing how strange, even discourteous, that must have sounded. She forgave me because I didn't know any better and she never said a word. She called me Tirairaka, the fantail, a quick, curious little bird, always flitting about.

When I met her, she had been a widow for almost thirty years. Her children were grown and gone away and one of her granddaughters lived with her. Like all the women of her generation, she had had a great many children: ten, of whom five were still living. Of the five who died, she told me about two. One was a baby who died of dysentery while she was in the hospital miscarrying the next. No one told her until she came home, weak and empty-handed. The other was her youngest, a boy. There was a photo of him on the wall in her house, a slender, fuzzy-haired teenager with a shy smile, taken not long before he was killed in a car crash at the age of seventeen.

Nana Miri and my mother-in-law had known each other most of their lives, and in later years they were next-door neighbors. Their houses sat side by side on the flat, facing out to sea— identical timber boxes with flaking paint and a sheet of corrugated iron for a roof. They each had a living room that doubled as a kitchen, two little bedrooms on one side, and a bathroom tacked on at the back. There was electricity and propane gas for cooking and cold running water in both houses, but there the similarities between them came to an end.

In Nana Miri's house there were pictures on the walls and china in the cabinet. The carpet was swept and the dishes were put away. Behind the curtains that separated the bedrooms from the main room, the beds were made and the clothes were folded. The living room had a couch against one wall and a wood stove, a counter, and a kitchen sink opposite. In the middle was a table where she served me tea with milk and sugar and biscuits on a plate. We took our shoes off at the door. It felt to me exactly the way my own grandmother's house might have felt—though, in fact, I had never known either of my grandmothers, both of whom died before I was born.

Next door, my mother-in-law's house looked like it had been hit by a tornado. A large woman with a big voice, she lived surrounded by the wreckage of her energy. The majority of her children, including Seven, inherited from her this total disregard for order. There was not a single clear surface in the place; everything had a pile of something on it: piles of newspapers under the couch, piles of towels on the back of a chair, piles of clothing, piles of shoes, piles of papers. Some of the piles were a mixture: fishing tackle and hair-brushes, hammers and magazines. Part of the problem was that there were too many people in the household and not enough drawers—my mother-in-law had also had ten children, all of whom had survived and most of whom had produced children of their own. But a bigger part was that no one ever threw anything away. Her daughters tidied periodically, mainly by shoving more things under the furniture and pushing every-thing to the edges of the room. I tried once or twice to help them but it was like trying to discipline entropy itself.

Whenever I was in Mangonui, I used to escape to Nana Miri's and sit with her at her table, eating biscuits and drinking tea.

"I don't know how they stand it over there," she would say, shaking her head. "They're always yelling."

"I know. Sometimes I think they're all mad."

We were two of a kind, Nana Miri and I.

Strictly speaking, Nana Miri had no rights to the land on which she lived. She had been born in Te Hapua, about a hundred miles north, and orphaned at the age of three when both her parents died in the pandemic of 1918. In Te Hapua, as in other isolated Maori communities, influenza spread like fire through dry grass. The people coughed, grew chill, then burning, and complained that their heads were being crushed between two stones. They had sudden nosebleeds, and when they coughed, they brought up a bloody, frothy phlegm. They were overcome with weakness and lay down where they were with parched throats and aching bones, alternately shivering and throwing off the blankets. The ones that went blue died first, a thin, bloody trickle seeping from their nose and mouth. Others lingered, fighting the pneumonia that followed hard on the heels of the *mate uruta*, the death cold.

The flu killed both the young and old, but many of its victims were men and women in the prime of life. In Te Hapua, as in other places, it left orphans by the score, and Nana Miri was sent to live with relatives on the other side of Parengarenga Harbour. *Parengarenga* means "the place where the *renga* lily grows," but *rengarenga* also means crushed, destroyed, beaten, and scattered about, which is how the people of Te Hapua must have felt at the end of 1918.

When she was seventeen years old, she married and moved with her husband to Waipapakauri, where they worked digging kauri gum. It was hard, backbreaking work and they were up to their knees in the swamp for hours at a time. But Nana Miri thought she must have been meant to live a long time since the flu hadn't taken her when it took everyone else. Her husband was less lucky. Every year he grew more gaunt, and when he died of tuberculosis at the age of forty-three, he left his wife and ten children in a community to which they had ties neither by marriage nor by birth.

It is rare, even now, to find someone in Mangonui who does not belong to the *iwi*, the tribe, who is not, as they say, "of their bones." The land on which Nana Miri lived belonged to Seven's father, who gave it to her when she was widowed and said it was hers to keep for as long as she liked. It was part

of a parcel of some four hundred acres, all that was left of the
thousands to which Ngati Rehia had once laid claim. Of these,
the most spectacular fifty—across the peninsula on the open
sea—were leased to the Pakeha for ninety-nine years. Another
two hundred acres were farmed by the Mangonui Corporation; a hundred or so of cabbage tree, manuka, and gorse
remained undeveloped; and the last fifty, on the inlet side of the
peninsula, were occupied by the village of Mangonui.

The arcane rules in Mangonui governing the placement of
houses and other property rights, and the ways in which
history was recollected differently by different people, gave
rise to feuds lasting generations over what belonged to whom.
My father-in-law had certain privileges owing to the fact that
he was the local minister and to his uncontestable line of
descent. He himself was the sole survivor of several children
and the son of the son of the son back to Tareha himself. So no
one argued with him when he gave Nana Miri the house and
said it was hers until she died.

Nana Miri and her husband had first come to Mangonui in
the years before the Second World War, following an apostle
of the prophet Ratana, a Maori farmer who, in that terrible
year of 1918, had been visited by the Holy Ghost and told to
unite the Maori people. Wiremu "Bill" Ratana was forty-five
in the year of the pandemic, a temperamental fellow with a
taste for football, fast horses, and drink. He caught the flu
when it came to Wanganui and recovered, only to find that of
the twenty-four members of his generation, just three remained. A week later he was sitting on the veranda of his
house when a cloud rose from the surface of the sea and began
to move toward him. Out of the cloud a voice spoke, saying,
"Fear not, I am the Holy Ghost. Cleanse yourself and your
family as white as snow, as sinless as the wood-pigeon. Ratana,

I appoint you as the Mouthpiece of God for the multitude of this land." Later an angel appeared and repeated the message, telling Ratana that he was to turn the people from fear of roosters and owls and belief in ghosts and spirits hidden in sticks and relics of the dead. He was to preach the gospel, heal the sick, and bring the people to Jehovah.

Out of the ashes rises the bird of hope. There had been others like him in the previous century—men like Te Kooti Rikirangi and Te Whiti o Rongomai—prophets who gathered the people in time of trial. And now, at the end of the Great War, in the wake of the pandemic, the air was full of "thought-storms and semi-heathen superstitions." The apostles fanned out from Ratana's home with instructions to gather up the *morehu,* or survivors, and take them to the places where the Maori had been strong. Nana Miri and her husband were among the thousands drawn to the movement. They knew the past was a time of death and they looked to Ratana for a new beginning, for unity and strength. And that is how they came to Mangonui, an old place, a place with *mana* from the old days, a place where they could start again.

"It was beautiful then," Nana Miri told me, staring out the window over a cup of tea. "Mangonui was just a camp. A mudflat over that way, a marsh over there. The old people came back from Waimate, no one had lived here for years, and we built our houses there where the oyster farm is now."

And then, as if she thought she might have given me the wrong impression, she looked at me sternly. "It was hard, you know, not like these days. We didn't have houses like this. We didn't have running water. You couldn't turn your lights on with a switch. We had houses made of *raupo,* you know, reeds. We got our water from the spring. But we had what we needed. *Kai moana, kumara* . . . You see those old trees?" She pointed through the window to a line of ancient peach trees and a scraggly lemon tree at the edge of the bush. "We planted them. We planted fruit trees all over this place—plums, peaches, lemons. Your father-in-law's mother made the best peaches in Mangonui. Beautiful golden peaches in big glass jars. You ask your husband, he'll remember."

Sometimes when I left Nana Miri's I'd go for a walk down the beach, past the *marae*, and back up toward the main road. There was a turnoff to the right that led to the cemetery, a small, weedy plot with a loose wire fence and a creaky metal gate on crooked hinges. I liked to look at the old stones, especially the ones with the Ratana symbols, a five-pointed star balanced in the cup of a crescent moon, the image of the prophet and two whales, the twin square towers of the Ratana church, looking, I thought, vaguely Lutheran.

I was never sure whether it was OK for me to be there, so I tried to make myself inconspicuous. The family who lived next door to the cemetery had a rottweiler who guarded the place closely. He was chained, mercifully, to a house post, but whenever I came to look at the graves, he leaped out of the shadows, barking furiously and baring his teeth. No one from the house ever appeared, though I often thought I saw the curtains stir. I imagined them inside, "Nah, it's just Seven's missus, you know, the Pakeha, in the cemetery again."

Nana Miri's death came as a surprising blow. It would be wrong to say that I knew her intimately, but I always felt as though there were a bond between us. I was an outsider and she was something of an outsider too. She had taken an interest in me in Magonui, and I had come to think of her as a sort of surrogate grandmother. It was no accident that it was to her, and her alone, that I blurted out the secret of our marriage.

The last time I'd seen her in Mangonui, winter had been coming on and I had taken her to buy some clothing. She lived on very little money and rarely bought anything for herself, and I wanted to give her something that would be both smart and warm. We went to a store in Kerikeri that sold women's clothing and picked out a pair of heavy black trousers and a patterned sweater in black and gray.

"There," I said. "That should keep you cozy."

"Oh, Chris," she said, giving me a hug.

She was already old when I first met her, though she was still climbing up and down the embankment at the age of seventy-eight. I knew, of course, she couldn't live forever, but I hadn't expected her to die—not yet, and not when I was so far away.

12

HAWAIKI

DURING THAT YEAR in Boston I struck up a correspondence with an old friend of my parents. They had all grown up together in the thirties in Southern California; I have a picture of the three of them as teenagers, standing shoulder to shoulder on the beach. They stayed in touch over the years, despite ending up on opposite sides of the country, but it was I, in the end, who had the most in common with Henry. Although we saw each other only rarely, we became frequent correspondents.

Henry had been born wealthy and had never had to work. He did have one job, though: not long after the Second World War he served briefly as governor of American Samoa. He was a curious choice by any measure, young and completely inexperienced, but his father was politically well connected and I imagine he wanted something for Henry to do. As it turned out, the experience had a profound effect on him.

In Samoa he met the girl he was to marry, an American administrator's daughter, young, good-looking, stylish, a little bored, no doubt, with the limited society of the islands. They celebrated their wedding on the veranda of the governor's house, the men in navy dress whites, the women in silk cocktail dresses in shades of magenta and plum. They had only been married a year when they moved back to California. Henry, I think, might have stayed, but his wife was understandably unwilling to start her family in such a remote place. It had not been her choice, after all, to go there. So, back they went to Los Angeles, where they settled into a large, handsome house with a pool and an aviary that had been given to them as a wedding present by Henry's father.

But that was not the end of it, at least for Henry. For the next fifty years he collected books and journals on the places and peoples of the Pacific, until he had one of the finest private libraries of its kind. He never went back to Samoa but instead bought a large piece of land in a remote corner of the Hawaiian Islands and built a house there, modeled on a Samoan *fale*, with a high, pitched roof and an airy feel and a wide, cool balcony facing the sea. He filled the house with books and artifacts and furniture made from rare Hawaiian wood. The tiles on the floor were blue like the ocean, the walls were white, and the roof beams were dark, and below the house were gardens and potting sheds filled with palms and orchids and every kind of bromeliad you can imagine.

I had known Henry all my life and Seven and I often saw him, in Hawaii or California, when we traveled back and forth. But it was not until that year in Boston that Henry and I started writing to each other. I was missing the Pacific and he— his wife by then had passed away and his children were grown—seemed to enjoy the exchange. As we came across subjects of mutual interest, Henry and I traded notes. I would send him the publications list of the National Research Institute in Boroka, Papua New Guinea; he would send me articles on ethnobotany, or political tidbits from *Pacific Islands Monthly*, or gossip from the *Maui News*. We both subscribed to the *Journal of the Polynesian Society*, though he was the more thorough reader.

"Dear C," he wrote. "Just in case your subscription to *JPS* hasn't caught up with you, I copied this article." Enclosed was a photocopy of "The Early Human Biology of the Pacific: Some Considerations" by Philip Houghton of the University of Otago in which the author makes the case for the action of natural selection upon voyaging proto-Polynesians. "In the historical record," Houghton writes, "a picture of a large-bodied, strongly muscular people distributed over a wide expanse of the Pacific is repeated almost monotonously." Henry had made a slight mark in the margin beside this passage. This was sort of a joke between us, Seven being such a classic example of the type.

The gist of the article was interesting. Throughout Polynesia, in Samoa, Tonga, Tahiti, New Zealand, Hawaii, the Cooks, the Tuamotus, and the Marquesas, the prehistoric record provides strong evidence of a distinctive Polynesian body type: heavily muscled with a long torso, proportionally short legs, and a round or brachycephalic head, all of which are suggestive of cold-climate adaptation. The larger, stronger, and more compact the body, the better it conserves heat. But, asks Houghton, does this make sense? One might expect this sort of body type in the Arctic or on the steppes of central Asia, or in North Dakota for that matter, where people are exposed to cold temperatures and strong winds. But the vast majority of Polynesians live in the tropics. Their islands are warm, even sultry in some seasons, leading many early European visitors to conclude that indolence and luxury were a Polynesian way of life.

But if we think more creatively, suggests Houghton, we will see that Polynesians are not so much an island as an oceanic people, and that the environment that has shaped them is not the solid one on which they live but the watery one through which they had to travel. No matter how warm it seems in the tropical Pacific when you are on dry land, it is cold when you are wet and exposed to the wind on the open ocean. And these are precisely the conditions to which every early Polynesian voyager was exposed. "Whatever the mean air and water temperature," he writes, "the environment of Remote Oceania is effectively the coldest to which *Homo sapiens* has adapted."

Dear Henry,
Thanks for the article on Polynesian morphology. Who knew that what was really going on was selection for the perfect rugby player! Remember Jonah Lomu, the six-foot-five, 266-pound Tongan who ran the 100 meters in 10.8? I remember watching him crash through the South Africans in the 1995 World Cup. He was absolutely unstoppable. Good genes, yah?

Seriously, though, I wonder if Houghton's take on this is widely accepted. It makes sense, but how fast can that kind of adaptation occur?

Hope the orchids are blooming.

Yours as ever,

C

The Polynesian triangle stretches from Hawaii in the north to New Zealand in the south, and from Tuvalu in the west to Rapa Nui (a.k.a. Easter Island) in the east, an area of ten million square miles. So far apart are some of these islands— Easter Island is nearly 900 miles from the nearest speck of land, Hawaii is 750 miles from its nearest southern neighbor—that for a long time European scholars refused to believe that they were intentionally colonized. Right through the 1960s a handful of historians insisted that the people who became Tahitians,

Marquesans, Cook Islanders—not to mention the far-flung Hawaiians, Maoris, and Easter Islanders—must have drifted to these islands accidentally, having been blown out to sea by storms and lost their way. The distances were too great, the technology too primitive, the environment too unpredictable, they argued. How could a neolithic people possibly accomplish such a thing?

But the idea of accidental colonization is surely even more preposterous. Almost every habitable island in the eastern Pacific, and there are hundreds of them, shows signs of Polynesian occupation at some time. Could they plausibly have drifted to them all? And did these accidental voyagers just happen to have with them all the domesticated plants and animals—the dogs, rats, pigs, chickens, taro, *kumara*, paper mulberry—that also migrated to these islands? Did they have women and children? Priests and gods? Did they set out to go fishing with everything it takes to reconstitute a civilization?

Today it is accepted that, for reasons that will forever remain obscure but that probably had to do with tribal conflict, overcrowding, perhaps climate change and a shortage of resources, as well as curiosity and "the wandering spirit," the ancestors of modern Polynesians began island-hopping eastward from the western edge of Oceania about three thousand years ago, eventually reaching Tonga, Samoa, and Fiji. Then, in roughly the first millennium (from about A.D. 100 to 800), a people who can be clearly identified as Polynesian from the similarity of their languages, myths, and technology made a series of daring exploratory voyages eastward into central Polynesia—to Tahiti, the Cooks, and the Marquesas. These were followed in time by the truly radical forays that led them to Rapa Nui, Hawaii, and New Zealand, until, as Cook observed in astonishment, they had succeeded in spreading themselves across "a fourth part of the circumference of the Globe."

There are marvelous accounts of crossing the Pacific written by Europeans who sailed in ships in the eighteenth and nineteenth centuries. The sentiments they express are a mixture of wonder and fear, amazement at their own insignificance, humility in the face of the sublime. For the voyaging European, the Pacific was a vast, inscrutable emptiness, an endless horizon, a sky full of light. It was the opposite, in every respect, of the place he called home, a cozy, terrestrial cluster of cities and farms, busy with human activity. The Pacific, by contrast, seemed dreamlike, a liminal space, a place of clouds and shadow. "We may now consider that we have nearly crossed the Pacific," wrote Darwin, as he made the long passage from Tahiti to New Zealand.

It is necessary to sail over this great ocean to comprehend its immensity. Moving quickly onwards for weeks together, we meet with nothing but the same blue, profoundly deep, ocean. Even within the archipelagoes, the islands are mere specks, and far distant from one another. Accustomed to look at maps drawn on a small scale, where dots, shading, and names are crowded together, we do not rightly judge how infinitely small the proportion of dry land is to water of this vast expanse. The meridian of the antipodes has likewise been passed; and now every league, it made us happy to think, was one league nearer to England. These antipodes call to one's mind old recollections of childish doubt and wonder. Only the other day I looked forward to this airy barrier as a definite point in our voyage homewards; but now I find it, and all such resting places for the imagination, are like shadows, which a man moving onwards cannot catch.

To the voyaging Polynesian, however, it must have been quite different. The oldest words in any Polynesian language, the core that every migrating group carried with it from the ancestral lands—the elemental lexicon—are words for sea creatures, fishing techniques, various parts of canoes. One might almost reconstruct a complete history of the Polynesian diaspora on the evidence of fishhooks alone. For early Polynesians, the ocean, far from being a "trackless waste," as so many Victorians had it, was crisscrossed by sea roads and pathways. Over every horizon lay islands, some near, some far, some big enough to colonize, some barely big enough to offer respite on the way to somewhere else. For two thousand years knowledge of these islands, where they lay and how to reach them, constituted the core of their arcana. Traveling in large, double-hulled sailing canoes, they navigated by the stars and the ocean currents, the winds, the swells, the birds, the look and feel of the sky and water. They knew hundreds of constellations, identified dozens of winds, could feel the interaction of as many as five different swells through the deck of an oceangoing canoe. They knew which birds flew out from land in the morning and returned to it at dusk. They knew that a high island would disrupt the trade winds, and that the lagoon of a low island would cast a greenish glow on the underbelly of the clouds.

They traveled over the ocean the way we traveled over the land, with all our belongings bumping along beside us, with our breeding stock and our favorite seedlings, a Bible and a change of clothes. They carried paste made from taro and breadfruit, dried fish, young coconuts, and water stored in gourds. They shipped cargoes of flintstone and seed tubers, sacred stones and feathers, parrots and piglets and dogs. Stories in the Maori tradition tell of babies born on long voyages, of disputes that erupted over sailing directions, of canoes that were wrecked on atolls or wandered into danger-ous regions of the sea. Few of the voyages are without incident: canoes get sucked into giant whirlpools, swamped by terrible storms, cast away upon islands that have since disappeared beneath the surface of the sea. Sometimes the voyagers are guided by whales or birds, or by *taniwha*, mythical sea monsters. Often there are supernatural components, and yet the detail of these stories is too prosaic—words to be said while bailing water, lists of members of the crew—to be mistaken for myth.

And then, about six or seven hundred years ago, long-distance voyaging ceased. Although Polynesians continued to build canoes and make short, interisland and coastal voyages, they never ventured out onto the sea roads again. *Ka kotia te tai tapu ke Hawaiki*, they say in New Zealand: "The tapu sea to Hawaiki is cut off." All over Polynesia the specific memory of where they had come from and how to get there disappeared, leaving no more than an echo, a myth of an ancestral homeland reachable only by supernatural means. In the Maori tradition this land is known as Hawaiki, a name that was carried throughout the islands by the earliest migrants and appears in every Polynesian language in some cognate form. The land of Hawaiki is an otherworldly place, sometimes in the east, sometimes in the west, sometimes in the sky or underwater. It is a land of origin and a source of life, a place of plenty, a paradise. But it is also a place of death and separation, and those who pass over to Hawaiki are lost to this world.

In three places the name has been given to actual islands. The first is Savai'i in Samoa, thought to be the original of them all, in part because Samoans are the only Polynesians who do not describe themselves as having originally come from someplace else. The second is a highly *tapu*, or sacred, island in the Society Islands commonly known as Ra'iatea, the island from which Omai came. And the third is the Big Island of Hawaii. Settled late in Polynesian prehistory, Hawaii (or Hawai'i, as it is properly known) is not the Hawaiki of myth but an echo or reflection of it. Like Plymouth or Essex or New England, it was named, perhaps hopefully, perhaps nostalgically, in remembrance of a former home.

When Aperahama was six months old, we moved again, this time from Boston to Honolulu, where I had a one-year postdoctoral fellowship at a research institute called the East-West Center. We were completely strapped for money, paying three quarters of my stipend in rent for a run-down, three-room bungalow on the side of Punchbowl Hill. The built-in cupboards had been eaten by ants and the bathtub was stained, but the floor was a curious and wonderful kind of polished concrete, silky smooth and cool, and we sat high enough on the hill to catch the trade winds and to see the lights of Waikiki.

The house was stuccoed and solid, with large rectangular windows and a wide, overhanging roof that kept out the sun and the rain. For such a small house, it was elegantly conceived. The front door opened directly onto a large airy room that stretched the full width of the building. On the back wall were two doors: one to the left that led into the kitchen, and one to the right for the bedroom and bath. In back the house butted up against the hill, but in front it had been terraced with black lava-rock walls, so that between the house and road was a perfectly level lawn, which ended abruptly in a drop of six or eight feet to a tangle of weeds and creepers. Then there was another eight-foot drop to street level. A narrow stone staircase with an iron gate led up to the house, which was entirely invisible from the road. It was our private sanctuary, hidden from the world.

Dear Henry,

Hawaiki nui, Hawaiki roa, Seven has discovered the ancestral homeland! He is learning to surf and has found an ancient brown Ford LTD wagon to carry his board around. Last week he rode his bike down Punchbowl with Aperahama in the seat behind him. What a maniac! I, on the other hand, have taken to walking (not wanting to drive the LTD) up and down Punchbowl with the groceries, carrying an umbrella to ward off the sun. The only other people who do this are elderly Asian ladies. We nod genteelly to one another as we pass.

You'll be glad to hear that the monetary crisis has eased. Seven has found a part-time job in an office with a bunch of big Hawaiian ladies who talk about him in Hawaiian—or at least they did until they heard him laughing and realized he could understand what they said. Mother is throwing in her social security check. My father says, "Consider it a grant from the federal government." So, between the three of us, we'll meet the rent.

We love Hawaii and can already imagine how sad we are going to be when we have to leave. It will be like being sent forth from paradise—again!

Thanks for the piece by Marshall Sahlins, always an interesting guy.

Henry's reply came almost by return post.

Dear C,

Your address indicates that you are located across the street
from where a friend of mine once had an apartment. She
lived in the big condominium on the *makai* side of Prospect.
I remember looking down on the bungalows across the
street and imagining that they must be inhabited by old
Chinese-Hawaiian grandmothers whose families would
come and stay there when they were in Honolulu for the
night. With your umbrella you might almost resemble one of
them—at least from above.

Not long after we arrived in Honolulu, Seven and I paid a
visit to the Bishop Museum, an institution founded in 1889 in
honor of the last descendant of the royal Hawaiian family. We
wandered through the rooms looking at paddles and grinders,
the ubiquitous fishhooks and lures, and some more exotic-
looking objects, including a necklace of braided hair. Eventually, we found ourselves in a picture gallery. There were a
series of landscapes: romantic views of Manoa Valley, a pond
with a few waterfowl, some desultory coconut palms, the
jagged outline of the mountains with their deep ravines. We
saw a sketch of Diamond Head from Punchbowl, seen from
just about where we lived, and a curious painting called *View
of the Smallpox Hospital, Waikiki*. The story was all there, in
pictures, the views of vessels lying at anchor, the canoes plying
back and forth, the Honolulu Fort, circa 1853, with its neat
companies of red-coated royal guards and Governor Kekua-
naoa in a cockaded hat.

Rounding a corner we came upon a little alcove hung with
mid-nineteenth-century portraits of Hawaiian royalty. On the
opposite wall a young queen in a high-necked black silk dress
with a lace collar looked out at me from the canvas.

"Seven, look! She looks exactly like Kura."

The resemblance to Seven's sister was uncanny. The same heavy-lidded, protuberant eyes with their golden-brown irises. All our boys have been born with eyes as black as night. It was never possible with any of them to see where the pupil stopped and the iris began. But Seven's eyes are not dark. His hair is black, but his eyes are a warm honey color, just like the Hawaiian kings and queens.

We walked around the alcove studying the portraits. Here was King Kamehameha IV and Queen Emma, posed and painted exactly as if they were burghers or Puritans or well-to-do benefactors (which, in fact, they were). Their severe but elegant costumes and serious expressions suggested something melancholy, as though they were looking down the barrel of time at what it had all come to. Beside them hung a sentimental portrait of their son, the young Prince Albert Edward Kaui-keaouli Leiopapa a Kamehameha. The last child born to any of the Hawaiian monarchs, he died in 1862 at the age of four.

It was odd to see this family resemblance and yet it made a kind of sense. Maoris and Hawaiians are not as closely related as, say, Maoris and Cook Islanders, or Hawaiians and Marquesans. But Polynesian populations have never been large and they must all have been quite closely related at one time. One study suggests that a single canoe-load of twenty young adults could theoretically have produced a population of a hundred thousand Maoris or Hawaiians by the time the Europeans arrived. This is probably not exactly how things happened, but the founding populations of any island group might have been quite small. And while they probably maintained contact with the islands they came from, there is no evidence to suggest contact with anyone from outside the Polynesian triangle.

Unless you ask Seven, of course.

There were several things Seven and I disagreed about: whether aliens had landed on Earth; whether the dead visited the living; whether buying life insurance was "asking for it." But one of our recurring disputes had to do with the origins of the Polynesian people. It began one night when we were watching an anthropological program on TV. They were discussing the peopling of the Pacific and the curious fact that all the domesticated plants and animals found in the Pacific originate in Southeast Asia—with one crucial exception: *kumara*, the sweet potato, a staple of the Maori diet, a plant so central to Maori life that myths of Hawaiki sometimes claim that the very cliffs are made of it. *Hawaiki nui kai*, they call it, a land of milk and honey, "Hawaiki of much food." *Kumara* comes indisputably from South America. And so the question presents itself: how did it get to Polynesia?

In the late 1940s a Norwegian adventurer named Thor Heyerdahl set out to demonstrate experimentally that Polynesia might have been originally populated by Mesoamericans who drifted there on balsa wood rafts. He called it the Kon-Tiki Expedition and he did, in fact, manage to make landfall on an island in the Tuamotus after a harrowing voyage of 102 days. The experiment did not prove that this was the way Polynesia was settled and, as it ran contrary to all the other archaeological and linguistic evidence, the theory did not take hold. But it helped keep alive the question of whether there was ever any contact between the people of Polynesia and those of the Americas.

"The circumstances which brought the first Mesoamerican high culture into existence are not fully understood," intoned the documentary's narrator. "All we know is that it happened about three thousand years ago and the evidence for it is monumental." And then the screen was filled with the image of a massive stone head, one of twenty-one such sculptures, thought to be portraits of Olmec rulers. It had a stern and beautiful face, with wide, sightless, almond-shaped eyes, a broad nose, and full lips that turned down at the corners.

"Hey," said Seven, "that looks like Tu!"

The likeness to Seven's eldest brother was, in fact, striking. It was the lips, I think, that were so persuasive, that beautifully curved, characteristically downturned mouth, and the broad, flat plane of the face, and the sense of heaviness. But for Seven it was more than that. It was proof that some kind of link existed between the steamy, lowland jungles of Central America and the Land of the Long White Cloud. The accepted thesis is that if Mesoamericans and Polynesians share any ancestral roots, they are not less than thirty thousand or forty thousand years old and they share them with most of Asia. There is no hard evidence for contact between the Olmecs or anyone else in the Americas and Seven's ancestors. But Seven was never one for received wisdom.

"And the *kumara*?" he would say when we argued. "How did we get the *kumara*? Tell me that. If we could sail to Easter Island, I don't see why we couldn't go all the way. Maybe those Olmecs were really Polynesians . . ."

It was during that year in Hawaii that Seven's father died. His death was unexpected; he was not an old man, and at first we imagined that his cancer might be treatable. Perhaps, If he had lived in a city, gone regularly to the doctor, been willing to undergo the indignities of treatment, who knows, maybe it would have been different—for a while. But his disease was already well advanced by the time anyone knew about it.

Seven flew home just in time to see his father before he died, taking the baby with him. Because Aperahama had been born in the United States, his paternal grandfather had never seen him. The family wanted him christened, if possible, before his grandfather died. Seven's father was too weak to perform the ceremony, but one of the uncles would do it and he would be there to bless the child.

There was no question of my going with them. We barely had enough money as it was for the airfare, and it just seemed like one of those occasions on which I wouldn't know what to do. With all the brothers and sisters gathered, not to mention the cousins and uncles and aunts, I knew it would be a dense and private affair. Of course, I would have been welcome, but I also thought it was something Seven should do alone. That said, it was not easy letting them go. Aperahama was only just old enough to go without me and I gave Seven a thousand instructions about what to do.

"Make sure you dress him warmly. I know it's summer, but it's not Hawaii, is it? It might get cool at night. And try not to lose his blanket. I think you should be careful how much *kina* you give him. And don't take him over to Harry's; I swear that house has bugs. If you need anything, ask Hera. She'll know what to do. And call me, OK? when you get there."

I spent the week alone in Honolulu, sitting in the living room, alternately reading and waiting for the phone. I was stunned at the silence and the sudden absence of things that needed my attention. I took my umbrella and walked all the way to Manoa. I got a few books from the library and walked back. The sun shone, the clouds gathered over the Pali, the evening fell abruptly, like a blind being suddenly drawn. I sat on the step and watched the moths and the giant cockroaches fling themselves at the light above the door. One of the books I got from the library was a collection of Maori laments. Maori songs are hard to follow because they are extremely allusive.

They are packed with references to people and places and events of the past; almost every phrase is metaphorical and requires a huge body of traditional knowledge to decode. But eventually I found one I could make sense of. I could even make out a few words: *mate*, death; *haere*, come or go; *taonga*, something of value, a treasure of some kind.

Haere, kua uhia koe ki ou taonga, ki nga kakahu o tenei hunga o te mate.

I could almost hear my mother-in-law's voice, could almost see them sitting with the body, could almost hear the quiet murmur of noise in the *marae*. I read the lament aloud, in English, alone in the empty house.

You have been wrapped in the precious clothes of this thing,
    death;
you have been clothed in the words of farewell; and
immersed in an endless spring of tears;
these greetings we have given you.
So, leave us now, farewell! Go, descendant of the ancestors,
go, the sheltering *rata* tree,
go upon your land,
go upon your waters,
borne on the words we have spoken for you,
to the dark night, the deep night, the dense night.
Go to Antares, to the star of summer,
to the gathering of the thousands,
Forsaking love, go!

A week later I went to pick them up at the airport. Seven had lost the blanket but he'd brought back a beautiful flax kit made by his auntie and a stuffed kiwi that he'd bought for Aper-ahama in the airport on the way home. He was very tired but he didn't seem what I would call sad. He *was* sad, but he was also calmer than any sad person I'd ever known. He wasn't in shock or trying to hold himself together. He wasn't in denial. He was just the way he had always been, except a little subdued.

He didn't have much to tell me. Just that his father had died, there had been a funeral, it had lasted for several days, and a great many people had come to bid him farewell. On the last night there had been a storm. Seven and his brothers had gone up the hill and were sitting looking out over Mangonui when a hole opened up in the clouds right over the *marae*.

"Look at that," said one of them. "Must be the exit."

"Yeah," said another. "The old man's on his way to Hawaiki now."

"Well, then," said Seven, "guess I'll see him there."

13

ONCE WERE WARRIORS

WHEN WE LEFT Hawaii, it was, by my count, the ninth time I had crossed the equator in less than seven years. I had flown every possible airline, made every possible stopover, tried every combination of long and short legs, and I was beginning to think of myself as an Old Pacific Hand. We were headed south, back to Australia, but this time we were bound for Queensland, where I had another fellowship for two years.

The far north of Australia occupies roughly the same position, culturally and semantically, as that of the Deep South in the United States. It is hot and tropical—about half the state of Queensland lies within the Tropic of Capricorn—and famous for its reactionary politicians, most notably Joh Bjelke-Petersen, who was premier of Queensland for nearly twenty years and whose positions included, among other things, support for the white minority government of apartheid South Africa. Tucked into the southeast corner of a state four times the size of Texas, Brisbane belongs in many respects to the metropolitan corridor of Sydney-Canberra-Melbourne that stretches down Australia's eastern coast. But, unlike these other cities, there is—or was—something of the frontier about it still.

With Aperahama and Seven's sister Kura, who had come over from New Zealand to live with us, we made quite a little family. We all lived together in a poor-man's Queenslander, a charming style of house with high-ceilinged rooms and windows made of louvered glass. Like all such houses, it was set about six feet off the ground both to discourage insects and to allow the cool night air to circulate underneath. There was a big mango tree in the backyard, which attracted a squeaking crowd of bats at dusk, and beneath the house lived a large but innocuous blue-tongued skink.

Across the river, a five-minute ride by passenger ferry, was the University of Queensland. It was set on nearly three hundred acres of landscaped grounds and was far and away the most beautiful campus on which I'd ever worked. The walk up to my office from the ferry took me through a maze of gardens, past an ornamental lake, and on up through an avenue of purple jacarandas to the Great Court, a large green lawn surrounded by monumental sandstone buildings. It was, in many ways, idyllic. I had colleagues that I liked and an office of my own, but I was hard-pressed to support the four of us on my tiny postdoctoral salary and so, as soon as we were settled, Seven set out to get a job.

He had never had any trouble finding work before, despite moving almost yearly to a new city. In Boston he'd built titanium bicycles; in Hawaii he'd been a dispatcher for the American Automobile Association. In Brisbane his first thought was to go back to foundry work, which, in that somewhat less sophisticated economy, seemed to hold out the best hope of a decent wage. He answered an ad in the paper for a jobbing molder, and they told him to come in for an interview the next day. But when he got there, they said, sorry, the job was filled. Two days later the ad was back in the paper.

Outraged, I rang up the office of equal opportunity.

"What does it take," I asked, "to file a claim of racial discrimination against an employer?"

"Did they tell him they wouldn't hire him because he was black?" asked the woman on the other end of the line.

"No, of course they didn't! They just told him there was no job. But there clearly is a job because they're continuing to advertise."

"Well, I'm sorry, but it has to be spelled out, either verbally or in writing, that they are not hiring him for reasons of ethnicity."

"That," I said, "is the stupidest thing I've ever heard."

Kura, meanwhile, had enrolled in school. She was twenty-three years old and had the equivalent of a tenth-grade education and I was adamant that she go back and finish high school. We found a day care for Aperahama and Seven continued to look for work. He talked about becoming a taxi driver and worked for a while as a janitor in a factory where they made salads for supermarket chains. He did a stint as a laborer for a builder, who was himself only intermittently employed, and then one day he came home and announced that he had taken a job selling vacuum cleaners door-to-door.

"I hope you're kidding," I said.

When I was a very little girl, according to my mother, I had what I described as a nightmare. I dreamed that I lived in a little house with a picture window. Inside the window there was a table and on the table there was a lamp. "That was it," said my mother. "Isn't that funny? I don't think you were more than five."

I don't remember having this dream but I know exactly what kind of house it must have been. Between the place where I grew up and the city of Boston there was a town through which we used to drive. It was full of little houses with metal screen doors set close to each other and to the road. They were houses like a child might draw: a peaked roof with a chimney, a door, and a picture window through which I could often see the flickering blue glow of a television as we drove past in the night.

As a child, I felt that there was something sad about these houses, though I wouldn't have been able to put my finger on what it was. They seemed poor to me, not with the desperate, bombed-out poverty of places like Harlem, through which we sometimes drove when we went to New York, but in a strained, respectable sort of way. They were like places I could almost imagine living, places I might have ended up in, if things had gone another way. To me they represented the sort of poverty into which one might actually fall.

I felt about these houses exactly the way I felt about a traveling salesman who used to come to my family's house once or twice a year when I was young. He was the only traveling salesman I ever knew—it was the end of the traveling salesman era—and I still remember the feeling I had when his car pulled into our driveway and I saw him get out and make his way slowly across the driveway to the front door. He must have come in early spring or late autumn because I can only see him crossing the gravel on some bleak and chilly day. He was a sad little man with a toupee and a face that fell in fleshy folds. Even as a child I thought his life must be miserable and I was embarrassed that we lived in a nice warm house while he had to be outside, going from door-to-door.

My mother always invited him in and he would nod and thank her and scrape his feet and lug his sample case full of linens into the dining room, where he could open it up on the table and show her what he had. I was always worried that my mother would say no, there was nothing that she wanted. But she always looked through everything carefully and picked out

something, a set of embroidered pillowcases or handkerchiefs
for my father. I now wonder how she paid him—did she give
him cash?—and I wonder, too, when he stopped coming and
when it was we finally realized that he wasn't going to call on
us anymore.

I never quite got over the feeling I had about him. When I
was a little older, I took to disappearing whenever he arrived.
But even that didn't help, because the very idea of him, the
shabby clothes, the stringy hair, the pathetic occupation, made
me feel depressed. And so, when Seven announced that he had
taken a job as a door-to-door salesman, I felt the memory of
this man wash over me and, for the first time in our marriage, I
despaired.

I told him he wouldn't be any good at it. He had never sold
anything in his life; he gave away everything, including our
cars. And while it was true that he could lie like the devil when
he wanted, he would never be able to cheat anyone out of their
money, which was what, I told him, this kind of selling really
was. What was even more worrying was the fact that after
attending a single training session he had been completely
indoctrinated with the view that this overpriced appliance was
superior to every other vacuum cleaner on earth. I knew he was
very susceptible to quackery, not always having a good basis
on which to evaluate competing claims. And besides, I wondered, since when had he become an expert in vacuuming?

Up to that point, I had viewed Seven's various occupations
with a mix of humor and something like pride. There was a
certain undeniable glamour in being a bicycle messenger—it
required such tremendous stamina and strength—and even his
work as a foundryman had a kind of masculine integrity. I
didn't care that his work wasn't white-collar; I even found it
kind of a relief. There hadn't been a blue-collar worker in my

family for a hundred years—we were all businessmen and engineers and professors—and I was always drawn to the unfamiliar. Besides, I was no more interested in money than he was. I, after all, had had all the opportunity in the world, and I hadn't exactly chosen a lucrative career. But, for me, this business of the vacuum cleaners crossed some kind of line. I found it weirdly humiliating and I begged him not to take the job.

Seven thought I was being completely ridiculous and for years he continued to sing the praises of this particular brand of vacuum cleaner. But I was right about one thing: he couldn't sell. He lasted in the job about two weeks before he realized he wasn't going to make any money and, to my inexpressible relief, he gave it up.

Perhaps more than any other episode in our life together, this incident forced me to acknowledge the issue of class. Of course, I had always known it was there between us, but I never paid it much attention, perhaps because it was easier for me to think dispassionately about the differences between Pakeha and Maori than about those between the privileged and the poor. But there were moments—days when I would come home from the university to find Seven and Kura stretched out on the floor watching monster trucks on TV— when I would look at them and think, *you people*. Then I'd do a double take and think, *what, do I want them to be just like me?* Of course I didn't. But the reality was that I was never going to be just like them either.

The place I really struggled with this was with Seven's sister, who was almost ten years younger than I and whom, I felt, I was in a position to influence. On the one hand, it was perfectly clear to me that if she didn't get an education, she was doomed—at the very least to a lifetime of poverty, but also, in my mind, to something more serious. Without a foundation of skills and knowledge, she would have no chance of discovering what she was good at or experiencing the satisfaction of making choices for herself. Being a girl, her prospects were even more limited than those of her brothers. She would remain within the narrowly circumscribed world of her family and there would be this great big universe around her that she would never know. And yet it was also clear to me that by encouraging her to become independent, I was, in effect, indoctrinating her with my own white, middle-class values.

It is a "basic Pakeha misunderstanding," writes the philosopher John Patterson, "that deep down, Maori and Pakeha are very similar." In fact, he argues, deep down, Maoris have very different ways of understanding the world. Some of these ways may look familiar—Maori respect for the natural world may look, for example, like environmentalism—but they stem from quite different systems of understanding. The basis of Pakeha concern for the environment is essentially utilitarian— we value the earth for what it can give us—while the Maori view is, at least originally, genealogical. They value the earth because it is effectively their kin.

In the old days, everything was genealogical for Maoris. The idea of family was so essential, joked the anthropologist J. Prytz Johansen, that if Kant had lived among them, he would have added kinship to his fundamental categories of knowledge, time, and space. In the classical view, the whole Maori cosmos unfolds itself as a great web of ancestral relations "in which heaven and earth are first parents of all beings and things, such as the sea, the sand on the beach, the wood, the birds, and man." In theory, any Maori can trace his descent back through a chain of historical figures like Tareha or Hongi Hika to the legendary navigators who arrived in canoes from

Hawaiki and beyond them to the gods of sea and forest and wind, to the first parents, Ranginui and Papatuanuku, Sky Father and Earth Mother, and beyond them to the great night, the nothingness, *Nui te Po*.

Admittedly, this conceptual framework may feel less than pressingly real to many contemporary Maoris, but it still permeates their lives in subtle ways—just as the Judeo-Christian ethos affects even atheists like me who have grown up within its ambit. Maori values are tribal values: what is good for the group is good for the individual, whereas the reverse does not necessarily hold true. In the ideal Maori community, there is a sharing of both resources and obligations. Sacrifice is often demanded; loyalty is highly prized. Competitiveness—unless in sports—is generally discouraged, while greed and selfishness are openly despised. The result is a society in which everyone is cared for, but also one in which individual achievement is the exception rather than the norm. One consequence of this is that, from the Pakeha point of view, Maoris often look unambitious, while Pakehas, seen from the Maori perspective, look ruthless, isolated, and cold.

I had seen, firsthand, how this worked in Boston, where Seven's lack of ambition struck my family as, well, *odd*.

"What does he want to *do*?" my father would ask me, meaning, what future did he envision, what plans did he have, what ladder did he see himself ascending?

"I don't really know, Dad. I'm not sure he wants to *do* anything at all."

I supposed this dynamic must have played itself out in reverse when it came to Seven's family, and I sometimes wondered if they saw me as hopelessly self-absorbed and striving, dragging my family around the world in the pursuit of some crackpot career. But it didn't help me one little bit to see both sides of the problem. When it came to Kura—or any of my own children, for that matter—I could never resist the imperatives of my own upbringing. They could lie on the floor and watch monster trucks all they liked, but as long as she was living with me, I was going to make sure she went to school.

At some point during that year I met an Aboriginal writer and activist named Sam Watson. I had scheduled an interview with him to discuss his novel, *The Kadaitcha Sung*, but as we were wrapping it up he said something to me that went home— *whump!*—like an arrow into a bale of hay. It was hard, he said, for people who had not experienced sustained, persistent discrimination to understand what it was like to be suspected every single day, by someone, somewhere, of having done something wrong or underhanded, of having nicked something, or lied, or broken the law. It was exhausting, he said, having to defend yourself against this barrage of suspicion. "It just wears you down after a while."

I think that, like a lot of white people, I had envisioned racism as a series of distinct, objectionable, even violent acts— the scary end of the spectrum—and had not really grasped that it was also, perhaps primarily, a relentless, wearying drone of negativity from which there was no escape. Of course, the reason I had not understood this was that, until then, I had never experienced it firsthand.

Right next door to us lived an old lady who regularly regaled Seven with stories about the Aborigines who used to live across the street. "Dirty buggers," she'd say to him, leaning across the fence, while he pushed the lawnmower back and forth. I was astonished by her behavior, not just that she would say such things, but that she would say them to Seven, who, as a Maori— Maoris being to New Zealand precisely what Aborigines are to

Australia—could not possibly fail to be offended by her remarks. But she clearly had some way of parsing reality so that he was included with her on her side of the divide, while the lazy, shiftless, thieving Aborigines remained securely on the other. Seven, to my further astonishment, ignored her comments. He said he felt sorry for her, living all alone in her little house, and he helped her with things that needed fixing and continued, for as long as we lived there, to mow her lawn.

But suburban Brisbane had its share of people like our next-door neighbor and you never knew when one of them would cross your path. There was one Saturday morning when we all piled into the car and set off to investigate the garage sales in our neighborhood. We owned almost nothing in the way of furniture or appliances, just a few beds, a kitchen table and some chairs, and we had no money to buy anything new, so we often went looking for what we needed at the weekend garage sales.

The first house we came to had a long side yard with a gate at the sidewalk and a garage at the back. We wandered around for a while looking at things and Seven bought a two-dollar sprinkler from a woman in the garage. As we were leaving—he was walking ahead with Kura, carrying Aperahama on his shoulders, I was coming along behind—a man in a lawn chair at the gate suddenly accosted him.

"D'you pay for that?" he demanded.

Seven just looked at him. "No," he said, and walked on through the gate.

This time, I could see that he was angry. "Bloody old bastard," he muttered, as we got back in the car.

I asked him later if he'd experienced that sort of thing much in New Zealand.

"No," he said. "Not really. The rednecks over there are too scared to say anything."

But when I pressed him on the subject, it became clear that he shared with many New Zealanders the view that their society was actually less racist than many, including both Australia and the United States. This may, in fact, be true, but no matter how well integrated New Zealand is comparatively speaking, statistically it is still a country with a clear racial divide.

Life expectancy at birth for Maoris is about eight years less than for other New Zealanders. Two out of five adult Maoris have no educational qualifications; nearly half live on an income of less than twenty thousand dollars a year. Maoris are twice as likely as non-Maoris to be unemployed. They are more likely to receive public assistance, to live in a house that is overcrowded, to rent rather than own. They are more likely to smoke, to be classed as "hazardous drinkers," to develop asthma, high blood pressure, and diabetes, to live without access to a telephone or car. Maoris are more likely than other New Zealanders to be arrested, convicted, and incarcerated, and, while they make up only 15 percent of the general population, they account for fully half of those in jail.

There is an argument, just under the surface of polite discourse, that would explain these figures in terms of Maori characteristics. Maoris, it goes, are just *like* that: they fight and get into trouble, they're lazy and don't go to school. Obviously, this is a racist argument, but because it dovetails with a pair of long-standing clichés—warlike Maoris on the one hand, languid Polynesians on the other—it is difficult to explode. What is equally obvious, however, is that the underlying issue is economic. What, after all, does the cluster of social indicators that includes low life expectancy, poor health, high unemployment, and low levels of educational attainment suggest, if not poverty? And what is the root cause of Maori poverty, if not colonization?

It would be hard to dispute that what these numbers, taken as a whole, reflect is the demoralizing effect on an indigenous people of having been colonized—which is to say, sidelined and impoverished in a country where they were once both sovereign and strong. This is, in fact, precisely what one sees over the course of the later nineteenth and early twentieth centuries in New Zealand: increasing white settlement and prosperity matched by corresponding Maori decline. "It was what we lost," says a character in Alan Duff's novel *Once Were Warriors*, "when you, the white audience out there, defeated us. Conquered us. Took our land, our *mana*, left us with nothing."

I met Duff that same year in Queensland, not long after I'd met Sam Watson. Duff was by then the author of at least two novels and a collection of essays, but the one that interested me most was his first. A bestselling novel in New Zealand, which was also made into an internationally successful film, *Once Were Warriors* was the first book to address the reality of what it was like to belong to the most alienated and dysfunctional segment of New Zealand society—unemployed, undereducated, landless Maoris. It was the same slice of society as that depicted in the article my father's cousin had sent him, which was, not accidentally, titled, "One Night Out Stealing" in a direct reference to another of Duff's books.

Once Were Warriors is an ugly tale of deprivation, brutality, and abuse, and New Zealanders of all stripes reacted strongly to it when it first appeared, some saying they were *shocked*, they'd had no idea, while others accused Duff of hanging out their dirty laundry. The central character in the novel is a tough guy named Jake Heke who beats his wife and bullies his kids and sees everyone "in terms of their fighting potential first, before he saw anything." Here is Jake, in the pub, feeling his power:

> And he stood there, waiting while the jugs were filled, aware of people's awareness of him; he felt like a chief, a Maori warrior chief—no, not a Maori chief . . . an Indian chief, a real Injun . . . Jake pouted his lips ever so slightly and pulled the corners of his mouth down by the use of the cheek or jaw muscles . . . he flared his nostrils like a, you know, a bull—I know! Like Sitting Bull. Chief Sitting Bull. And he part lidded his eyes . . . so he stood there swelled with pride and vanity and this sense of feeling kingly and inside a voice was going: Look at me. *Look* at me, ya fuckers. I'm Jake Heke. Jake the Muss Heke. LOOK AT ME (and feel humble, you dogs).

Duff's point about Jake and those like him is that they are but vain, weak, ignominious echoes of what Maoris used to be. "We used to be a race of warriors," says a character in the novel, but that was a long time ago and all that's left now of the warriors thing is a brutal sort of stoicism that Duff calls "toughness." "Us Maoris might be every bad thing in this world, but you can't take away from us our toughness."

According to Duff, Maoris have allowed themselves to sink into a morass of dissipation and self-pity, and while the root cause of this decline may, in fact, be colonization, it does them little good to lay the blame for their plight at the foot of the Pakeha. That is the sort of thinking, he argues, that "has turned us into a race of people that says it's okay to be a loser, it's okay to beat my wife, it's okay to go and get drunk three or four times a week with the last of my money . . . because the whites have colonized and dispirited me." He doesn't deny that racism and bigotry are out there, he just thinks it's something you have to factor in. "I know it's harder for me to get a job, so I've got to try twice as hard," he says. "Don't cry about it. Someone's got to be in the minority."

When it was first published, the novelist Witi Ihimaera (author of *The Whale Rider*) called *Once Were Warriors* "the *haka*, the rage" of the Maori people. A *haka* is an action song performed by men as a prelude to battle, or, these days, at the opening of a rugby match. The term is usually translated as "war dance," though Cook perceptively referred to it as "a show of courage by insult." This is precisely what Duff's work is: a challenge, an insult, and a goad. It is calculated to bring the wrath of almost everyone down upon his head—Maori activists who see him as an apologist for the Pakeha; Pakeha liberals who think he's a right-wing crank; traditionalists who view him as an embarrassment. But it's easy to get so distracted by Duff's aggressive posturing that you forget what his message really is.

Duff has an almost evangelical faith in the transformative power of education, discipline, and hard work. But his exhortations to Maoris to read, to go back to school, to get off the dole and start working have often been interpreted as a call for assimilation to mainstream Pakeha society—a charge that fills Duff with rage. "I have never ever said assimilate to a Pakeha!" he said in an interview with Vilsoni Hereniko. And, anyway, he argued, "It's not a Pakeha world. It's a universal world. In fact, it's Asian now." Still, one would have to be blind not to see that Duff himself is a kind of cultural hybrid. The peculiar mix of attitudes and aspirations he embodies, of Maori means and Pakeha ends, represents not exactly the fusion of two sets of values but a sort of furious oscillation between two points of view.

Duff comes from what he himself describes as a "starkly contrasting background"—"Maori mother, European father. Father educated, mother uneducated. Father rational, mother . . . volatile," as he put it to me—and is known for writing out of his own experience of stints in borstal, or juvenile detention, and a generally disordered youth. Duff's father, a scientist and the brother, incidentally, of the well-known anthropologist Roger Duff, had what he describes as "a profound influence" on him. "But it took a little while to undo the damage that was done in my childhood," he said. "My mother and her brothers simply got enraged at something and the table went up and everybody fought and it was considered normal. And then everyone kissed and everyone got drunk and the next day or the next week they were doing the same. That's why I had that sort of theme in *Warriors*."

If *Once Were Warriors* was a *haka*, it was also clearly a lament, both culturally for the "fierce pride" of a warrior people and personally for a childhood sacrificed to "unthinkingness" and neglect. It was powerful precisely because it combined these different kinds of sadness, which were related, though not in any simple way, and because, in so doing, it encapsulated what is perhaps the most painful and difficult aspect of colonization: that more has been lost than has been gained and, yet, what is there to do but soldier on?

I shared Duff's view about the fundamental value of education, and for years I talked to Seven about going back to school. I didn't want to push him—I think it's pointless to try to change the people you love—but I did want to encourage him if he showed any interest at all.

Academically speaking, he had a lot of catching up to do: algebra, geometry, expository writing. He had been steered into trade school at the age of fifteen, which meant that he didn't even have what I considered a complete high school education. It made me furious when I thought about it: all those Maori kids shunted into the labor pool as teenagers when they should have been studying chemistry and French.

Eventually—this was some years later—he enrolled in a community college. He took some math and technology classes and a class in painting and one in composition, in which they read short stories, poetry, and plays. The drama text that semester was Sophocles' *Oedipus Rex*. The assignment was to write about Oedipus's fatal flaw and I was trying to get him to find different ways of talking about the king, without writing the paper for him.

"You need to find some other ways to describe him," I told him. "What are some other words for 'anger'? His irrational hostility, his intemperate aggression . . ."

"I wouldn't say that," he said. "I'd say 'violent,' maybe."

"Think of your uncle, your cousin—they're angry men. Think about them, the way they yell and throw things, the way they bully people. You've got some firsthand experience of this sort of thing."

Seven seemed to find this funny. "Once were warriors," he said.

14

Gu, Choki, Pa

LONG BEFORE HE was born, I knew our second child was going to be a boy. He was always kicking, squirming, elbowing me in the ribs. We could see his knees and elbows, or maybe those were his fists, pushing out against the walls. He's a fish, I thought, a fast-swimming, deep-diving, fighting fish, a marlin, a kingfish, a tuna.

I was hardly surprised, then, to see what kind of a baby he turned out to be. Strong and solid, he was the most heavily muscled infant I had ever held. He had a head full of black hair and dark, ruddy skin, and two blue-black Mongolian spots on his buttocks. Our first child had been so fair as to pass for white; only the inky blackness of his irises and something about the shape of his face might have told you that he was not entirely Caucasian. But this one would certainly pass for Maori. There was even something of Seven's mother about his face.

I imagined then that he would be like his cousins, Seven's brothers' and sisters' boys, one of whom, a handsome round-faced child with shining hair, had once met us at the airport by leaping out of the crowd and launching into a *haka*. He was about five years old at the time and fearless, slapping his thighs and stamping his feet and shouting, "*Ka mate, ka mate, ka ora, ka ora!*" to the astonishment of everyone at international arrivals.

When I tried to imagine Seven's childhood, I always thought about these boys. It required no effort whatsoever to insert them into the stories he told. Like the one about the time he and his brother rode down the big hill in Mangonui on a bike with no seat, no pedals, and no brakes. There was a ninety-degree turn at the foot of the hill and his brother, being older and in control of the bicycle, jumped to safety at the last minute, while Seven flew straight into a fence post and ended up with fifty stitches in his knee.

Or the time when he went out fishing, this time with a different brother, and threw out his line and hooked his own leg. They had just rowed out to the mouth of the inlet and neither one of them wanted to row all the way back in. Their first idea was to cut out the hook, but the knife was dull and so they decided to cut the line instead, leaving the hook where it was until they had finished fishing. Eventually, they got Seven to a doctor who tried to numb his leg by injecting an anesthetic into the bottom of his foot. But Seven had almost never worn shoes in his life and the calluses on his soles were so thick they broke the needle.

All his stories were like this: tales of risk and survival, often with a darkly comic twist. He bore no grudge against the brother who'd jumped off the bike. He would probably have done the same thing; it was just his bad luck not to be steering. And there was something in the story of the fishhook that made a gentle mockery not only of his ineptitude in hooking his own leg but of the doctor's in trying to jab the foot of a ten-year-old Maori boy from the country. They were often absurd, these stories of scrapes and mishaps and bad decisions, and the humor lay in the ratio of the teller's nonchalance to the severity or magnitude of the event.

The most extreme example of this I ever heard was a story that was told to me by one of Seven's cousins. It had to do with a dog that had fallen off the back of a truck and was dragged by a rope for a quarter of a mile before anyone realized what had happened. The cousin seemed to find this uproariously funny. "It was a good dog," he said when he finally stopped laughing. "It crawled off and licked itself clean." Although I suspected at the time that this story was being told for my benefit, even so, I thought it was revealing. It *was* a good dog, in the cousin's estimation, because it had suffered and survived, against all odds and with no help from anyone else.

There is a word they use in New Zealand that I've never heard used quite the same way anywhere else. "*Staunch*" in ordinary English, means "trustworthy" or "loyal." But when it is used in New Zealand, particularly by Maoris, it means something rather different. I would have said "strong," or "fearless," or maybe "unexcitable." But, according to Seven, there were shades of meaning that I'd missed.

"What does it mean," I asked him, "when you say that someone is *staunch*?"

"It means . . . holding their own ground," he said. "Having a presence."

"Is it the same as fearless?"

"Not really. People who do extreme sports are fearless. They're not staunch."

"OK, so it's not a matter of physical bravery. How about strong?"

"Any kind of person can be staunch. Big people, little people . . ."

"So it's not a matter of being physically imposing. It's an attitude."

"That's it. It's like a kind of power someone has that makes other people respect them."

This reminded me of something that happened, way back at the very beginning, when Seven had first come to Melbourne and we were just getting to know each other. We were walking together on a crowded sidewalk and I noticed that as people approached us, they veered out of our way. Nobody had ever done that when they saw me coming, so I said something like, "Gee, it must be good to be so big." And Seven laughed and told me that he had a certain way of walking that made people get out of his way.

"Really? Are you trying to intimidate them?"

"Nah," he said. "I just like walking in a straight line."

To be staunch in New Zealand, I eventually realized, is to have *mana*. *Mana* is variously translated as "authority," "influence," "prestige," and "power," but, in truth, we have no English word that fully expresses it. In the old days, writes Anne Salmond, *mana* was inherited at birth, but from then on "men were engaged in a contest for relative *mana*, and according to performances in war, marriage, feasting and on the *marae, mana* rose and fell." It was associated with sacredness, like a divine touch or the idea of selection, and yet the path to achieving it was remarkably democratic.

There is no necessary link between *mana* and physical power—some of the most feared and successful Maori leaders of the historical period, Hongi Hika for instance, were physically unprepossessing men—but it is historically bound up with violence through the concept of *utu*. *Utu* is another word for which we have no good translation. It refers essentially to the principle of reciprocity, the idea being that one is obliged to pay back in kind any slight to one's *mana*. Usually, writes Salmond, "*utu* was exacted on the battlefield, where it was difficult to mete out precisely the right amount of punishment, and after every such encounter, new *utu* accounts were established. As a consequence groups were forever skirmishing; villages had to be fortified and in the more embattled areas people lived in constant expectation of attack."

Cultures, seen from the outside, often seem to have a pattern to them, a shape, an ethos, a characteristic spirit, a disposition. I once looked up the word *"belligerence"* in an American dictionary and found the following sentence illustrating how the word was used: "among the Native American tribes of the Colonial period, the Iroquois were known for their *belligerence*." If this dictionary had been written on the other side of the world, it might have said "Maori" instead of "Iroquois." But the thing about stereotypes is that, while they contain some information—the extent to which pre-contact Maori or Iroquois cultures enshrined the act of war—they also obscure all those qualities that might contradict or complicate the dominant idea: the value of *aroha*, or love, for instance, the importance of children, respect for the aged, all that pertains to the domestic side of life, the gentler virtues of friendship, kindness, charity, and cooperation.

One of the men in my experience who exemplified these other qualities was Seven's father. I had heard that in his younger days he was more of a terror, but I always found him gentle and reserved. Seven, although much bigger and stronger, seemed to take after him in this respect (his size came from his mother's side of the family, as did, perhaps, the fiercer temperament of some of his siblings). He was mild in much the same way as his father, and he often played this mildness off against his strength.

At some point Seven's stories about his youth stopped being about bikes and fishhooks and started being about fights. He liked these stories and told them often, but as if they were part of some mythic past—like the one about the time all the boys at school gathered in a ring down on the playing field to watch him fight a notorious bully. With his big hands, long arms, and fast reflexes, he was a formidable opponent and he often seemed to attract the attention of large, belligerent men. Once, when we were traveling in Australia, we were sitting in a restaurant in some country town and a big guy walked up to him and tried to step him out.

"Does that happen to you often?" I asked, when the man had finally given up and gone away.

But Seven wasn't, in essence, a fighter. He had the capacity but not the impulse, the ability but not (or at least not often) the desire. He was potentially quite dangerous but, unless he were exceedingly angry, to be with him felt completely safe. He was, I used to think, like the flip side of the coin, a reminder that things are always more complex than they seem.

This also seemed to me true of Matiu, our second son. I had thought briefly of calling him Mao Mao, when I was still thinking of fish; or Makoare, a family name that might almost be rendered "Macquarie" in English; or Kingi, which is a fairly common Maori name (there is also a girl's name Kuini, which sounds to English ears like "Queenie"). But in the end we called him Matiu—the Maori form of Matthew, pronounced like Machu in Machu Pichu—because I liked the sound.

Some very physical babies are always straining, squirming, pushing away, as though they cannot bear to be constrained. But Matiu was never physical in that way. He was a profoundly powerful baby—he could hold his head up and sit and stand long before he should have been able to—but he had a deep, physical kind of calm. He would go all soft and quiet when you held him and nestle into the crook of your arm and lie there for hours with his head under your chin, listening to the thump-thump of your heart. We used to take him with us to parties and pass him around so that all the women could take a turn at holding him and carry on about what a lovely, snuggly baby he was.

It was clear as he grew older that he would never be a fierce child, a fighter. He was gentle and cooperative, affectionate and kind. He was like his father and his grandfather and, for all I knew, his great-grandfather before them. And yet he had the physical power, the quick reflexes, the heavy muscles, the big bones. He would always be able to throw his weight around if he wanted, though it seemed unlikely to me that he ever would. Then, every once in a while, out of the blue, there'd be a flash of something almost atavistic.

One day when Matiu was about three years old, he came home from preschool, planted himself with his legs apart, punched the air, and shouted, "*Gu! Choki! Pa!*"

I was sitting in the kitchen with my next-door neighbor and we just looked at each other and laughed. Neither of us had the slightest idea what he was doing.

There were hand motions that went with the words. *Gu* was a fist stuck straight out. *Choki* was two fingers in a V. *Pa* was the hand open, palm outward, fingers spread wide. Each gesture was made with the arm extended out in front of the body.

"It's the Maori in him," said my neighbor. "He's a born warrior."

It did look like a *haka* when Matiu did it, but, as we found out some time later, it was just rock-paper-scissors in Japanese.

There wasn't a new baby in our family every time we moved, but each time we had a baby we were in the process of moving. Matiu was conceived in Queensland, but by the time he was born, we had moved back to Melbourne. I had been offered a

job there as an editor and, though it meant leaving my fellowship early, it was too good an opportunity to pass up. Kura had
finished her course and Seven was not unhappy to be leaving
Brisbane. He had never succeeded in finding work that he liked
and, to add insult to injury, he'd hurt his back at the salad
factory and was spending weeks at a time lying on the living
room floor growing increasingly despondent.

We drove down from Queensland—Seven, Kura, Aperahama, and me, stopping for a box of Bowen mangoes at the
state line and camping in a park full of kangaroos along the
north coast of New South Wales. It was spring and at first the
temperature was lovely, cool in the mornings, hot in the
afternoons, brilliantly clear and sunny. But as we traveled
south, the weather deteriorated and, by the time we reached
Victoria, it was raining and cold.

We had arranged to take a serviced flat not far from the
university while we looked for someplace to live. Knowing
the city as we did, we figured it would take at most a
couple of weeks. But it had been years since we lived in
Melbourne, and the real estate market had changed: there
were fewer places to rent and the prices were higher. Plus,
there had only been two of us the last time; now we were
four, almost five. That meant three bedrooms, which put
all the neighborhoods we'd lived in previously completely
out of reach.

We looked and looked and I got more and more worried and
then, one day, I had an idea. We would take the house of an
academic on sabbatical, a short-term lease, just a semester or, if
we were lucky, a whole academic year. It would be entirely
furnished, down to the sheets and crockery, which was helpful,
and, because of the length of the lease, would be offered at a
below-market rate. We could get our three bedrooms in any

neighborhood we liked, so long as every six or twelve months we were willing to pack up and move.

And so, for the next four years, we lived in a series of other people's houses. One belonged to a chemical engineer, another to a lecturer in accounting, the third was owned by a woman who made films, the fourth by a man who was leaving the university to work for some corporation overseas. They took their families, their pets, and their personal belongings, but they left everything else: their furniture, their appliances, their pots and pans, their gardening tools, their towels and bedding, even their videos and books.

It was always peculiar at first. We crept round the houses, opening drawers and cupboards, trying to figure out where everything was: which sheets belonged on the trundle bed and which were for the double; where they kept the hammer and the corkscrew; which pots fit comfortably in the cupboard and which were better underneath the stove. It was like learning the Dewey decimal system: the only sense it made was internal and the only way you could understand it was to surrender yourself to its logic. There was no point in trying to impose one's own order on a house that was already so completely inhabited, albeit by people who were no longer there. The trick was not to resist them but, rather, to try to figure them out, to do things the way they would have done them. After a while we got used to it, not only to each of the houses in turn, but to the process of serial adaptation.

Up until the time I went to college, I had lived my entire life in a single house—the house my parents continued to live in and the one that Seven and I had visited when he first came to the States. The only exception was a year when my family went to live in Switzerland for what must have been my father's own sabbatical. It was the year that I turned eight, and it is the only year of my childhood that I can remember distinctly. I remember the school I went to and the row in which I sat. I remember the daffodil-colored coat I wore at Easter and the smell of the shop downstairs in our building that sold candy and cigarettes. It is all still perfectly crisp and vivid, like a stone lodged in the middle of a stream, while the rest of my childhood seems like an unbroken flow of experience in which I can hardly pinpoint a single detail.

This, I suppose, is one of the advantages of moving: the creation of these spatiotemporal markers in the mind. But there is a reason these markers get created; it is not simply a matter of the difference between one place and the next. Moving is inherently traumatic, and one of the reasons we remember it is that it is always a kind of shock.

Matiu was born in the second of these houses; Aperahama began school in the third. By the time we faced our fourth it was clear that we couldn't keep going in this fashion. It was one thing to schlep ourselves about, or even ourselves and a baby, but it was another thing entirely to move school-age children. Aperahama had gone to kindergarten in a nice little school just down the road from the house we'd been renting when he turned five. But as he approached his sixth birthday, and the beginning of first grade, the owners returned from abroad. I was resigned to moving—I didn't much like the house anyway—but I really didn't want my son to have to start changing schools.

Of course, I had seen this coming and all the summer we had looked for someplace else to live. But the rental market was the worst I'd ever known it. There was nothing out there: nothing that we could afford, nothing that we couldn't. Two weeks before the start of school I was on the verge of panic. And then, out of the blue, someone called who'd seen a sign I'd posted near the school. They were just about to move to England. Would we be interested in renting their house while they were away?

It was a godsend. The house was wonderful, with a beautiful garden, a bright, open kitchen, and central heating (a bonus in Melbourne that we'd never enjoyed). It was a solidly middle-class dwelling and a huge step up from the cavernous, drafty, unrenovated Victorian we'd been rattling around in for the past year. Best of all, it was just blocks from Aperahama's school. But for how long would we have it? The owners had said a year, maybe two, maybe three if we were really lucky. But there was not much point in getting attached to it. Sooner or later, we were going to have to move.

At first, moving back to Melbourne had felt like coming home. But time had done its work and things had changed. Surprisingly few of our friends had children, and the fact that we had no extended family—apart from Kura, who was now going to college and living in a shared house full of students—made everything more difficult. There was no one to babysit for us or pass on hand-me-downs, no one to get together with for holidays or help with celebrations.

Few things are harder than raising children in a vacuum. I was already worried about the fact that we were raising the boys outside New Zealand. On the one hand, this meant that they would not have to deal with the domestic politics of being Maori, but then there was the problem of all the things they wouldn't know. They would never learn to do a *haka*; they wouldn't know how to behave on the *marae*. They would never have a proper accent in Maori or hear the sound of the language in their heads. They would be strangers when they went back to New Zealand; they wouldn't know any of the customs or protocols and would make all the dumb mistakes that I had made. But there was little that I could do about any of this so long as Seven didn't mind.

I often tried to encourage him to speak Maori to the children and to teach them some of the things he knew. Once, I suggested he show Aperahama how to fish with a hand line like the one I'd seen him use in Mangonui. It was just a circle of plastic on which a fishing line was wound, but the way he could throw it out was marvelous. "Oh," he said, "I don't even know where to get one of those. And, anyway, it's easier to fish with a rod." I think the idea of trying to re-create the world he'd grown up in struck him as silly. He was never one to fetishize his own culture, not when, as he pointed out, there was a perfectly good alternative to hand. I think he agreed with Sir Paul Reeves, the former governor-general of New Zealand, who once said, "There are as many ways of growing up Maori as there are Maori themselves"—and one of them is not to grow up Maori at all.

But there was something else I hadn't anticipated, which had to do with the way that *I* had been raised. One has no idea, in advance, how much one is going to draw upon one's own experience of childhood in order to raise children. And yet, I too was "out of culture." The Australian school system, for example, was foreign to me and, although I could make sense of it from year to year as my children progressed through the grades, I had no memory of how it went, no overview, no sense of where it was going, no model for what was coming up. Nor did I really understand the other mothers, who had, for the most part, grown up right there, sometimes in that very suburb. I didn't know what to make for children's birthday parties or what to bring for the school potluck. I didn't have any loyalty to the local football club. I didn't belong to any neighborhood organizations. I didn't even go to church.

Some of this awkwardness might have had to do with the particular neighborhood in which we were living. There were places in Melbourne where I might have felt more at home—where the mothers might have been more like me, though the fathers would, of course, have been even less like Seven—but we couldn't afford to live in any of them. The curious thing was that, in the past, I had never minded this sense of dislocation. On the contrary, I'd always been happiest swimming in some strange sea. But once I became responsible for my own children, I no longer enjoyed the feeling of being out of my depth. How was I supposed to know what to do with them if I couldn't follow the only templates that I had?

It was a classic immigrant's problem and, of course, it could have been very much worse. Melbourne wasn't *that* different from what I was used to—everyone spoke English, after all—but it was different enough to be disorienting. And that, combined with my growing sense of insecurity about finding anywhere to live, made me feel that, although we had come back to a place where we'd been happy, we had not necessarily come back to a place we could call home.

And then an arrow dropped in front of us, just as Seven always said. It came in the form of a telephone call from my mother. My father was in the hospital again; it was serious though not immediately life-threatening. But he was nearing eighty and I had to ask myself: did I want to do what Seven had done and go back for the funeral, or was it, maybe, time to go back home?

15

MATARIKI

I REMEMBER WAKING in the middle of the night on my very first flight across the equator and looking out the window of the plane. There, low on the horizon and much smaller than I'd imagined, was the Southern Cross. This constellation is to the southern hemisphere what the Big Dipper is to the north, a bright, familiar figure in the night sky that any child can point to. It is made up of four bright stars with a fifth, smaller star floating in the lower right-hand quadrant. To the lower left is an area of darkness long thought to be "an opening into the awful solitude of unoccupied space." In fact, it is a dark cloud of hydrogen gas nearly five hundred light-years away.

A circumpolar constellation, the Cross rotates through the southern sky with its long axis always pointing to the pole, and it is as useful to the navigator in the southern hemisphere as Polaris, the North Star, is to the sailor in the north. While, technically, I might still have been north of the equator at that moment—for the Cross is just visible within the Tropic of Cancer and can be seen low on the horizon from Hawaii and the Florida Keys—for me, the presence of that little cluster of stars was not merely an indication that I had crossed over the line. It was a sign, *the* sign, that the world of things I knew was dipping out of sight behind me, while before me rose a world of things I'd never seen.

When I made my final journey a decade and a half later, it was along this same pathway in reverse. I had Seven, Aperahama, and Matiu to keep me company, and a third child on the way. We allowed ourselves five weeks to enjoy what we knew would likely be our last big trip, at least for sometime to come. There are many things you can do with one child that are difficult, if not impossible, with three, and moving back and forth across the world is certainly one of them.

We stopped off in New Zealand to say good-bye, making the rounds of Seven's siblings in Auckland and Kaitaia and Whangarei. We slept on people's couches and in their guest rooms and once we pitched a tent in someone's yard. But after ten days or so of constant moving (the tent was rather damp), we decided to rent a house for a week on a beachfront not far from Mangonui. It was a tiny place, extremely rustic, but it looked out on the most spectacular bay. It was autumn, the off-season, and the weather was unsettled: one day of brilliant sunshine followed by two of scudding clouds.

The beach was on the ocean side of a long branching peninsula that reached out into the sea. It was remote and extremely quiet, just a little cluster of houses, several of which were shuttered up. A stream ran into the ocean at one end of the beach, and each tide brought new pools and eddies for the children to play in. At the back of the cove there was a steep hillside that led up to the crest of the ridge, and once or twice I clambered up to the top with a cell phone to ring my mother. To our mutual amazement the connection was perfectly clear, and I felt as though I were describing a parallel universe when I tried to explain to her where I was.

"Well," I said, "I'm sitting on a rock in a paddock. There's a fence behind me and a couple of cows and a lot of prickly-looking gorse. But looking out the other way it's quite incredible. I'm up on a bluff overlooking the Pacific, and from where I'm sitting I can actually see the curvature of the earth. I think if you set off from here and sailed in a straight line, you wouldn't hit land again until you came to Valparaíso." There was a strong swell coming in from the east and the breakers down on the beach shone brilliantly whenever the sun broke through. "The color of the sea? Hmmm. I think maybe I'd call it Prussian blue."

The other important stop on our farewell journey was, of course, Hawaii. It had been years since we lived in Honolulu, but we had never gotten over our fondness for the place and Seven often talked about returning. We stayed in a little flat on the university campus and took the boys to Ala Moana to show them the break where Seven liked to surf. We went up over the mist-shrouded Pali and down to the beach at Sans Souci. We showed them the basketwork gods in the Bishop Museum and walked them round the portraits of the Hawaiian monarchs whose resemblance to their Maori aunties and uncles was so plain to see. And, as a sort of coup de grâce, we took them to visit Henry.

Henry, who was the same age as my father, was having some trouble getting back and forth, and he told us we were lucky to find him there; it was probably the last time he'd be able to make the trip from California. I had brought him a book by Ben Finney on the off chance that he didn't already have it. It was the story of the journey of the *Hokule'a*—a reconstructed double-hulled voyaging canoe—from Hawaii to New Zealand and back again, a journey, including side trips, of some twelve thousand nautical miles. Henry knew a good deal about experimental voyaging—journeys undertaken in traditional vessels using only traditional knowledge and tools—and had followed the fortunes of the *Hokule'a* since her maiden

voyage to Tahiti in 1976. Although he was mildly allergic to
the idea of reinvented tradition, and disliked the hordes of New
Age tourists who came to pray to the goddess Pele, he was
intrigued by these efforts to rediscover the ancient navigational
techniques.

"*Hokule'a*," he said, "is the Hawaiian name for Arcturus,
Hawaii's zenith star. Arcturus is a bright star. The brightest, I
believe, in the northern hemisphere and its line of declination
happens to be precisely the same as the latitude of the Big
Island. Some people think the old Polynesians deduced the
existence of an island beneath it on the principle that every
bright star ought to mark something important. Sirius, the
brightest star in the heavens, passes directly over Tahiti. But
you know, if you were hunting for Hawaii, you might also find
the Pleiades useful. Makali'i, the 'little eyes'—or by some
accounts the 'eyes of god,' though I think that may be a late
interpretation—travels over us as well."

Henry leaned back in his chair and looked out the great glass
windows at the sky.

"I know that one," said Seven. "We call it Matariki. We
sometimes used to use it to find north. But I never knew it was
over Hawaii."

When our third son was born about six months later—on
Columbus Day, as it happened—my mother jokingly asked if
we were going to call him Cristobal.

"Ha ha," I said. "No. We're going to call him Dani. Nice
and simple, don't you think? But his real name is Dani
Matariki. A pointer to the northern hemisphere. A north star
for the south."

Each time we moved it was logistically more difficult and each
time the stakes were higher. We had, in spite of all our

problems, begun to put down roots in Australia. My entire professional career had been spent in the Pacific; everyone I knew or had ever worked with was there. Seven, who'd gone back to the messenger business, had a network of very close friends. Our children spoke with Australian accents. I had gone so far as to become naturalized and carried two passports: one with an American eagle and one with an emu and a kangaroo.

And, yet, when the call came about my father, we barely hesitated. He was ill and old and there was too much for him to look after, too many leaves, too much grass, too much snow. We, for our part, had too little money. No matter how hard we worked, it seemed it was always one step forward and two steps back. Maybe, I thought, in America, we could pool our resources: my mother could cook, I could clean, my father could pay the bills, Seven could do the heavy lifting. *From each according to his ability*, I joked, *to each according to his need*.

We shipped three trunks of clothes and bedding, two trunks of toys, a titanium bike, a case of tools, and forty boxes of books and papers. It was the most we'd ever amassed in the way of belongings, but it was still not much for a family of almost five. We had no furniture at all and no kitchen equipment to speak of. I did own one good knife, which I wrapped in a towel and packed in my suitcase, and there was a frying pan I was fond of that had been given to me by a friend, but I left it behind with Seven's sister, along with everything else, including the car. We promised our friends we'd be back in a few years but they just looked at each other and said, "Well, we'll wait and see."

We had, typically, given almost no thought to the question of where we were going to live. Our first thought had been to stay with my parents until we sorted ourselves out. But we soon found that Boston was even dearer than Melbourne. Jobs were hard to come by; salaries were low; health insurance and child care were astronomical; and house prices and rents were, as usual, completely out of reach. But we did have one thing we hadn't had in Australia, and that was help.

The advantages of living in a multigenerational household are apparent to vast numbers of people around the world, but in America, affluence has enabled a culture of isolation and the idea of living with one's extended family strikes most people as quite mad. *How can you stand living with your parents?* my friends asked me, while my parents' friends asked them, *How can you stand living with your kids?* Actually, it was quite easy. There were many more people to do all the things that needed doing—shoveling, cooking, babysitting, putting on and taking off storm windows and screens—and while we brought a certain degree of mess and chaos, we also brought life and energy to a house that was growing quieter with every passing year.

It wouldn't have worked for everybody, but it worked for us. Everyone sacrificed something—privacy, control—but everyone benefited. Seven and I were able to raise our children in a place much nicer than anything we could afford. My parents had company and help with the arduous task of looking after a house in New England on three acres of land. And, as for the children, it was entirely win-win: an array of devoted adults to look after them, a safe and beautiful environment, a nice little public school.

Which is not to say that there weren't problems. My parents objected to Seven's truck, a hulking red Ford with a rusting snowplow that he thought he might someday learn to use, and complained about the quantities of junk that he brought home from the dump—broken snowblowers and television sets, bent ski poles and baby strollers, lamps, radios, bicycles, any kind of remote-control car. It was symptomatic of their differences: his inventiveness versus their refinement. And reminded me of the anthropologist Nicholas Thomas's argument that the close proximity of two cultures—on, for instance, a colonial frontier—does not necessarily result in cultural synthesis. On the contrary, he writes, "closely connected things can remain utterly different."

Seven and my parents could agree to disagree and, so long as they respected each other's boundaries, everything was fine. For me, the problem was different; it was the feeling of having been displaced in time. Everywhere I went there were echoes of my own history: there was the field where I used to go riding; there was the gym where I'd broken my arm; there was the house where my brother was married. I had grown up in this very place with these very people and I knew it all like the back of my own hand. But it was a life I associated with childhood, and there were times when I felt like a subject in a psychology experiment in the erasure of adult memory. My parents were still in their room; my children were in the room I'd occupied as a child; Seven and I were in the guest room. It was like not knowing where in your life you were.

But, then, wasn't this sense of disorientation precisely what I'd always sought? I told myself that I had simply embarked on a new adventure, filled with minivans and soccer fields and bank over-drafts, which to the prejudiced observer might have seemed like the antithesis of a voyage of discovery, a kind of antiexpedition, an unadventure, but which—looked at from the right angle—was as challenging and peculiar as anything I'd known.

There was one person for whom it really was an adventure, however. Seven was no longer the innocent he'd been when he first came to America, but he had never lived anywhere quite like the place to which we had now moved.

The town in which my parents lived was one of those New England villages with a flower pot, a white church, and a common in the center, and a small, grudging concession to commerce in the form of a bank, a post office, a supermarket, and a gift shop about a mile away. Although it was only about fifteen miles from Boston, it had retained much of its original character, thanks to the implementation of a radical two-acre zoning policy in the late 1950s. Thus, while all the towns around it had grown denser and more suburban, my parents' town had remained remarkably pristine.

There had been demographic changes, however. The people who had moved out from Boston in the late 1950s and early 1960s—my parents among them—were attracted to the area by the prospect of cheap land. They were mostly middle-class people, professionals and businessmen, but also a number of academics like my father. As the value of the land went up, however, the professions of the inhabitants changed. Professors could no longer afford to live there, and by the time Seven and I arrived, the town was filled with venture capitalists and financiers.

In this small and affluent community, Seven was difficult to miss. Everything about him was different: the way he looked, the car he drove, his accent, the things he wore. Soon it seemed that everybody knew him. Although I had the advantage of having already lived there, within a matter of months more people knew Seven than knew me.

One day I went to the local library to get some books for a talk about New Zealand that I'd been asked to give at the preschool. When I got there, I found that some other group was doing a project on the antipodes and all the books on New Zealand were already out. I explained the situation to the librarian.

"You know," she said, leaning across the counter confidentially, "there *is* a Maori in town that you could talk to."

"I know," I said, trying not to smile. "I'm married to him."

As the years went by and we showed no sign of returning to the Pacific, people began to ask me if Seven was happy in the States and whether he ever wanted to go home.

"Don't you want to go back to New Zealand?" I would ask him.

"Not really," he always said.

For some reason, everyone, including me, expected him to be homesick. But when I thought back on my own decade and a half away, it struck me that I had rarely been homesick in all those years. I had enjoyed the freedom that came with being far away and had liked being the only one of my kind wherever I lived. Now that I was back in Boston, I could appreciate the ways in which *belonging* was useful. I understood the landscape and the weather; I got a higher percentage of the jokes. But I still sometimes found it claustrophobic and I imagined that Seven was probably enjoying the freedom to reinvent himself that I, by coming home, had given up.

One of the things he did was to take up tennis, a sport no Maori where he came from played. He was athletic and picked up sports easily but, until he learned to control the ball, his strength was something of a liability.

He had signed on at one of the local clubs where they gave each of the members a ranking and booked partners for them at the appropriate level. Seven, being a novice, was added to a doubles group consisting of three middle-age women. I can only guess what they thought when they saw him coming—with his long black ponytail and his powerful dark arms and his gleaming tennis whites. But, after he nearly knocked his partner out with a badly aimed forehand to the back of the head, he was never matched with that kind of group again.

Eventually, Seven became quite a good tennis player. One year he even took first place in the doubles tournament on the Fourth of July. The prize was a plastic water bottle with the words *Suburban Tennis League* printed on the side.

"I'm going to take a picture of you with that," I told him, "and send it to your brothers."

"Ha ha. Very funny," he said.

16

THIEVES AND INDIAN-KILLERS

J UST BEFORE WE left New Zealand on our way to the
States, we had gone with a bunch of Seven's brothers and
sisters to the pub in Kerikeri where Seven and I had first met. I
was feeling a little nostalgic and, under the influence of a
couple of beers, I confessed to one his brothers that I was
concocting a plan.

"You know what I'm going to do?" I said to him.

"What's that, Sis?"

"I'm going to write your family story."

"Write your own first," he said without missing a beat.

I thought about this when I got back to America. For years I
had been obsessed with Seven's history—or, more properly,
with the history of the Maori people—but I had never given my
own history much thought.

By a strange coincidence, not six months after we arrived in
Boston, a slim bound volume came unexpectedly in the mail.
Titled *The Descendants of George Abbott of Rowley, Mass, in
the Single Line to Everton Judson Abbott, Followed by All the
Abbott Descendants of the Twentieth Century*, it was a gen-
ealogy of my mother's family, compiled by one of her cousins
in Minnesota. The story of the family's origins in England and
their arrival in the American colonies was a confusing one,
involving obscure parliamentary records, false interments, and

missing wills. But there was one point that leaped out at me: the eponymous American ancestor, George Abbott of Rowley, Yorkshire, had taken possession of a house lot of two acres in Rowley, Massachusetts, in 1642.

This fact, when I discovered it, set off a clanging in my head. What are numbers? Accidents, symbols, ciphers—they are meaningless in themselves. And yet, there it is: an American beginning and, in perfect synchronicity, a Maori end, as though history, like electricity, leaped across the breach from one conductor to another.

The Yorkshire Abbotts were dissenters, but they seem to have been a cautious lot, not given to precipitate gestures. Still, they no doubt watched with growing concern as England gradually emptied of their brethren. George Abbott, I imagine, followed the fate of the reformists closely as, parish by parish, they packed their things and set out for America in the hope of "laying a foundation for the advancement of the Redeemer's kingdom" in those wild and inhospitable regions. News came back across the sea: the New England settlements prospered. At last he made up his mind and, putting behind him all that was familiar in life, he joined the trailing end of the Great Migration, shipping for the colonies just as England lurched toward civil war.

There is much to be said for the daring of emigrants, but one wonders whether any of these tradesmen and shopkeepers and farmers fully realized where they were going. Rowley, Massachusetts, in 1642 was a place in which chairs were uncommon, china and porcelain not to be had, and tea the rarest of luxuries. Men lived to an average age of forty-three and children often succumbed to contagious diseases. Accidents were not uncommon: people drowned and froze and were scalded and got lost in the woods. Fires consumed houses; barns were struck by lightning and sometimes maliciously set alight. One might be publicly whipped for shooting fowl on the Sabbath Day or have one's ears cut off for seditious speech. The possession of any books at all and more than three sets of clothing was a sign of affluence.

The boundaries of Rowley town lay eight miles from the meetinghouse in any direction. Beyond that was wilderness: to the east a tangle of salt marshes, to the west the forest primeval, filled not only with moose and bears but with wolves in such numbers that a bounty was offered for every head nailed to the meetinghouse wall. Above all, there were Indians—Agawams, Pennacooks, and Pawtuckets—whose uncanny ability to appear and disappear, along with their shifting and uncertain loyalties, kept the colonists in a state of perpetual nervous tension. The town's public institutions reflected the settlers' hopes and fears, being about evenly divided between the functions of life and those of death, with a grist mill, saw mill, and meetinghouse on the one hand, and a watch house, powder house, training ground, and cemetery on the other. It would be years before they could even think about a school.

George Abbott was granted a house lot in the first distribution on the corner of Kiln Lane and the High Way, next door to Sebastian Briggam. Like other settlers, he received a wood lot, a meadow lot, and a planting lot from the common lands. He built a wood-frame house with clapboard sheathing and erected a fireplace made of stone. He planted rye, peas, beans, and corn, and a small apple orchard, which he laid out on the slope that ran down behind his house. There he lived with his wife and four sons until the early winter of 1647, when, in the course of repairing his chimney, he fell from the roof of his house and died. His effects at death included a satin cap, thirty books, and two black gowns, which showed him to be a man of some consequence in the colony. Despite his premature death, his descendants married well and prospered, numbering no fewer than twenty-three in the second generation.

The land on which the town of Rowley was established belonged, as did all the land lying between the Merrimack and Bass rivers, to Masconnomet, Sagamore of Agawam. No payment was made for the title—beyond the eight hundred pounds paid to some settlers of Ipswich and Newbury who had previously laid claim to acreage that was now within Rowley's boundaries—until sixty years later, when three of Masconnomet's grandsons sued for compensation. The basis of their claim was a deed to the neighboring town of Ipswich, signed by their grandfather in 1638, in which he had relinquished "all the right and interest I have unto all the havens, rivers, creeks, islands, huntings, and fishings, with all the woods, swamps, timber, and whatever else is, or may be, in or upon the said ground to me belonging" in the Bay of Agawam (later known as Ipswich) for the sum of twenty pounds.

The relationship between settlers and natives waxed and waned as rumors swirled in the unstable atmosphere of the new colony. Reports circulated among the colonists of Indian conspiracies to murder them in their beds. Warrants went out for the arrest and disarmament of Indian leaders, only to be rescinded when they proved unfounded or impossible to effect. A set of military watches and alarms was established in every township, and men were ordered to furnish themselves with powder and shot and to keep their muskets ready. A sense of anxiety hung over the general population. John Winthrop records a chilly night in September 1642 when a traveler, having lost himself in a swamp and hearing the howls of wolves in the distance, cried out for help in the darkness. A nearby settler heard the cries, but believing that Indians were torturing the man, he dared not go to his rescue. Instead, he fired his musket in the air, setting off alarms from Dorchester to Salem.

But although the colonists feared and even hated the Indians, they were confident of one thing: in the long run the natives would disappear. Settlers spoke of the terrible epidemics that swept the coastal region even before the Pilgrims had landed at Plymouth, describing these outbreaks as mysteriously providential. "It seems God hath provided this country for our nation," one wrote, "destroying the natives by the plague, it not touching one Englishman, though many traded and were conversant among them." In some places "the Contagion hath scarce left alive one person of an hundred," wrote another, while elsewhere the plagues "utterly consumed man, woman and child, so that there is no person left to lay claim to the soil which they possessed."

My mother was fond of saying that we were descended from pickpockets and thieves and, more recently, from Indian-killers. The "pickpockets and thieves" was a backhanded reference to the family's early arrival in the colonies and to the fact that every settler society contains its share of rogues. The "Indian-killers," on the other hand, was a direct reference to her great-uncle Colonel Henry Hastings Sibley, who led the campaign against the Santee Sioux, which ended in the mass hanging of thirty-eight Indians at Mankato, Minnesota, in 1862, the largest mass execution in U.S. history.

It was a bitter joke because, although we understood the truth of it, none of us could say with complete honesty that we wished it had been any other way. Privilege comes at a cost and it was the Dakotas and Pennacooks and Pawtuckets who paid the price of our family's prosperity. This, of course, was true of everyone on the leading edge of a colonial frontier. But the unhappy irony that my mother's wealth was directly linked to the dispossession of America's natives, while my husband's poverty was directly linked to an identical and simultaneous act of dispossession by people exactly like us who had simply set out in the opposite direction became inescapable once I finally focused my attention on our side.

The story of my mother's family had always seemed to me rather glamorous when I was growing up. There were things in our house that had belonged to her relatives: a small silver box with an enameled lid that had been given to one of her aunts as a party favor, a Georgian coffeepot with a wooden handle, a set of gold encrusted goblets, a writing desk with secret drawers. These objects suggested the sort of world that, as a child, I'd read about in books, a world in which girls and boys were orphaned and sent to live in big houses with people they hardly knew, a world of nannies and parlor maids, of coded behavior and strict decorum, a world in which appearance and reality seemed, at least to a modern child, to mask each other in mysterious ways.

My sense of this world was wholly imaginary and therefore much more elemental than that of my mother, whose feelings about her family were mixed. She had made a concerted effort to escape them, marrying a Californian with no money, moving away to the East, pursuing a modern, cosmopolitan lifestyle. And yet she belonged inescapably to them and often talked about her relatives, recalling their provincial grandeur and self-conscious refinement with a mixture of horror and pride.

In recent generations, the Abbotts had belonged to the haute bourgeoisie of St. Paul, Minnesota, a middle-western capital settled by Yankees who retained an aura of gentility that was presumed to have come directly from England itself. St. Paul society at the turn of the twentieth century consisted of a cluster of families—Ramseys and Archers and Sibleys and Steeles—who managed big houses on private incomes and gave parties and traveled and occasionally worked. None of the Abbotts had done much of anything for two generations by the time my mother came along, and the fabric of the family was already unraveling. Her parents were entirely preoccupied with their own problems and could not be bothered with their children, whom they farmed out to various members of the clan.

My mother was sent to live with her grandmother and three maiden aunts in a large house on Grand Avenue in St. Paul. They dressed for dinner and had breakfast in bed and were waited on by Irish girls who ironed the antimacassars and used a different entrance to the house. It all took place long before I was born, but my mother carried with her into the twenty-first century a set of habits and customs, many of which no longer had any practical application. *When the finger bowl is placed before you, lift the bowl and remove the doily from the plate. Place the doily to the right of your table setting, then place the finger bowl on it. This will leave your plate free for dessert.* She told me once about a foreigner who thought the water in his finger bowl was a clear kind of soup and drank it, eating the gardenia petals as a garnish.

Her grandmother Abbott was an ample woman who had raised five children without ever changing a diaper or cooking a meal. Once a year she would descend to the kitchen and have an apron tied about her by one of the maids. Then she would stand in front of the stove with a long wooden spoon, stirring a great pot of jam. "Mama is making the marmalade," they

would say. One of her sons was a doctor like his father, the
other, my grandfather, was dissolute. None of the daughters
ever married, though the eldest was vivacious and gay and was
said to have been disappointed. Why the second never married
I don't know, but the youngest and prettiest of the three was
hurt in an accident as a child. Racing downhill on her bicycle,
she got her skirts caught in the spokes and fell, hitting her head
on a granite curbstone. She was deaf after that, as well as odd,
and it was a queer kind of justice that permitted her to live
longer than anyone else and to use up, in a highly eccentric
fashion, a sizeable chunk of the family money.

They were not alone among their generation, my mother's
maiden aunts. There were girls like them in almost every
family. In the years when they were young, there was a
shortage of eligible men in places like St. Paul. Some of them
died in the Great War of dysentery or mortars, some died of
flu, some simply went away and never came back, having
discovered New York or California. Meanwhile, the Misses
Abbott stayed on in the big house with Mama, doing good
works and visiting and gradually growing old. After their
father died and their brothers married, it was just the four
of them. Five, if you count Great-aunt Clara, Grandmother
Abbott's sister, who lived as a dowager in the Commodore
Hotel and kept up a running dispute with her friend Mrs.
Griggs as to which of them was the richest woman in Minnesota.

It is hardly creditable how fast this society formed or how
rigidly it was cemented, given that Minnesota had only just
emerged from the pioneering period. Grandmother Abbott
herself had come out to the territory as a girl on a flood tide
of frontier settlement that swept the upper Mississippi in the
1850s. At the start of that decade there were only 6,000 settlers

in Minnesota, and a traveler heading to St. Paul might still have given the name "Pig's Eye" as his destination. Ten years later the number of settlers had swelled to 170,000, the dream of statehood had become a reality, and the process of social stratification had well and truly begun.

Meanwhile, the Indians were steadily retreating westward as treaty after treaty was signed ceding portions of their lands. They were known to themselves as Dakota but the white men called them Sioux. A hundred years earlier the French, who were the first Europeans in the region, were told by the Ojibwa (or Chippewa), with whom they traded, that the people to their west were "Nadouessioux," meaning "little viper" or "lesser enemy." They were "lesser" because, in Ojibwa eyes, the "greater viper" was the large and dangerous Iroquois confederation to the east. This name, shortened simply to "Sioux," was picked up by British and American traders and then by the settlers who began arriving in droves in the mid-nineteenth century.

Choctaw, Chippewa, Iroquois, Sioux—they were names to jump rope to by the time my mother was a girl. Among the ladies of her aunts' circle were two sisters of whom it was said privately that they could never be married because they had *Indian blood*. But where the Indians themselves had gone to was no longer a question of much interest. I asked my mother if she had ever seen any Indians when she was growing up. She looked a little confused, as if it were a trick question.

"They were a subclass," she said.

"But there must have been Indians somewhere." I persisted. "Maybe not in St. Paul, but in the country, on reservations. Didn't you ever see any Indians anywhere?"

"We went to powwows sometimes, and we saw Indians there."

"What did they look like?"

"They were dressed up—like Indians. You know, they danced and beat drums."

"Was that for the white people? Were they dressing up for you or for themselves?"

"I don't know."

"Did you give them money?"

"I certainly didn't. But perhaps my father did. I just don't know."

A few days later my mother added, "You know, I started thinking about the Indians and I remembered something else."

One summer when she was about fifteen years old, my mother went with her aunts to visit Mrs. Griggs at her summer compound, a vast estate of log-house buildings dotted along the shore of a lake. Mrs. Griggs had built a community center in the nearby town where films were sometimes shown on Saturday nights. On this particular night the movie was *Cimarron*, a popular western that had won the Oscar for Best Picture in 1931 and was described by a reviewer some decades later as delivering the social message that "Indians are people too." The hall was packed with Indians, whom my mother remembered as "a lot of overweight women in housedresses and men in checked shirts." The film was exciting and there was lots of cheering and laughter until suddenly the camera cut to a scene in which a train, shot head on, seemed to come hurtling out of the screen toward the audience. All the Indians shrieked and dove under their chairs.

Seven was in the room when my mother told this story and, since I could sort of tell where it was going, I kept my eye on him to see what he would do.

"You know," he said equably, "I bet if the room had been full of Maoris, they'd have done exactly the same thing."

*   *   *

It's easy to be critical of pioneers, as easy as it was a hundred years ago to worship them. Where once we saw their bravery, their self-sacrifice, their intrepid spirit, we now see only their greed, their brutality, their cunning manipulation of the truth. But a frontier is not that simple. It is less like a line than a zone of shadow, an area of give and take. It evolves and changes and the people who are in it change too: how they think and what they say and what they mean when they say it.

In 1850 Henry Sibley, then a territorial delegate to the U.S. Congress from Minnesota, wrote a letter to Senator H. S. Foote:

> The Indian is here in his forest home, hitherto secure from the intrusion of the pale faces; but the advancing tide of civilization warns him that ere long he must yield up his title to this fair domain, and seek another and a strange dwelling place. It is a melancholy reflection that the large and warlike tribes of Sioux and Chippewas who now own full nine-tenths of the soil of Minnesota must soon be subjected to the operation of the same causes that have swept their Eastern brethren from the earth unless an entirely different policy is pursued by the Government towards them.

Sibley was known as a "friend to the Indians," in part because of his long association with the Dakota through the medium of the fur trade. He had come out to the territory in the late 1820s, when he was only a teenager and it was still a wilderness, and had taken a job as a trader for the American Fur Company. He was quickly promoted to clerk and not long after to partner with sole responsibility for the Dakota trade. He learned the Dakota language and was known among the Indians as *Wah-pe-ton Houska*, or Long Trader. In 1835 he built a large limestone house in Mendota and embarked on a political career. He was the first justice of the peace west of the Mississippi River, a congressional representative for the Territory of Minnesota, a member of the Minnesota legislature, and finally, the first governor of the state. A staunch defender of the natives' interests, Sibley always kept a room in his house for Indians who might need a place to sleep. It could only be reached by an outside stair, and when my mother was young, she heard the rumor that the Dakota who stayed there were not always men.

A tall man with a high forehead and thinning hair that he combed across the crown of his head, Sibley had a rather delicate, heart-shaped face, small wide-set eyes, and a long mustache. In a photo taken in 1862, when he commanded Minnesota's military force against the Sioux uprising, he was fifty-one years old. His face is gaunt and hollow about the cheeks and he wears a startled, uneasy expression, about halfway between defiance and panic.

On most nineteenth-century frontiers there were two competing views about native peoples. The coarser view held that the natives should simply be exterminated to make way for the settlers, or, in its milder version, that they should forcibly be moved far away. The more progressive view held that "education and a course of moral training" in conjunction with "the influence and restraint of our benign laws" would eventually enable the native to "be placed upon an equality, socially and politically, with the whites." This was the view held by Sibley throughout most of his adult life and active political career. No one, it is worth mentioning, thought it possible that natives— *qua* natives—could coexist with pioneers. And indeed it is almost impossible to imagine how that might have worked, dependent as both parties were for their survival upon the same real estate.

Sibley was an assimilationist, which we now understand to mean that he idealized the gradual eradication not of the Dakota people themselves but of everything that made them Dakota. It now seems overtly genocidal, but at the time it was considered the alternative to genocide. In his address to a Congress preoccupied with the question of slavery, Sibley argued passionately that the "gentlemen seem not to be aware that there exists under the Government of this Republic, a species of grinding and intolerable oppression, of which the Indian tribes are the victims, compared with which the worst form of human bondage now existing in any Christian State may be regarded as a comfort and a blessing." But it was not a question simply of morality, there were practical matters to be considered. If changes were not made in the way that the government dealt with the Indians, there was going to be hell to pay on the frontier.

> The busy hum of civilized communities is already heard far beyond the mighty Mississippi . . . Your pioneers are encircling the last home of the red man, as with a wall of fire. Their encroachments are perceptible in the restlessness and belligerent demonstrations of the powerful bands who inhabit your remote western plains. You must approach these with terms of conciliation and of real friendship, or you must soon suffer the consequences of a bloody and remorseless Indian war.

It was clear, Sibley continued, that any such struggle with the Indians "must necessarily end in their extermination," but it could all be avoided if the government would only turn its attention to the problem of the West.

It did not and things went more or less as Sibley had predicted—but not without his being there to help them along.

One of the most frequently cited causes of the Dakota Conflict, the first in a cascading series of clashes that involved most of the Indians of the West and lasted almost three decades, coming to an end only in 1890 with the sordid massacre at Wounded Knee, was a trick played upon the Dakota at the 1851 signing of the Treaty of Traverse des Sioux. This was a major treaty opening up land for settlement on the western side of the Mississippi River. Although the Indians who signed it received only pennies an acre they were satisfied with the agreement, which provided the tribes with government annuities at a time when the decline in the fur trade and increasing scarcity of game, combined with growing pressure from would-be settlers, was causing them great hardship.

But after signing the formal treaty document, the chiefs at Traverse des Sioux were directed to place their mark upon another piece of paper that had not been discussed and that the chiefs later claimed to have thought was a duplicate of the treaty they had already signed. This second paper, which came to be known as the "traders' paper," allowed for the payment of individual Indians' debts to fur traders out of the general tribal funds owed them by the government in payment for the ceded lands. It was, you might say, a direct subvention of government money to entrepreneurial pioneers. Sibley, whose personal fortune had long been tied up with the fur business (by his own account he had lost $10,000 a year since 1842, much of it in credit to Indian traders), was a major player in these negotiations. In a letter to the then-territorial governor, Alexander Ramsey, he pressed the traders' case, arguing that if the Indians' debts were not taken into account, it would be "a gross injustice towards men who impoverished themselves in supplying the Indians, after 20 or 30 years of labor and exposure."

But it got worse. When, ten years on, the situation had so deteriorated that the Sioux, now starving and almost completely landless, were forced into open revolt, who should be called upon to put down the uprising? None other than Henry Sibley, now a prosperous, middle-age landowner with a substantial vested interest in the stability of the state. Even allowing for a natural drift toward conservatism with age, it is a shock to read Sibley's words, written on the eve of the military campaign:

> Unless we can now, and very effectually, crush this rising the State is ruined, and some of its fairest portions will revert for years into the possession of these miserable wretches who, among all devils in human shape, are among the most cruel and ferocious . . . My heart is steeled against them, and if I have the means, and can catch them, I will sweep them with the besom of death.

Sibley was right in predicting that the Indians would be defeated. Within a month the war was over and Sibley had nearly 2,000 Indians in captivity. He appointed a commission to try the participants for "murder and outrages" committed against settlers. And over the next five weeks, 425 Indians were tried—as many as 40 in one day—and 321 were convicted, of whom 303 were sentenced to death. The personal intervention of Abraham Lincoln saved the lives of all but 38, who were hanged in Mankato on the day after Christmas 1862 before a crowd of spectators. The occasion was reported in the *St. Paul Pioneer Press*:

> Three slow, measured, and distinct beats on the drum by Major Brown . . . and the rope was cut . . . the scaffold fell,

and thirty-seven lifeless bodies were left dangling between heaven and earth . . . As the platform fell, there was one, not loud, but prolonged cheer from the soldiery and citizens who were spectators, and then all were quiet and earnest witnesses of the scene.

In 1843 Henry Sibley married Sarah Steele, who was my great-grandmother's aunt. She had been brought out to the territory by her brother Franklin Steele, an early Minnesotan pioneer with a canny eye for real estate. In the face of some stiff competition, Franklin Steele had laid claim to one of the choicest pieces of Mississippi River frontage—the Falls of St. Anthony at the river's navigable head—the instant it was ceded by the Sioux. Within a decade he owned the two biggest lumber mills in a state full of timber and in time he earned a place in the history books as the territory's first millionaire.

In the 1850s Franklin Steele wrote to his older brother John, a Pennsylvania doctor, encouraging him to come out and try his fortune in the West. John Steele, who was Grandmother Abbott's father, packed up the family—eleven in all, not counting the servants—and traveled out from Pennsylvania by boat, down the Ohio River and up the Mississippi. Like his brother, John Steele had a knack for making money and he quickly began to buy up property, much of it in St. Paul. The most significant of his holdings was a large, three-story, L-shaped building on the corner of Wabasha and Seventh streets. The "Steele Block," as it came to be known, provided an income for much of my family for many years. It supported Grandmother Abbott and her children, including my grandfather and the maiden aunts, right through the Great Depression, which, thanks to their holdings, they experienced vicariously, if at all.

It was after the Second World War that the problems started. The value of the property's leases dwindled, there were unpaid taxes and imprudent deals, and the building fell into disrepair. There are confusing accounts as to who made which bad decisions but, in the end, there seems to have been little choice. The family was forced to cash in its last asset, and the year after I was born, the Steele Block was sold and my mother received a final check for her share.

"What did you do with it?" I asked her.

"*What did we do with it?* We built this house, of course." My mother dandled the youngest of my sons on her knee. "Just think, darling," she whispered to him, "one day all this will be yours."

17

One Summer

MY CHILDREN ARE Abbotts, but they are also members of the Ngati Rehia *hapu* of the Ngapuhi tribe of Waimate and the northern Bay of Islands. The New Zealand white pages lists ten people with my children's surname in New Zealand. Of these, one is their grandmother, two are uncles, two are aunts, and the rest are cousins. There are more, of course, some without telephones and a few in Australia. In the current generation it is a large and flourishing family—my children's Maori grandmother has nearly thirty grandchildren; their Pakeha grandmother has only six.

But one has only to go back a little way before the picture changes. It was 1921 before the Maori population had recovered to the level of the 1850s, which were themselves catastrophic by the standards of only a generation before. Throughout the nineteenth century and into the twentieth, epidemics of measles, influenza, and whooping cough periodically decimated Maori communities, while tuberculosis, unknown in New Zealand in 1814, was by the end of the nineteenth century considered "the curse of the race." It is a family tree with many phantom limbs. I feel for my children a kind of survivor's guilt. For myself I feel something of the guilt of the perpetrator.

*　　*　　*

That first summer after we returned to America, a summer, as I remember it, that came upon us suddenly, preceded by no spring, I signed a paper for a half million dollars' worth of life insurance. It wasn't that I expected to die; on the contrary, I was a good risk, so good that I qualified for a reduced premium—or so the salesman told me. The insurance was for my children, the three of them, all still little boys at the time. I had just turned forty and had almost no money. Seven had gotten a job, but it was not much of one, and I had my grants and some freelance income. But it amounted to almost nothing when you consider what it costs to live.

In fact, the underwriters queried my application: why does she need $500,000 when she only makes $15,000 a year? *Oh that*, I told them. *We're in something of an unusual situation just now*. What I didn't tell them is that we'd been in this unusual situation, or one just like it, for most of the past fifteen years. Another thing the underwriters wanted to know was why it was me and not my husband who was taking out insurance. That was harder to explain. I couldn't say to them: *He's a Maori. He doesn't like to talk about death*. But that was the truth of it. The idea of actually preparing for death, going eyeball-to-eyeball with the beyond, was so much more than Seven could handle that I didn't even tell him what I'd done. He was the beneficiary of a half-million-dollar policy that he didn't know anything about.

But whatever financial security we had, it was never going to come from his side of the family. They had land in New Zealand, a little parcel of it, subdividable into an ever-increasing number of portions. It had all belonged to his family once, half the Bay of Islands, everything from Waimate to Marsden Cross. But that was two hundred years ago and everything had changed with the land sales and annexation and the fall of the Maoris from grace. Seven's family still owned something in Mangonui; it's just that it wasn't enough. Their piece had belonged to Seven's grandfather and his sisters, but the old man had had several children and the sisters five or six each, and all of them had had children, and everyone was equally entitled, though some, including Seven, were unlikely ever to come claiming their share.

No, whatever our kids were going to end up with, it was going to have to come from me. And there I was at forty with no house, no land, no portfolio. I didn't even have a decent car. I felt I'd done them a disservice in failing to accumulate the sorts of things that children have a right to expect, and I wasn't sure they would appreciate what they did have, which was an interesting personal history. I wasn't sure whether, in the end, that would seem like enough. So that's when I took out the policy.

It seemed to me I owed them some sort of explanation. And so I drafted a letter, or maybe a kind of manifesto, which I tucked alongside the policy in the folder marked *Met Life*. I expected they'd be grown up when they found it, perhaps at the very moment when they began to feel curious about such things.

"Dear Boys," it began,

in each of you is a little bit of the conqueror and the conquered, the colonizer and the colonized. Seeing us and seeing you, people have always commented: this one looks a little more Maori, that one a little more white. It seems to them not only a matter of skin tone but of abilities—this one is so coordinated, that one has such an analytic mind. The old assumptions are all still visible, like rocks poking out from under a thin layer of soil. Often people have found

themselves compelled to mention *hybrid vigor*, as if flatter-
ing us with observations about what good results cross-
breeding gives.

Two things on this score have always stuck in my memory. The first is your auntie Kura's remark that your grandmother always wanted her to *marry out*. It helps to
understand the size of their community and the fact that
they were all cousins on both sides of the road. Your
grandmother had a mortal fear of marriage among close
relations. I don't believe this was a personal idiosyncrasy.
There were people in the family who had married too
close—one of her uncles had married his own niece—but
it was one of those things nobody talked about. As far as
your grandmother was concerned, when it came to marriage
partners for her children, Maori was OK so long as it was
distant, but Pakeha was better because it was by definition
further away.

This was fully the opposite of what I'd expected. I'd
always imagined my English ancestry could only be perceived by your father's people as attenuating the family line.
I see now that this betrays a certain sentimentality. But it was
often hard for me to know what they were thinking. What
did Uncle Hone mean, for instance, when he suggested that
your father and I might not be as far apart as we looked?
"You know," he said to me one night in the pub, "there *was*
a Pakeha back there. An American, a sea captain. Set himself
up in Waimate with a couple of sisters for wives. Maybe you
two are really cousins."

"Maybe," I told him. "You think we should call the whole
thing off?"

On my side it was entirely different. On my side inbreeding was considered the lesser evil, the acceptable risk,

not nearly so dangerous as *marrying down*. In St. Paul, where your grandmother was born, the pool of possible marriage partners was almost as small as it was in Mangonui. So small that anyone with the right sort of pedigree was almost certain to be related in some way. So small that the combination of the Great War and the flu left a whole generation stranded. My mother had no fewer than three maiden aunts. Their brother, my grandfather, married his own cousin. They both committed suicide later—separately, mind you—by shutting themselves up in the garage and turning on the car. Though, of course, that doesn't prove anything.

The other thing I think about is Charles Darwin, who had his own reasons for pursuing the subject of cross- and inbreeding. He himself was the product of a Darwin-Wedgwood marriage, and in 1839 he married another Wedgwood, his first cousin Emma. They had ten children in seventeen years, of whom two died young, several were chronically unwell, and the last was in some way subnormal.

Darwin himself suffered from chronic intestinal disorders that no one was ever able to diagnose, and when his eldest daughter began to complain of stomach trouble, he was certain it was something he'd passed on. Over a period of months she grew sicker—feverish, headachy, less and less able to keep anything down. At last she began to vomit uncontrollably, bringing up not only the spoonfuls of brandy they fed her but a bright green bile. When she finally slipped into a coma and died, the doctor gave as the cause of death a bilious fever with typhoid character, but both he and Darwin firmly believed that she had succumbed to an inherited malaise.

Late in his life, Darwin began a series of experiments designed to verify his suspicions empirically. For ten years he collected data on the height, weight, vigor, and fertility of dozens of plant species—morning glories, foxgloves, orchids, petunias, Chinese primroses, French poppies—which he carefully cross-pollinated with a paintbrush and compared with plants that had self-pollinated. In 1876 he tabulated the results. His cousin Galton, the eugenicist, checked his statistics: the crossed plants were superior in every respect to those that were self-fertilized.

Make of this, children, what you will. There are many reasons to feel bad about what has happened: your father's people suffered more than their share, my people benefited, if not directly from their distress, then from the distress of others just like them. It's an ugly story and no mistake, but it's important to see it clearly and not to be sentimental about things that happened in the past.

Sometimes it seems that we are all just part of a great tide sweeping us forward from our separate streams into one vast, undifferentiated ocean. It is hard to know how to feel about this. When two cultures come together they do not blend in equal parts: one invariably dominates, the other often disappears. It seems the rule of nature: the dominion by the many of the few. And yet, although so much is lost, something is gained. The world gets smaller—or is it larger?—the boundaries that have been so troublesome begin to disappear.

Half-caste. It is the language of the last century, of Kipling and Conrad, and deeply out of vogue. But to me it is a word that smacks of daring. *Hapa*, they say in Hawaii, where almost everyone is part one thing and part something else, meaning simply a person with a foot in two worlds. When

you children were young and we used to shuttle back and
forth across the Pacific, following the erratic path of my
academic career, we often stopped in Hawaii. There was a
spot outside the university library that I particularly liked, a
cool stone bench beneath the green and humid canopy. I
used to sit there with my piles of books and watch the local
kids go by, *hapa haole*, *hapa pake*, *hapa pilipino*, with their
almond-colored skin and their long dark hair. In their
indeterminate exotic beauty they always reminded me of
you.

I hope you boys will not feel cheated out of what you
might have had—money, land, a *turangawaewae*, "a
place," as the Maoris say, "to stand." But you come from
a long line of nonconformists. Your maternal grandmother,
as you may recall, was a Communist in the thirties, a fact
which absolutely horrified the maiden aunts. And your
father's side goes back like an arrow to Tareha, who was
virtually alone among the northern chiefs in refusing to sign
the Treaty of Waitangi. This history is alive in you. It is your
birthright, your inheritance, a kind of shadow DNA, in
which the great house on Grand Avenue is encoded, with its
aspidistras and its soup tureens, along with the huia feathers
that your great-great-great-grandfather wore and the
carved canoes of the *tangata whenua*, the people of the
land.

I slipped the folder into the filing cabinet between *Mass.
Taxes* and *New Zealand Immigration*. I knew there were a lot
of people who questioned what I'd done in marrying a man
who could not have been more different from me if we'd set out
to embody the principle of Opposites Attract. And even I
sometimes wondered why I hadn't stayed home and married

a radiologist. But there it was, that *interesting personal history*, which was shorthand in my mind for all that mattered in life—for freedom, for adventure, for risk and the charm of the unexpected, for the gamble of not always knowing what was going on.

Epilogue: New Zealand, 1642

Always to islanders danger
Is what comes over the sea;
Over the yellow sands and the clear
Shallows, the dull filament
Flickers, the blood of strangers:
Death discovered the sailor
O in a flash, in a flat calm,
A clash of boats in the bay
And the day marred with murder.
The dead required no further
Warning to keep their distance;
The rest, noting the failure,
Pushed on with a reconnaissance
To the north; and sailed away.

—Allen Curnow, from "Landfall
in Unknown Seas" (1942)

IN THE WARTIME year of 1942, a little book was published
to commemorate the tercentenary of Tasman's discovery of
New Zealand. It contained three separate pieces: a poem
composed in honor of the event by the New Zealand poet
Allen Curnow; an essay on Tasman's place in history by the
great Pacific historian J. C. Beaglehole; and the text of Tasman's journal "of a voyage made from the city of Batavia in the

East Indies for the discovery of the Unknown South Land, in the year anno 1642."

It is a wonderful book: the poem, a severe, moving mediation on the relationship between the present and the past; the essay, expansive, thoughtful, and enormously well-informed; and the journal, intriguing and elusive as documents from the distant past so often are. Taken together they constitute as good an analysis of these events as can be imagined. And yet, you can read them all—and everything else ever written on this subject—and still not feel as though you really, truly understand what happened in New Zealand on December 18, 1642.

In part, this is because there is no record at all of these events from the Maori point of view. At least, no story that seemed to have its origin in Tasman's visit ever reached European ears. Five or six generations later, when Cook arrived, he could find no one in the vicinity of Murderers' Bay who knew anything about it. And by the time another fifty years had passed, the social upheaval associated with colonialism had so completely altered the makeup of the region that Ngati Tumatakokiri, the tribe that is thought to have lived there in Tasman's day, had effectively ceased to exist.

To the Maoris of the colonial era the place was known as Taitapu, meaning "sacred coast" or "sacred tide," a word with overtones of danger and prohibition. *Taitapu* is also an old word for "boundary," and some kind of boundary was certainly breached on December 18, 1642. For while, in a sense, nothing happened, no lasting settlements were made, no treaties signed, no flags raised to signal an intention, nevertheless, a crack was opened in the world, an almost invisible crack that no one would notice for over a century, but a crack nonetheless in the isolation in which the Maori people had lived for almost a thousand years.

Ironically, given what came later, it was the Europeans who fared worst in this first encounter. Tasman's instructions warned him about the sort of "rough wild" people he might find, arguing that, as experience in other parts of the world—namely America—had shown, "no barbarous people are to be trusted, because they usually think that the people who appear so exceedingly strange and unexpected come only to take over their lands." This was something many "barbarous people" had learned from painful and repeated experience, but the Maoris had never heard of Europeans and no one "strange" or "unexpected" had appeared on their shores for hundreds of years. Still, they clearly intended to attack; they were so quick to assemble, so ready with their plan. They had numbers on their side and no experience of firearms. From the Maori point of view it must have looked an easy victory.

And yet, if we think about how outlandish the Dutch vessels must have seemed, with their great wooden sides and the strange pale faces peering down from them, if we think about the sound of cannon fire and the flash of guns, it is almost impossible not to wonder what the Maoris were thinking. It is sometimes said that Maoris and other Polynesians mistook the arriving Europeans for ghosts or gods or some other kind of supernatural being, though it is hard to know even how to frame such an argument, given the Maoris' routine acceptance of the presence of the supernatural in their lives. But either way, they must have recognized the extraordinariness of the event. And so the question naturally arises: Were the Maoris of Taitapu responding to the astonishing arrival of Dutch ships with equally exceptional behavior? Were they motivated by dramatic tension, by an urgent need to display their strength? Was it the very strangeness of the situation that inspired them? Or were they treating their visitors conventionally, as they would any tribal enemy caught trespassing within their territorial bounds? Were they acting out of an inverse terror or a brazen and belligerent poise? Was ambush and massacre a last resort or a first?

At this distance we will never know, so slight is the documentary record of what happened on the day when New Zealand swam into European view. But history often gives no answers to the most interesting questions. What it does tell us is that such moments, however murky or absurd, eventually become mythic, archetypal. They are the beginnings of a new story, the first notes of a new tune, the first turns of a rope that binds people together. This is not, of course, how they at first appear. At first, they are just things that happen. But before long they acquire a special status as reference points against which all subsequent contacts must be measured.

With hindsight we can point to the use that was made of Tasman's story by later Europeans, to the way this first contact encounter shaped the perception and experience of those who followed in his wake, and to the monumental consequences this had for the Maori people. But we can also look back and see a day like any other, a day of wind or no wind, of rain or no rain, a day, for the Dutch, of surprise and anxiety, for the Maoris a day of triumph, but also surely of doubt.

The past, they say, is a strange country, but I think it's more like a place we lived in as children and left while still young, a place warped and twisted by memory but one that, at some level, we still know. History repeats, and yet it doesn't—not quite. The same scenarios crop up again and again, the same splits, the same structures, but each time the details have all changed and it's a different story. What matters is both the way it changes and the way it stays the same: the particularity and the pattern, the dancer and the dance. What matters is that we understand the past as something familiar and recognizable and, at the same time, something so foreign that we can barely make sense of it—like the sound of a conch-shell trumpet, Moorish and yet not quite Moorish after all.

ACKNOWLEDGMENTS

THIS BOOK WAS a long time in the making and many people have helped me on the way. I'd like to thank the Literature Board of the Australia Council and Arts Victoria for a pair of grants that got me started and Hazel Rowley who read some very early drafts. My old friend Peter Craven gave me an early vote of confidence when he included a version of two chapters in *Best Australian Essays*. I also want to thank the members of my writing group—Ann Cobb, Terry Butler, Maryel Locke, Gwynne Morgan, Henriette Power, Jeanne Stanton, and Meg Sinnott Rubin—whose generous enthusiasm, good fellowship, and admirable professionalism kept me going through the long middle slog. Many other people read bits and pieces and listened patiently to me; although I cannot name them all, I would like to mention my friends Tessa Fisher and Birgit Larsson.

There are two people, though, without whom this book would never have become a reality. The first is my agent, Brettne Bloom, to whom I owe an enormous debt of gratitude, not only for taking on the project in the first place, but for the unflagging enthusiasm, warmth, and generosity she brought to it at every stage. And the second is my editor, Gillian Blake. They say that no one edits anymore, but, if my experience is anything to go by, that is utterly untrue. Were it not for Gillian's firm, insightful guidance and editorial acumen, I would still be sitting at my desk with a work forever in the process of becoming.

Finally, I want to thank the members of my family. It was my parents' unqualified generosity over more years than I care to enumerate that enabled me to undertake a project that must have seemed astonishingly self-indulgent at times. I could not possibly have done it without their assistance and my only regret is that, after helping me out for so many years, my father did not live to see it finished. Lastly, but only because I owe him so much, there is my husband, Seven. My constant companion for two decades, he has ridden out these last few years with remarkable (even for him) equanimity. Although I've tried to juggle my various obligations as wife, mother, daughter, editor, teacher, and writer without dropping too many balls, both he and I know just how many have gone flying. I'd like to take this opportunity to thank him for quietly, generously, and uncomplainingly picking them up.

A Note on Pronunciation and Spelling

BASIC MAORI IS comparatively easy for English speakers to read and pronounce. There are five vowels (*a, e, i, o, u*), which are pronounced more or less as in Italian:

- *a* (ah) as in "father"
- *e* (ay) as in "rain"
- *i* (ee) as in "meet"
- *o* (oh) as in "store"
- *u* (oo) as in "food"

There are eight consonants in the language (*h, k, m n, p, r, t, w*). All the consonants are pronounced as in English with the exception of *r*, which is rolled as in Italian or Spanish and which, when it falls in the middle of a word, can sound more like a soft "d." Thus, the name *Kiri*, for example, can sound like "Kiddy" to the English ear.

There are also two consonant combinations which sometimes give English speakers pause: *wh*, which is pronounced as "f," and *ng*, which is pronounced as in "song" but which can also come at the beginning of a word such as *nga*.

Vowels in Maori may be either long or short and this also affects the way they are pronounced. Current standard practice in New Zealand is to indicate a long vowel in written Maori with a macron (a straight line over the letter). Thus, the correct form of the word *Maori* is actually *Māori* and *pa* is actually *pā*.

But Maori has been a written language for barely two hundred years and there is considerable variation in the way it has been written over time. During certain periods, for example, it has been conventional to indicate the long sound by doubling the vowel, as in *paa* for *pā* and *Maaori* for *Māori*, while in the very earliest texts there is often no indication of vowel length at all.

In the interest of consistency, I have decided not to use either the double vowel or the macron. A reader with little or no exposure to Maori can, in most cases, approximate the correct sound simply by sounding out the letters according to the guidelines above. Anyone wanting a more detailed account of the language should visit the Māori Language Commission Web site (www.tetaurawhiri.govt.nz).

Another decision I have had to make is how to pluralize Maori words appearing in an English text. In Maori, changes of number, tense, etc., are not shown by any change in the word itself—the way, for example, we add "s" to nouns in English. Although, in my experience, many Maori speakers will, in fact, add "s" to certain common Maori words when they are speaking English, I have decided not do this. Thus, the word *marae* may refer to one meetinghouse or to more than one. The only exceptions are the words *Pākehā* and *Māori*, which I use as loan words, that is, English words borrowed from Maori, adding a plural "s" when necessary.

Finally, a note on English spelling. Several of the sources used in this book were written in the eighteenth century when idiosyncratic spelling and capitalization were common, even among highly educated English writers. I have taken the liberty of regularizing the spelling of many words—"posable" to "possible," "hade" to "had," "oyther" to "other," and so on—as well as standardizing capitalization and punctuation.

GLOSSARY

aroha love
fale (Samoan) house
haere mai come here
haka dance or action song
hangi earth oven
hapa (Hawaiian) part or fraction (a loan from the English "half");
    a person of mixed ancestry as in *hapa haole* (part-Caucasian),
    hapa pake (part-Chinese), *hapa pilipino* (part-Filipino)
hapu adj. pregnant; n. subtribe
iwi bone; tribe or nation
kai food
kai moana seafood
kete woven flax bag or basket, often called a "kit"
kina sea urchin
kūmara sweet potato
makai (Hawaiian) toward the sea
mana power, authority, influence, prestige
Māori adj. normal; usual; ordinary; n. native of New Zealand
marae meetinghouse
mate death
mate uruta death cold; influenza
mere short flat weapon made of stone
moko tattoo
mokomokai preserved head
mōrehu survivor; remnant
nui big; great
ora life
pā fortified village

Pākehā   person of European descent

patu   *n.* a weapon; *v.* to beat

paua   abalone

pipi   a type of shellfish

pō   night

pūha   a kind of edible wild green

rangatira   chief

rata   a kind of tree

raupō   bulrush

rengarenga   *adj.* crushed; *n.* rock lily

roa   long

taiaha   weapon of hardwood about five feet long

tangata whenua   the people of the land; indigeneous people

taniwha   mythical creature; sea monster

tapu   *adj.* forbidden, sacred; *n.* ceremonial injunction (source of the word "taboo")

taua   war party

te   definite article ("the")

tupuna   ancestor

turangawaewae   a place from which to speak; a place to stand (i.e., on the *marae*)

umu (Hawaiian)   earth oven

utu   the principle of reciprocity

wahaika   fiddle-shaped weapon of bone or wood

whare   house

whare kai   kitchen (of the *marae*)

Selected Bibliography

O NE BOOK HAS influenced me above all and that is
Bernard Smith's pioneering study of art and history,
European Vision and the South Pacific, which framed so many
of the questions that it seemed important to ask. I am also
deeply indebted to a generation of scholars whose lively,
authoritative histories set a standard for work in the field that
will not soon be surpassed: J. C. Beaglehole (1901–1971),
E. H. McCormick (1906–1995), and O. H. K. Spate (1911–
2000). Other writers I would like to mention include Nicholas
Thomas, whose brilliant, flexible thinking has long been an
inspiration to me; James Belich, whose seminal study of the
New Zealand Wars should be required reading for anyone
interested in New Zealand; and Anne Salmond, whose work
on contact between the Maori and European peoples brought
the knowledge of two disciplines together in a wonderfully
useful and interesting way.

PROLOGUE: NEW ZEALAND, 1642

Abel Janszoon Tasman and the Discovery of New Zealand. Wellington: Department of Internal Affairs, 1942.

McCormick, E. H. *Tasman and New Zealand: A Bibliographical
Study*. Wellington: Government Printer, 1959.

Sharp, Andrew. *The Voyages of Abel Janszoon Tasman*. New York:
Oxford University Press, 1968.

Walker, James Backhouse. *Abel Janszoon Tasman: His Life and Voyages*. Hobart: Government Printer, 1896.

1. PAIHIA

Colquhoun, David. "'Pakeha Maori': The Early Life and Times of Frederick Edward Maning." M.A. thesis, University of Auckland, 1984.

Darwin, Charles. *The Voyage of the Beagle*. 1839. London: Dent, 1959.

Gibson, Ross. *The Diminishing Paradise*. Sydney: Angus & Robertson, 1984.

Lansdown, Richard, ed. *Strangers in the South Seas: The Idea of the Pacific in Western Thought*. Honolulu: University of Hawaii Press, 2006.

Lee, Jack. *The Bay of Islands*. Auckland: Reed, 1983.

Reed, A. W. *The Reed Dictionary of New Zealand Place Names*. Auckland: Reed, 2002.

Stefansson, Vilhjalmur, ed. *Great Adventures and Explorations*. New York: Dial Press, 1947.

Stroven, Carl, and A. Grove Day, eds. *The Spell of the Pacific: An Anthology of Its Literature*. New York: Macmillan, 1949.

Williams, Glyndwr, and Alan Frost, eds. *Terra Australis to Australia*. Melbourne: Oxford University Press, 1988.

2. ABOMINABLY SAUCY

Banks, Joseph. *The* Endeavour *Journal of Joseph Banks*. Edited by J. C. Beaglehole, 2 vols. Sydney: Angus & Robertson, 1962.

Beaglehole, J. C. *The Discovery of New Zealand*, 2nd ed. London: Oxford University Press, 1961.

———. *The Life of Captain James Cook*. Stanford, CA: Stanford University Press, 1974.

Cook, James. *The Journals of Captain James Cook on His Voyages of Discovery*. Edited by J. C. Beaglehole. Vol. 1, *The Voyage of the* Endeavour *1768–1771*, Hakluyt Society Extra Series, no. 34. Cambridge: Cambridge University Press, 1955.

Dunmore, John. *The Fateful Voyage of the* St. Jean Baptiste. Christchurch: Pegasus, 1969.

The Expedition of the St. Jean-Baptiste *to the Pacific 1769–1770: From Journals of Jean de Surville and Guillaume Labé.* Edited and translated by John Dunmore. London: Hakluyt Society, 1981.

Historical Records of New Zealand. Edited by Robert McNab, 2 vols. Wellington: Government Printer, 1908–1914.

Reed, A. H., and A. W. Reed, eds. *Captain Cook in New Zealand,* 2nd ed. Wellington: Reed, 1969.

Salmond, Anne. *Two Worlds: First Meetings Between Maori and European 1642–1772.* Auckland: Viking Penguin, 1991.

Sissons, Jeffrey, Wiremu Wi Hongi, and Pat Hohepa. *The Puriri Trees Are Laughing: A Political History of Nga Puhi in the Inland Bay of Islands.* Auckland: Polynesian Society, 1987.

4. TERRA INCOGNITA

Conrad, Joseph. *Tales of Hearsay and Last Essays.* 1928. London: Penguin, 1944.

———. *Tales of Unrest.* 1898. London: Penguin, 1977.

Favenc, Ernest. *The History of Australian Exploration, 1788–1888,* facsimile ed. Gladesville, NSW: Golden Press, 1983.

White, Patrick. *Voss.* Harmondsworth: Penguin, 1981.

5. PRESENT PERFECT

Bougainville, Louis de. *A Voyage Round the World.* Translated by John Reinhold Forster. 1772. New York: Da Capo, 1967.

Grace, Patricia. *Baby No-Eyes.* Auckland: Penguin, 1998.

Lovejoy, Arthur O., and George Boas. *Primitivism and Related Ideas in Antiquity.* New York: Octagon, 1965.

News from New Cythera. Edited by L. Davis Hammond. Minneapolis: University of Minnesota Press, 1970.

Robertson, George. *The Discovery of Tahiti: A Journal of the Second Voyage of H.M.S.* Dolphin *Round the World, Under the Command of Captain Wallis, R.N., in the Years 1766, 1767 and*

1768. Edited by Hugh Carrington. London: Hakluyt Society, 1948.

Smith, Bernard. *European Vision and the South Pacific 1768–1850: A Study in the History of Art and Ideas*. London: Oxford University Press, 1960.

Spate, O. H. K. *Paradise Found and Lost: The Pacific Since Magellan*. Vol. 3. Canberra: Australian National University Press, 1983.

6. THE VENUS

Bentley, Trevor. *Captured by Maori: White Female Captives, Sex and Racism on the Nineteenth-century New Zealand Frontier*. Auckland: Penguin, 2004.

———. *Pakeha Maori: The Extraordinary Story of the Europeans Who Lived as Maori in Early New Zealand*. Auckland: Penguin, 1999.

Campbell, I. C. *"Gone Native" in Polynesia: Captivity Narratives and Experiences from the South Pacific*. Westport, CT: Greenwood Press, 1998.

Earle, Augustus. *Narrative of a Residence in New Zealand; Journal of a Residence in Tristan da Cunha*. Edited by E. H. McCormick. London: Oxford University Press, 1966.

Hallowell, A. Irving. "American Indians, White and Black: The Phenomenon of Transculturalization." *Current Anthropology* vol. 4, no. 5 (December 1963).

Malinowski, Bronislaw. *Argonauts of the Western Pacific: An Account of Native Enterprise and Adventure in the Archipelagoes of Melanesian New Guinea*. 1922. New York: Dutton, 1961.

Marsden, Samuel. *The Letters and Journals of Samuel Marsden 1765–1838*. Edited by John Rawson Elder. Dunedin: Reed/Otago University, 1932.

McNab, Robert. *From Tasman to Marsden*. Dunedin: J. Wilkie, 1914.

O'Brian, Patrick. *Joseph Banks: A Life*. Boston: David R. Godine, 1993.

Parkin, Ray. *The Great Endeavour: H. M. Bark Endeavour*. Melbourne: Melbourne University Press, 1997.

A People's History: Illustrated Biographies from the Dictionary of New Zealand Biography, Vol. 1, *1769–1869*. Wellington: Department of Internal Affairs, 1992.

Robson, L. L. *The Convict Settlers of Australia*. Melbourne: Melbourne University Press, 1965.

Sherrin, R. A. A. *Early History of New Zealand*. Auckland: H. Brett, 1890.

Spate, O. H. K. *Paradise Found and Lost: The Pacific Since Magellan*. Vol. 3. Canberra: Australian National University Press, 1983.

7. A Natural Gentleman

McCormick, E. H. *Omai: Pacific Envoy*. Auckland: Auckland University Press, 1977.

Melville, Herman. *Moby-Dick*. 1851. New York: W. W. Norton, 1967.

Spate, O. H. K. *Paradise Found and Lost: The Pacific Since Magellan*. Vol. 3. Canberra: Australian National University Press, 1983.

8. A Dangerous People

Banks, Joseph. *The* Endeavour *Journal of Joseph Banks*. Edited by J. C. Beaglehole, 2 vols. Sydney: Angus & Robertson, 1962.

Cook, James. *The Journals of Captain James Cook on His Voyages of Discovery*. Edited by J. C. Beaglehole. Vol. 1, *The Voyage of the* Endeavour *1768–1771*, Hakluyt Society Extra Series, no. 34. Cambridge: Cambridge University Press, 1955.

Crosby, Alfred W. *Ecological Imperialism: The Biological Expansion of Europe, 900–1900*. Cambridge: Cambridge University Press, 1986.

Darwin, Charles. *The Voyage of the* Beagle. 1839. London: Dent, 1959.

The Expedition of the St. Jean-Baptiste *to the Pacific 1769–1770: From Journals of Jean de Surville and Guillaume Labé*. Edited and translated by John Dunmore. London: Hakluyt Society, 1981.

Hawkesworth, John. *An Account of the Voyages Undertaken by the Order of His Present Majesty for Making Discoveries in the Southern Hemisphere and Succinctly Performed by Commodore Byron, Captain Wallis, Captain Carteret and Captain Cook*. 3 vols., 2nd ed. London: W. Strahan and T. Cadell, 1773.

Historical Records of New Zealand. Edited by Robert McNab, 2 vols. Wellington: Government Printer, 1908–1914.

Lovejoy, Arthur O., and George Boas. *Primitivism and Related Ideas in Antiquity*. New York: Octagon, 1965.

Maning, F. E. *Old New Zealand: A Tale of the Good Old Times and a History of the War in the North Told by an Old Chief of the Ngapuhi Tribe*. 1887. Auckland: Golden Press, 1973.

McLeod, Rosemary. "One Night Out Stealing." *North & South*, December 1994.

Pearson, W. H. "Hawkesworth's Alterations." *Journal of Pacific History* 7, 1972.

Salmond, Anne. *Hui: A Study of Maori Ceremonial Gatherings*. Wellington: A. H. and A. W. Reed, 1975.

9. SMOKED HEADS

Burns, Barnet. *A Brief Narrative of a New Zealand Chief*. Belfast: R. & D. Read, 1844.

Cook, James. *The Journals of Captain James Cook on His Voyages of Discovery*. Edited by J. C. Beaglehole. Vol. 1, *The Voyage of the Endeavour 1768–1771*, Hakluyt Society Extra Series, no. 34. Cambridge: Cambridge University Press, 1955.

Crosby, R. D. *The Musket Wars*. Auckland: Reed, 1999.

Horatio Gordon Robley: Soldier Artist in the Bay of Plenty 1864–1866, a catalog of his paintings displayed at Baycourt, August 1990. Tauranga, NZ: Tauranga Historical Society, 1990.

Maning, F. E. *Old New Zealand: A Tale of the Good Old Times and a History of the War in the North Told by an Old Chief of the Ngapuhi Tribe*. 1887. Auckland: Golden Press, 1973.

Marsden, Samuel. *The Letters and Journals of Samuel Marsden 1765–1838*. Edited by John Rawson Elder. Dunedin: Reed/Otago University, 1932.

Robley, H. G. *Moko: The Art and History of Tattooing*. 1896. Twickenham, UK: Tiger Books, 1998.

Vayda, A. P. *Maori Warfare*. Wellington: A. H. and A. W. Reed, 1960.

Yate, William. *An Account of New Zealand and of the Church Missionary Society's Mission in the Northern Island*. 1835. Shannon: Irish University Press, 1970.

10. TURTON'S LAND DEEDS

Bulter, John. *Earliest New Zealand: The Journals and Correspondence of the Rev. John Butler*. Compiled by R. J. Barton. Masterton, NZ: Palamontain & Petherick, 1927.

Lee, Jack. *The Bay of Islands*. Auckland: Reed, 1983.

Maori Deeds: or Old Private Land Purchases in New Zealand, from the Year 1815 to 1840, with Pre-emptive and Other Claims. Together with a List of the Old Land Claims and the Report of Mr Commissioner F. Dillon Bell. Wellington: Government Printer, 1882.

Marsden, Samuel. *The Letters and Journals of Samuel Marsden 1765–1838*. Edited by John Rawson Elder. Dunedin: Reed/Otago University, 1932.

Pool, D. Ian. *The Maori Population of New Zealand, 1769–1971*. Auckland: Auckland University Press, 1977.

Sinclair, Keith. *A History of New Zealand*, revised ed. Harmondsworth: Penguin, 1980.

Sissons, Jeffrey, Wiremu Wi Hongi, and Pat Hohepa. *The Puriri Trees Are Laughing: A Political History of Nga Puhi in the Inland Bay of Islands*. Auckland: Polynesian Society, 1987.

11. NANA MIRI

Crosby, Alfred W. *America's Forgotten Pandemic: The Influenza of 1918*. Cambridge: Cambridge University Press, 1989.

Henderson, J. McLeod. *Ratana: The Origins and the Story of the Movement*. Wellington: Polynesian Society, 1963.

Rice, Geoffrey. *Black November: The 1918 Influenza Epidemic in New Zealand*. Wellington: Allen & Unwin, 1988.

12. HAWAIKI

Davidson, Janet. *The Prehistory of New Zealand*. Auckland: Longman Paul, 1984.

Darwin, Charles. *The Voyage of the* Beagle. 1839. London: Dent, 1959.

Evans, Jeff. *Nga Waka O Nehera: The First Voyaging Canoes*. Auckland: Reed, 1997.

Finney, Ben. *Voyage of Rediscovery: A Cultural Odyssey Through Polynesia*. Berkeley: University of California, 1994.

Forbes, David W. *Encounters with Paradise: Views of Hawaii and Its People 1778–1941*. Honolulu: Honolulu Academy of Arts, 1992.

Heyerdahl, Thor. *Fatu-Hiva*. Harmondsworth: Penguin, 1976.

Houghton, Philip. "The Early Human Biology of the Pacific: Some Considerations." *Journal of the Polynesian Society* vol. 100, no. 2 (1991).

Kyselka, Will. *An Ocean in Mind*. Honolulu: University of Hawaii Press, 1987.

Lewis, David. *We, the Navigators: The Ancient Art of Landfinding in the Pacific*, 2nd ed. Honolulu: University of Hawaii Press, 1994.

Man on the Rim. Directed by John Oakley and Robert Raymond, written by Alan Thorne and Robert Raymond. Videocassette. ABC, 1989.

Nga Moteatea. Collected by A. T. Ngata, translated by A. T. Ngata and P. Te Hurinui. 3 vols. Auckland: Polynesian Society, 1972, 1974, 1990.

Orbell, Margaret. *Hawaiki: A New Approach to Maori Tradition*. Christchurch: Canterbury University Press, 1991.

Rose, Roger G. *Hawai'i: The Royal Isles*. Honolulu: Bishop Museum Press, 1980.

Thorne, Alan, and Robert Raymond. *Man on the Rim: The Peopling of the Pacific*. North Ryde, NSW: Angus & Robertson, 1989.

13. Once Were Warriors

"Alan Duff: The Book, the Film, the Interview," *Meanjin* vol. 54, no. 1 (1995).

Duff, Alan. *Once Were Warriors*. Auckland: Tandem Press, 1990.

Hereniko, Vilsoni. "An Interview with Alan Duff." *Inside Out: Literature, Cultural Politics, and Identity in the New Pacific.* Edited by Vilsoni Hereniko and Rob Wilson. Boulder, CO: Rowman & Littlefield, 1999.

Johansen, J. Prytz. *The Maori and His Religion in Its Non-ritualistic Aspects*. Copenhagen: Ejnar Munksgaard, 1954.

Patterson, John. *Exploring Maori Values*. Palmerston North, NZ: Dunmore Press, 1992.

14. Gu, Choki, Pa

Witi Ihimaera, ed. *Growing Up Maori*. Auckland: Tandem Press, 1998.

15. Matariki

Finney, Ben. *Voyage of Rediscovery: A Cultural Odyssey Through Polynesia*. Berkeley: University of California, 1994.

Kyselka, Will. *An Ocean in Mind*. Honolulu: University of Hawaii Press, 1987.

Kyselka, Will, and Ray Lanterman. *North Star to Southern Cross*. Honolulu: University of Hawaii Press, 1976.

Thomas, Nicholas. *Possessions: Indigenous Art/Colonial Culture*. London: Thames & Hudson, 1999.

16. Thieves and Indian-killers

Abbott, Thomson Steele. *The Descendents of George Abbott of Rowley, Mass., in the Single Line to Everton Judson Abbott, Followed by All the Abbott Descendants of the Twentieth Century*. Grafton, WI, 1997.

Brown, Dee. *Bury My Heart at Wounded Knee: An Indian History of the American West*. New York: Bantam, 1972.

Freeman, Victoria. *Distant Relations: How My Ancestors Colonized North America*. South Royalton, VT: Steerforth Press, 2000.

Gage, Thomas. *The History of Rowley, Anciently Including Bradford, Boxford, and Georgetown, from the Year 1639 to the Present Time*. Boston: Ferdinand Andrews, 1840.

Jewett, Amos Everett. *The Early Settlers of Rowley, Massachusetts*. 1933. Somersworth, NH: New England History Press, 1981.

Kennedy, Roger G. *Men on the Moving Frontier*. Palo Alto, CA: American West Publishing Company, 1969.

Lass, William E. *Minnesota: A History*, 2nd ed. New York: W. W. Norton, 1998.

Shortridge, Wilson Porter. *The Transition of a Typical Frontier, with Illustrations from the Life of Henry Hastings Sibley, Fur Trader, First Delegate in Congress from Minnesota Territory, and First Governor of the State of Minnesota*. Menasha, WI: Collegiate Press, 1922.

Winthrop's Journal 1630–1649. Edited by James K. Hosmer. 2 vols. New York: Charles Scribner's Sons, 1908.

17. ONE SUMMER

Desmond, Adrian, and James Moore. *Darwin*. London: Penguin, 1992.

EPILOGUE: NEW ZEALAND, 1642

Abel Janszoon Tasman and the Discovery of New Zealand. Wellington: Department of Internal Affairs, 1942.

Salmond, Anne. *Two Worlds: First Meetings Between Maori and Europeans 1642–1772*. Auckland: Viking Penguin, 1991.

A NOTE ON THE AUTHOR

Christina Thompson is the editor of *Harvard Review*. Her essays and articles have appeared in numerous journals, including the *American Scholar*, the *Journal of Pacific History*, *Mānoa*, and in the 1999, 2000, and 2006 editions of *Best Australian Essays*. She lives near Boston with her family.

A NOTE ON THE TYPE

The text of this book is set in Linotype Sabon,
named after the type founder, Jacques Sabon. It was
designed by Jan Tschichold and jointly developed
by Linotype, Monotype, and Stempel, in response
to a need for a typeface to be available in identical
form for mechanical hot metal composition
and hand composition using foundry type.

Tschichold based his design for Sabon roman
on a font engraved by Garamond, and Sabon
italic on a font by Granjon. It was first used in
1966 and has proved an enduring modern classic